Acclaim for Rachel Pruchno's

SURROUNDED BY MADNESS

"An important, poignant voice rooted in one family's experience. Will help move communities beyond dialogue to action."

MICHAEL J. FITZPATRICK, M.S.W.
Executive Director
National Alliance on Mental Illness

"A heart rending but honest story ... [that] will help others avoid the self-blame and diminish the heartbreak that severe mental illness can impose."

PETER V. RABINS, M.D., M.P.H.
Professor of Psychiatry and Behavioral Sciences
Johns Hopkins University School of Medicine
Co-author of *The 36 Hour Day*

"Reading Surrounded By Madness is like watching the inevitable train crash that you can't stop from happening. Poignant, vivid, tragic, yet ultimately resilient."

STEPHEN P. HINSHAW, PH.D.
Professor, Department of Psychology
University of California at Berkeley
Vice-Chair for Psychology, Department of Psychiatry
University of California at San Francisco

"Dramatic insights into the plight of families. Humanizes a difficult problem. A must read."

GERALD N. GROB, PH.D.
Henry E. Sigerist Professor of the History of Medicine Emeritus
Institute for Health, Health Care Policy, and Aging Research
Rutgers University

"A report from the front lines of the daily battles of mental illness and a first-hand account of loss, this is a compelling book for clinicians, scholars, and family members trying to understand chronic mental illness."

MICHAEL A. SMYER, PH.D.
Professor of Psychology & Provost
Bucknell University

"Honest and heartbreaking and sure to initiate important conversations about mental illness – the first step toward reducing stigma."

CHRISTINE FERRI, PH.D.
Associate Professor of Psychology
The Richard Stockton College of New Jersey

"The heavy-hearted memoir of a woman who lost her mother and daughter to the bitter grip of mental illness.

"Penned in a vivid, literary style that bleeds anguish, Pruchno's story is a mother's worst nightmare. Since the book centers on a young person and leaves such a powerful impression, it would make a solid supplementary text for a college psychology course. Pruchno's feelings of desperation and powerlessness speak more to the reality of mental illness than an academic case study ever could.

"An unvarnished look at the destructiveness of mental illness as told by a person who suffered at the hands of someone else's demons."

KIRKUS REVIEWS

Surrounded By Madness

First published by Dog Ear Publishing
4010 W. 86th Street, Ste H
Indianapolis, IN 46268
www.dogearpublishing.net

ISBN: 978-1-4575-2559-9

This book is printed on acid-free paper.

Printed in the United States of America

Surrounded By Madness

A Memoir of Mental Illness and Family Secrets

Rachel Pruchno, Ph.D.

In loving memory of
Gladys Ehrenreich Pruchno
(1924 to 1975)

Dedication

For my husband and life partner, whose love, analytical thinking, and wonderful sense of humor helped me traverse this emotional journey.

For my son, who continues to bring me joy.

For my daughter: if only love were the answer, mine would have saved you. I hope someday you understand how much I love you, how hard I fought for you, and why in the end I had to let you go.

For families struggling with mental illness: I hope reading my story encourages you to tell yours.

About the Book Cover

Amber Christian Osterhout is a talented artist and the creator of the Gaining Insight campaign. After her younger brother developed paranoid schizophrenia, Amber found herself immersed in a continuing cycle of grief most often characterized by feelings of sadness and depression. To aid in her healing, Amber called upon both her creative and scientific backgrounds. By examining the relationship between mental illness and social stigma, Amber developed artwork to educate others about the realities of mental illness and help end its stigma.

What started out as an art therapy project soon turned into a personal journey. As a result of creating the Gaining Insight exhibit, Amber has had the pleasure of speaking at various mental health events, meeting many inspiring individuals in her travels. By honoring her brother and millions of others who live with mental illness, Amber hopes to replace fear with empathy and shame with courage.

Disease Onset is one of the six images comprising the Gaining Insight exhibit and it appears as the background art used in the cover design for this book.

Visit www.gaining-insight.com to learn more.

Contents

Author's Note

I have changed the names of some people and all of the healthcare institutions because my purpose was to tell this story, not to hurt anyone. Sadly, however, the facts have not been altered.

Preface

Approximately 25% of adults and 10% of children and adolescents in the United States experience a mental illness severe enough to cause problems in their thinking, feeling, mood, ability to relate to others, or other aspects of daily life. For every person experiencing a serious mental illness – such as depression, schizophrenia, obsessive-compulsive disorder, post-traumatic stress, bipolar disorder, or borderline personality disorder – there are family members who suffer as well. In the United States alone, where 11.4 million people struggle with severe mental illness, the lives of close to 100 million mothers, fathers, wives, husbands, siblings, and children are touched by severe mental illnesses.

Scientists know little about the causes of these mental illnesses, and treatments to ameliorate their symptoms are inadequate. Even less attention has been paid to understanding the devastating and far-reaching effects that mental illnesses have on families.

My early years were defined by secrecy, stigma, and fear caused by growing up with a mother diagnosed with manic depression. Some forty years later, I watched in horror as my adopted daughter's racing thoughts, impulsive behavior, and spiraling emotions – symptoms of the ADHD, bipolar disorder, and borderline personality disorder with which she was eventually diagnosed – rendered her unable to concentrate in school, a target of sexual predators, and vulnerable to fits of mania and anger.

More than chronicling the challenges of a family struggling with mental illness, *Surrounded By Madness* is testament to the resilience of families and the destructiveness of secrets. Whether families are defined by biological ties or created through adoption, those touched by mental illness strive for accurate diagnosis and effective treatments. They fight the indignities of a healthcare system that is often unresponsive and uncaring. They look hopefully to medication regimens that are complex, difficult to adhere to, and fraught with horrible side effects. They contest laws giving persons with mental illness the right to make decisions about their care even when health professionals agree that they lack the capacity to do so. And they continue to love the person they knew before the strangling grasp of mental illness took hold, robbing them of a cherished and valued family member. Too often, family members succumb to stigma about mental illness and hide behind a cloak of secrecy.

With *Surrounded By Madness*, I give voice to one of the many families touched by mental illness. This book is a memoir and, as such, it recounts my memories and experiences. Sadly, however, my experiences are not unique. Similar tales unfold daily in the lives of millions of families. But, because of the novel perspective I bring to this story – having lived with mental illness as both a daughter and a mother, as well as having a thirty-year research career devoted to understanding the effects mental illnesses have on families – my hope is that this memoir will awaken a national dialogue leading to better understanding about the struggles facing families often decimated by mental illness.

From the time my husband Josh and I started building our family, I kept a running log of my thoughts. I saved, forgot about, and then discovered a box of letters my mother wrote to me when I was in college. Thanks to these resources, the wonders of archived e-mail messages, and the remarkable strategies Josh, my brothers, and I developed for remembering, I was able to reconstruct specific conversations I had with friends, family members, therapists, and teachers. I cobbled together these pieces, painstakingly trying to recreate the story accurately, just as my family and I had lived it.

I began this book when my daughter Sophie left home, hoping that writing it would be therapeutic for me. It was. It gave me the power over my out-of-control world that I needed as much as I need oxygen. It also taught me volumes about my marriage, my love for Sophie, and myself.

Prologue

As Sophie opened the front door, I was hit by a blast of frigid air. She picked up the three white plastic garbage bags she had hastily stuffed with her clothes and makeup, her toothbrush thrown in as an afterthought. She turned to look at me, her hazel eyes dancing with excitement. And then my daughter walked out of my life.

I watched as she descended the steps, her ponytail bouncing to the rhythm of her stride. Slipping on a small patch of ice, she steadied herself as she advanced toward the waiting car. In the moonlit darkness, I barely made out the car's driver, her latest can't-live-without-him boy, the twenty-one-year-old heroin addict she'd met just weeks ago in the psychiatric hospital. The tip of his cigarette glowed as he moved it to his mouth and then away. The smell of rancid tobacco from her clothes lingered in the hall. As the car pulled away, its one working headlight cast a shadow on the snow-covered driveway. Its muffler scraped the pavement. Shivering, I closed the door.

The antique clock my husband Josh's great-grandfather had handcrafted chimed eight times, its mellow peal signaling Sophie's departure. The odor from the fish I'd fried for dinner still hung in the air. While I wished she would change her mind and reverse the few steps she had taken, I knew she would not. This was, after all, the child who made one frightful decision after the next and never looked back. No, once Sophie set her mind to something, there was no turning back.

I glanced at the abstract image of the colorful neuron we had hung proudly on our dining room wall. Sophie had painted it for her senior art project just months ago. Her teacher insisted it was good enough to be displayed in The Museum of Modern Art. Not only was Sophie a talented artist, she also was lauded as an up-and-coming actress, and the poetry she wrote was exquisite.

Sophie's dog Dunkin shot back his big ears. He barked as he raced from the living room window to the dining room window and then back again, trying to alert me to the dangers awaiting her, beseeching me to stop her, to make her come home. Travis, our black Lab, took his cue from Dunkin and added his raspy yelp to the ruckus. As the car drove down the street, Dunkin howled.

In his soft tenor, Josh continued explaining the complexities of an algebra problem to our son Aaron. I sank into the blue leather sofa in the dimly lit living room, feeling hollow and bereft. Travis rested his head in my lap. My body shook uncontrollably as I sobbed into his coarse short fur. I hadn't experienced this mix of abandonment, fear, and sadness since my mother's suicide nearly thirty-six years ago.

CHAPTER 1

A Snowy Evening

March 1967. I am twelve years old.

Cautiously, I descended the steps of the school bus, looking first to my left, then to my right. Not seeing him, I took a deep breath and barreled toward my house, slowed only by the weight of the schoolbooks I carried. The late March air bore a hint of spring despite the remains of last night's snow on the lawns and bushes sparkling in the afternoon sun. I pushed my glasses back up my nose.

I thought about the English assignment for the evening: "Ask the person whom you admire most to describe an early memory that was life-changing. Then write a one-page essay describing the memory and your reaction to learning about it." Even while my teacher explained the assignment, I toyed with the idea of talking to my father. But I knew he would be unlikely to talk to me. For years, anytime I asked him about life in Lithuania before the war, his experiences in concentration camps during the war, or his life in Europe after the war, I always got the same answer: "I don't want to talk about it." I figured I'd talk with my mother. So much in my life changed in the seven months since we had moved to Southfield, one of Detroit's sprawling suburbs, and I suspected she was responsible for much of that change. Maybe I would actually learn something from this homework assignment.

"Hey Tits! Want to eat me?" It was the dickhead from down the street.

My pulse quickened as I looked up. Partially blinded by the sun, I squinted as I watched him taunt me with the snowball he tossed up and down in his bare hand. To most people, he was a skinny seventh grade boy with long stringy brown hair and thick black glasses. To me he was Danger, a bad boy who smoked behind the school between classes, a bully who took joy from tormenting me because he knew I had no friends. Part of me took comfort from the fact that he wasn't teasing me about my weight. Had he known me last year, before puberty caused me to lose twenty pounds and grow three inches, his torments surely would have included "fatso" and "porker." Maybe I should have been flattered that he noticed my boobs. But I wasn't.

"Get lost," I growled, quickening my pace, plowing forward with as much determination as I could muster, heartened that I was just steps from my front door. How I wished we'd never moved, that I was back in the shelter of my old neighborhood. There, no one ever teased me, even though I was a fat little kid with buckteeth and no fashion sense. There, I played jump rope, jacks, or Barbie dolls with my girlfriends. We raced or skipped down the tar path to school. There, I wasn't the last kid chosen when we played kickball, and I always had someone to talk to. There, I was safe. Though only five miles away, this new neighborhood may well have been in a different country.

"Oh, come on. You know you want it!"

What I wanted was for someone to tell me the move to Southfield had been a big mistake and that we were moving back to Detroit. What I wanted was for my mother to greet me joyfully every day after school, hum to the Saturday afternoon opera on the radio, and confidently settle squabbles between my younger brothers, nine-year-old Ben and seven-year-old Brian. What I didn't want was to live with the sad, whiny woman my mother had become. I was even willing to go back to being a fat kid if that's what it would take to make things the way they were before we'd moved.

I opened the front door and stepped inside, but not before the icy snowball struck my back.

"Hi Mom, I'm home," I called, shaking off the snow and my anger.

"Hi Rach. How was your day?" she asked, smiling broadly. The fact that her nose was splattered with flour and the house smelled like chocolate meant she'd made cookies for my brothers and me.

"Yum! Smells like you made my favorite!" I gushed, throwing down my coat and heading for the kitchen.

During the past few weeks, things at home had begun to feel almost normal. The sadness and anxiety that had all but paralyzed my mother, making her weepy and causing her to wring her hands and lament that she wasn't a good enough mother, had disappeared. She'd gained back most of the weight she'd lost, and her clothes no longer drooped on her slender frame. Her once pale cheeks had a healthy pink blush. Even her hair, fresh from a home perm, had regained its bounce. Yet I remained haunted by that first moment when I realized something was very wrong with my mother.

It was the third week of seventh grade, just six months ago. Frustrated by being the friendless new kid in school, I'd decided that, if I could spruce up my wardrobe, all my problems would disappear. After much pleading, I convinced my mother to buy me a pair of purple crushed velvet bellbottoms and a white Peter Pan collared blouse, much like the outfit I'd seen one of the popular girls wearing. I'd worn the blouse once and thrown it in the laundry basket. When I went to put it on that morning, it was three shades of pink. I hollered "Mom! What did you do to my new white blouse?"

Because she didn't answer, I went in search of her. I was fuming.

She wasn't in the kitchen where she usually spent the early morning reading the *Detroit Free Press* and drinking coffee. "Mom," I screamed. "Where are you?"

Still no answer.

I trudged back upstairs. The door to her bedroom was closed. She was sobbing. I held my breath and listened for a moment before knocking.

"Come in," my father said. There was an unfamiliar softness to his Lithuanian accent.

My mother sat on the bed, tissue in hand, trying to hide her tears. My father sat by her side.

"Mom," I said, rushing to her, forgetting about my blouse. "What's wrong?"

"I don't know, Rachel. I'm no good. I wish I could be a better mother. I can't do anything right."

Hoping for an explanation, I looked to my father. He was silent. Clearly he'd heard this before, but didn't know what to say.

"Mom, what are you talking about? You're a great mother." I wanted her to stop talking like this. It scared me.

"I'm not. I'm not. I ruined your pretty new blouse. I must have put it in the washing machine with Brian's red tee-shirt. I can't do anything right."

"It's just a dumb old blouse. Don't worry about it. We can buy another one."

Although my father and I were able to distract her that morning, over the next few months everything made her sad. Her sadness had me crying myself to sleep at night.

In the past few weeks, something had made her snap out of it. I didn't know what it was, but I hoped never to see that side of her again.

Remembering the evening's assignment, I said, "Mom, I have homework I need your help with."

"How can I help?" she asked, sitting down at the kitchen table and taking off her glasses. Even this past winter, when she was at her lowest point and getting out of bed was a chore, she always found the strength to help my brothers and me with homework.

"Tell me about an early memory that was life-changing," I said parroting the assignment.

Silence. The blood drained from her face. Her lips trembled. Her brown eyes stared at her glasses, trying to hide her tears from me.

"Mom? Are you okay?" How could my question have caused her such distress? "We don't have to do this. I can just make something up for my dumb old essay."

"No, I want to tell you. I guess I've always wanted to tell you, but I didn't know how."

Over the past several months I'd learned to do everything I could to be a good girl and not upset her. Now that she was acting normal, why did my homework question bother her so?

Regaining her composure, she spoke softly, measuring each word. "I was three years old. It was the winter of 1927. The snow was falling and I was standing in my living room looking out the big window toward the street. It was beautiful outside. Everything was covered in white. There was a man shoveling the snow. He looked very happy. I watched the snow accumulate on the sidewalk as the smiling man shoveled. Just then there was a clatter in the kitchen: I think a cup broke. The house was full of my relatives. Some of the grown-ups were crying and everyone talked in hushed whispers. I knew something was wrong, but I didn't dare turn my head to see what it was. Someone picked me up, hugged me, and put me to bed. I don't know who it was, but I had the feeling that whatever was happening meant my life was never going to be the same. I fell asleep to the murmur of Yiddish words I didn't understand. The next morning my father told me my mother was dead."

Tears rolled down my cheeks. Did this have anything to do with her sadness these past few months? And who was Grandma Rosie, the kind woman I always had believed was my mother's mother? What other secrets did my mother have?

"What happened to your mother?" I asked, choking the tears back.

"My father said it had something to do with her gall bladder, but I never knew much more."

I said nothing.

The front door flew open and Ben, out of breath from the daily race home from school against Brian, taunted, "Beat you again, sucker!"

CHAPTER 2

Wicked Stepmother

M om was pacing again.

Watching her, I remembered a family trip to the Detroit zoo. I was seven years old. The late spring morning sun warmed my face. Ben and I raced from exhibit to exhibit, stopping long enough at each one to insert our red Trunkey-the-Elephant into the keyhole of the yellow box. There'd been much begging and pleading on our part before Mom agreed to spend the fifty cents to purchase the key. Although Brian wanted to run with us, Mom said he needed to sit in his stroller. Ben, at four years old, was impatient. At each exhibit, he wanted to insert Trunkey into the keyhole, turn the key, and dart to the next exhibit. I wanted to stop and listen to the brief audio story about each animal the key unlocked. Because I was the big sister, we agreed to do it my way.

At the tiger cage, I froze. I watched the lone tiger pace back and forth. Although there were no physical bars, the tiger seemed to understand that he could walk only ten steps in one direction, turn, and then walk ten steps in the other direction. I asked my father why the tiger kept walking back and forth. He shrugged, exhaled the last puff of his Kent cigarette, stepped on its butt, and said, "I don't know. Maybe he's frustrated." Had my father's experience in the concentration camp been like the tiger's? What was it like to be nineteen years old, waking up a prisoner, wondering whether each day would be his last on Earth? How did he survive confined to a cold barrack, deprived of all but a pittance of moldy bread? Had he paced back and forth all day?

Now, years later, I watched my mother. She walked ten steps from her bed to her bathroom and then back. Then she did it again and again. Just like the tiger. I stared at the white carpet, expecting to see a gaping hole marking her path. She wrung her hands and shook her head. "I'm no good. I'm a horrible mother. I wish I could be a good mother like Muriel and Helen." The weariness in her voice crushed me.

"Mom, you're a great mother." I'd said these words at least a half dozen times that afternoon, hoping they would comfort her. This time my words felt hollow and meaningless. She was either unable to hear them or incapable of understanding them. Sometimes, when I talked to her, it was as if I were speaking a foreign language, a tongue my father, brothers, and I understood, but one that was nonsensical to her. "You've always been there for the boys and me," I pleaded, trying to cajole her, to no avail. The pacing and handwringing continued. Her breath smelled like rotting garbage, a sign that she'd reached the worst part of her annual cycle of depression. I was frustrated and angry. I wanted her to be normal so I could be a normal teenager.

When I was younger, there was no doubt she was a great mother. She tended to all of my needs as well as those of my brothers. She instilled in us a love of learning, taking us on weekly trips to the library, and reading to us each night before tucking us into bed. When we were sick, the smell of Vicks VapoRub pervaded the house and there was always a big pot of chicken soup simmering on the stove. She made my annual visits to the ophthalmologist special, taking me to Cunningham's soda fountain for an extra-thick chocolate malted while we waited for the drops the doctor put in my eyes to enlarge my pupils. She taught me to play piano and, when I was seven, she made matching multi-colored pastel silk shirtwaist dresses that we wore when we performed Moszkowski's "Spanish Dance" in our teacher's annual recital. Family vacations were thoughtfully planned, economical, and often educational. Summertime brought day trips to Kensington beach, the zoo, and – when we were especially good – to Kresge's five and ten cent store where she gave each of us a quarter to spend. The clothes she sewed for my Barbie doll made me the envy of the neighborhood girls. My friends coveted the green and white Barbie dress that matched the curtains in our kitchen. The chocolate birthday cakes, with butter cream frosting she decorated according to our wishes, ensured that our parties were the best of all.

When I was a child, my mother always smelled good to me. She had several different perfumes she sprayed on herself when she and my father went out in the evening. If I'd been good, she'd dab a bit on my arm and I'd fall asleep inhaling her scent. My favorite was Madame Rochas. It smelled like jasmine, roses, lemon, and narcissus all blended together. My father had given it to her for one of her birthdays. While her fragrances were different from one another, each was as familiar to me as her face and as characteristic of her as the pin curls she fastened with bobby pins after washing her hair with Breck shampoo. Sometimes her hands held the faintest hint of the garlic she chopped as she prepared dinner. In the middle of the night, when I had a bad dream and called for her, I was comforted by the remnants of the Merle Norman cold cream still on her face that she used to remove makeup before going to bed.

Even in the depths of her depressive cycles, my mother was a good mother. She read and corrected every paper my brothers and I wrote and helped with our homework. Her organizational skills were second to none; we often teased that her lists had lists. Before her first hospitalization in December 1968, for what I later came to know was manic depression, she cooked and froze food so we could have home-cooked meals while she was gone. She left step-by-step instructions in what we called the "Bible," ensuring we wouldn't miss a single piano lesson or dentist appointment and that we knew what to eat for dinner each night. And she insisted that my father bring our papers, tests, and quizzes when he visited her each evening at the hospital so she could continue to monitor our school progress.

For the past five years, the rhythm of Mom's emotions was easy to track. During the spring and summer, she flew high. Rising at four thirty each morning, she cleaned the house and made dinner before I woke up. She was a whirlwind – practicing piano, doing house projects, or reading. She read weighty books about the economies of foreign countries or thick volumes of classic literature, not the romance novels or psychological thrillers enjoyed by other mothers in the neighborhood. As fall approached, her mood plummeted. She stayed in bed for much of the day, often curled in a fetal position. She cried and was jittery and inconsolable. While always decisive and in charge during the warm months of the year, by late fall she waffled over such inconsequential decisions as what to wear or what to make for dinner. Late in the calendar year, her mantra of "I'm a terrible mother" played over and over like a scratched record. Vials of medicines lined the kitchen counter. By winter, I was petrified to leave her alone. My dad worried about going to work and leaving her alone. She'd already made two suicide attempts. One was earlier this month, the other about a year ago. Both times she swallowed too many pills and had to have her stomach pumped. Each time, she ended up spending weeks at "4S," the psychiatric unit of Detroit's Sinai Hospital. At least once they tried electroconvulsive therapy.

When I was a child, mental illness wasn't something people talked about. No professional ever talked to me or to my brothers about my mother's illness. In fact, no one even gave her illness a name. I didn't know what the doctors did for her when she was in the hospital, but I wondered how all the cutting boards, picture frames, and aprons she made while she was there could make her well.

My father, an engineer at Ford Motor Company, did the best he could to help me understand. But, because he himself didn't know what caused her overwhelming sadness and worry, he could provide little in the way of explanation to me. I imagine that Mom's illness frustrated my father as each of the strategies he came up with to try and make her happy – buying her a lamb's wool coat and a beautiful home in the suburbs, taking her on vacations, and complimenting her at every opportunity – failed to alleviate her pain. Her illness must have frightened my father and made him wonder whether mental illness – this unknown demon – would take his beautiful wife from him, as Hitler had robbed him of his parents and his older sister.

My parents' friends and even my father's brother were told little about her illness. They talked with my father, calling and offering to help when my mother was in the hospital, but none of them knew about the incessant crying, hand wringing, and pacing we witnessed on a daily basis when she was ill. They didn't hear her unremitting laments about not knowing what to cook for dinner, how to clean the house, or how to discipline my brothers and me. They didn't feel her anguish as she brooded about my father's inability to relax, Brian's reading problems, Ben's tendency to hem and haw when speaking, and my tendency to be sassy. To them, my mother was beautiful, smart, and reserved. Because they weren't allowed to see her pain, it never occurred to them to ask my brothers or me how we were doing.

Although no one ever prevented me from mentioning my mother's illness, somehow it became our family secret. Just as I knew not to ask my father about his life in Europe, I knew not to ask too many questions about Mom's illness. Secrets about my mother made me lonely. They kept me from inviting friends to our home, fearing they might witness some of her odd behaviors and forcing me to try to explain them. Yet this silence created a special closeness with my father and brothers; it became part of the glue holding us together.

And so I took it upon myself, beginning at age twelve, to figure out what I could do to fix my mother's problems. I talked to her, helped out at home, and did my best not to annoy her. I tried to reconcile the reality of her illness with my wish that she were healthy or, if she had to be sick, that she had an illness people could understand. Some nights, as I drifted off to sleep, I had conversations with God in which I bargained away her mental health demons for heart disease, cancer, or diabetes. Other nights I pretended I was Nancy Drew. Like the fictional amateur sleuth I adored, I cast myself in the role of my mother's savior. Just as Nancy solved the secret of the old clock and the puzzle of the broken locket, so too did I solve the mystery of my mother's illness. I sought refuge in my schoolwork, slugging through countless math problems and writing and re-writing chemistry labs until they were perfect, the work keeping my loneliness and fear of losing my mother under control.

Because my mother and I were alike in so many ways – intelligent, reserved, approval-seeking, and well-organized; yet neither of us a risk taker, artistic, or impulsive – I worried about whether I was destined to end up with her mental illness. Would I awaken at four thirty in the morning and frantically clean the house? Would I become so sad that I couldn't get out of bed?

This afternoon, though, as I watched Mom pace back and forth for the umpteenth time, I was angry that I had to stay home with her. Five years after we'd moved to Southfield, I finally had made friends. Sue, Lauren, and Lucy invited me to go to the movies with them to see *Play Misty for Me*, but Brian and Ben needed new winter coats and Dad told me to stay home with Mom while he took them to Hudson's annual sale.

The phone rang. It was Sue making a last-ditch attempt to include me in the afternoon trip to the movies. She said her mom could pick me up and bring me home. I wanted to go so badly, but I looked at my mom, sighed, and said, "Sorry, Sue, I wish I could go, but I have a bunch of math homework to do. Next time?"

I hung up the phone and glared at Mom. "Why didn't you go?" she asked.

"Because Dad said I had to stay home with you," I snarled.

"That's ridiculous. Go ahead. Call her back. You can go," she pleaded, resuming her pacing.

"I can't go anywhere. I can't have friends," I sobbed.

"What are you talking about? Of course you can have friends."

"No I can't. I can never invite anyone to come over here."

"Why not?" she asked. "We have such a beautiful home. What are you ashamed of?"

How could she not know?

The silence in the room was deafening.

"You!" I screamed. "How can I invite kids to come here when all you do is pace, pace, pace? You're like a clock. Tick-tock, tick-tock. Back-and-forth, back-and-forth. What would they think?"

My mother stopped pacing. She looked at me. I worried my anger would push her to do something dangerous. Heat bubbled in my gut. Had I pushed her too far?

And then she did something I never expected. She laughed.

"You've got to be kidding. You think it's because of me you don't have friends? Let me tell you what my sister Harriet and I had to deal with when we were kids. How'd you like to come home from school every afternoon and have to clean the house, because if you didn't, your wicked stepmother yelled at you or beat you? How'd you like to have to scrub the toilets and clean the floors and always be told you didn't do a good enough job? How'd you like to live in a dark, dingy apartment in New York where the only place kids could play when it was rainy or cold outside was a smelly, damp cellar?"

"Wicked stepmother? I thought you loved Grandma Rosie."

"It wasn't Grandma Rosie. She didn't marry my father until much later in life. I was close to thirty then. I was eight when my dad married Bertha. Harriet was ten. My mother had been dead for about five years, and Dad was alone with two little girls. I guess he decided we needed a mother. Bertha never loved us, and we hated her."

"Why didn't you ever tell me about her before?"

"I guess it never came up. It was a long time ago and it didn't seem to matter."

Somehow, even at age seventeen, without my doctorate in Human Development, I knew it did matter. A whole lot.

CHAPTER 3

Beef Stroganoff

December 2, 1975. I am twenty-one years old.

By the time I turned sixteen, I knew my mother would kill herself. Her pain was too unrelenting, her feelings of being a burden to my father, brothers, and me were too great, and her sense of determination was second to none. What I did not know was when.

And so I lived on the edge, consumed with worry. In high school, the first to arrive home in the afternoon, I worried about whether I would find her dead or alive. In college, if I telephoned and she didn't answer, my overactive imagination spun one tortured story after the next, each ending with her death.

Thanksgiving weekend of my senior year at Michigan State was the last time I saw my mother. She had muddled through the holiday, but she was depressed. Even so, we'd talked at length about my impending graduation and what I should do next. She advised me to pursue my interest in psychology and go to graduate school. I wasn't so sure. On Sunday afternoon, when I hugged her goodbye before catching a ride back to school, she whispered, "Don't worry about me; I'll be fine. Study hard and do well in school."

The following Tuesday, I called my mother to see how she was feeling. Getting no answer, I worried, but then comforted myself with the explanation that she'd taken Brian to an orthodontist appointment or was busy running errands.

My roommate Susan and I had been teaching ourselves to cook that semester. With our senior year of college coming to a close, we realized the importance of adding life skills to our repertoire of book knowledge. We had perfected spaghetti with meat sauce, Moussaka, and Chicken Parmesan. Our next challenge was Beef Stroganoff.

The smell of onions and garlic sautéing made my mouth water. Sound from the record player warmed the chilly December afternoon. Maynard Ferguson held a long delicious note on his horn. The record skipped and the doorbell rang. "I'll get the record; you get the door," Susan said.

Opening the door, I was startled to see my father and Brian. My father's face was grey. His eyes were red. Brian looked at the ground.

"Rachel," my father said, "we need to talk to you."

I led them into the bedroom I shared with Susan. My father gently closed the door and said, "Mom's gone. She died this morning. It was too much for her this time. She started the car with the garage door closed and let it run. She's dead."

I froze. This can't be happening.

I'm falling. I see the two Flying Wallendas plummet to their deaths as their high wire pyramid collapses at the Shrine Circus. I am eight years old. Pink cotton candy sticks to my fingers. Now I wait for my own crash. Within seconds, I'm swaying forty feet above the concrete coliseum floor, as the sole woman in the performance that evening had done, clinging to the wire while members of her family braced her fall and saved her life. Will anyone catch me or am I doomed? The grotesque circus clown standing in the center ring that fateful night pleads for order. Now I make my own plea. Make my mother be alive. Make this be a bad dream.

"Rachel, you need to pack your clothes so we can get on the road. We still have to pick up Ben." My father's hoarse voice shocked me back to the horrible reality unfolding in my room.

I bawled as the truth of my mother's death sank in. While I knew my mother would eventually kill herself, the reality of her death shook me. No, this wasn't supposed to happen. She's just fifty-one years old. She has to come to my graduation in June. She has to tell me what to do with the rest of my life.

Brian looked at his well-worn, black sneakers. Like them, he was beaten down and tired. He'd learned the grim news from my father when he returned home from school that afternoon. Listening to my father tell me what had happened, and then, later that evening, hearing him recount it for Ben must have been like rubbing salt in a wound.

My hands shook as I gathered together clothes, packing for our trip home, thinking about the funeral to come. Worry about studying for final exams – my main concern only minutes earlier – was gone.

Susan surely heard my cries and certainly was wondering what had happened. As I opened the bedroom door, her concerned look made me burst out my news. "My mother's dead." Speaking those words for the first time, the pain seared. She hugged me tightly.

My father, Brian, and I stepped out into a grey, bitterly cold evening. A piercing wind whipped across the parking lot and smacked me in the face. It smelled like snow. Brian carried the small suitcase I'd packed in haste. My mother's car, parked under the sole light in the lot, was covered with thick grey soot.

"What happened to Mom's car?" I asked.

My father unlocked the doors, saying nothing.

I opened the back door and was pummeled by the cloying smell of burnt marshmallows. The back of my throat was on fire. I gagged. "What's that horrible smell?"

"It's from the exhaust," my father answered with no further elaboration.

As I got into the car in which my mother had killed herself, I wondered what she'd thought as she opened the car door and sat in the driver's seat just hours ago. Did she have any regrets? Did she think about changing her mind once she had started the car?

Why did my father drive this car to pick me up? Why hadn't he taken his company car or Brian's car? Why hadn't he borrowed his brother's car? Why didn't he rent a car? I wanted to ask, but I didn't dare. We were all too fragile.

Despite the frigid temperatures of the December night, we sped along Interstate 96 at eighty miles an hour with all of the windows open, the car's heater running full blast. My teeth chattered. An hour later, we reached Ben's dorm at the University of Michigan in Ann Arbor.

I didn't want to get out of the car and watch my brother's heart break, but I had no choice. As the three of us walked down the dorm hall, Brian and I trailed, allowing my father to take the lead. Ben bandied with his friends at the end of the hallway. When he looked up and spotted us, he froze. He must have known why we were there.

As Ben heard the details of my mother's death for the first time, Brian for the third time, and I for the second, we wept. My father put his arms around his three grief-stricken children, our tears mingling. Then he said, "Ben, pack up. We need to go home. I still have to talk to the rabbi tonight." As Ben pulled clothes out of his drawers, I folded them and put them in his suitcase. Then we headed home, no longer a family of five.

As we drove, we talked. Dad said that a neighbor had called him in a panic when Mom failed to respond to a flurry of late morning phone calls. He raced home and found the car still running in the garage.

My father gripped the steering wheel and stared at the road. I sat behind him, watching the reflection of his eyes in the rear view mirror. His lips were rigid, his skin pale. He didn't know I was looking at him.

I imagined him racing into the driveway. Had he smelled the car's fumes before he yanked the garage door open? Did he scream her name? Did he know she was dead before he saw her? How long had he waited for the ambulance to arrive? I don't think he cried while he watched the futile efforts of the emergency responders trying to resuscitate his wife of twenty-two years because he never cried. What was he thinking as the police peppered him with countless questions designed to rule him out as a suspect in her death? How had he kept from crumbling? The shock of finding her must have reignited the grief he experienced when the Nazis slaughtered his mother, father, sister, and other family members.

The family secret of my mother's mental illness was extended to her suicide, as I wanted neither the pity nor the endless questions such knowledge would generate. To the queries of people who entered my life after my mother's death, I said simply that she had died in a car accident on an icy road.

Although I now knew the when, where, and how of my mother's death, it would be years before I understood the why.

To this day, I have never eaten Beef Stroganoff.

Chapter 4

Ten Years After

October 26, 1985. I am thirty-one years old.

Was it really bad luck for the groom to see the bride before the wedding? If so, we were in trouble, since Josh and I were dressing for our wedding in the same room. I panicked as the zipper on my size six wedding dress refused to budge, imagining myself marching down the aisle with my backside exposed. I hadn't gained weight since my last fitting; if anything I'd lost a few pounds as the excitement of our wedding day mounted. But my soon-to-be-husband Josh's calm prevailed as he removed a pin the dressmaker had forgotten.

The warm sun-blasted afternoon that had enabled Ben and Brian to fete Josh with his last round of golf as a bachelor yielded to a breezy twilight. The orange daisies, purple and white mums, white lilies, and pink roses adorning the top floor of Philadelphia's Bellevue-Stratford Hotel were stunning and their sweetness filled the room. The jazz band played a mellow, inviting rendition of "Sunrise, Sunset." The ushers had escorted family and friends to their seats. The photographer had finished snapping pictures of the wedding party, and the signatures on the *ketubah* – our Jewish marriage contract – had dried. Susan, my maid of honor, had straightened my veil for the last time and then strolled down the aisle, signaling the start of the ceremony.

From the back of the ballroom, I watched Josh's grandparents lead him toward the *chuppah*, the wedding canopy signifying the home we would build together. How lucky I was to have gone on that blind date eight months ago. Josh and I complemented one another in so many ways.

My father and I looked at each other, both of us nervous, keeping our promise not to cry. "You look beautiful," he whispered. "Just like your mother."

I smiled, fighting the lump forming in my throat. "Don't make me cry."

When I was young, my father was the supporting actor in our family. He went to work each morning before I woke up and came home in time for dinner. My brothers and I knew not to pester him until he'd had a shot of *Absolut*, his favorite vodka. Weekends were family time, which meant we did whatever Mom said.

While I never really understood what my father did at Ford, clearly it was something important. Every year there were fancy new cars whose colors my brothers and I took turns choosing. He was most proud of a project featured on the cover of the August 1976 issue of *Popular Science* magazine. Its headline proclaimed "Ford's New Variable Venturi Carburetor: Clever Engineering Matches Fuel Use to The Load, Saves Gas." My dad and his team had modified technology used in aircraft, figured out how to mass-produce it, and developed a carburetor design that yielded cleaner exhaust and better fuel mileage. Although this success coincided with the years when worry about my mother's mental illness consumed him, his colleagues never knew. It would be years later, long after his death, that I would understand how truly amazing it was that he'd been able to hold our family together and make such an important discovery.

"Ready?" he asked, a twinkle in his hazel eyes.

"Ready."

I took hold of my father's left arm and we inched toward the *chuppah*. A sea of faces smiled at us, but I thought only of my mother. The emptiness to my left, where she should have been, holding my hand on this important walk, muted the room's colors and sounds.

This wasn't the first important event in my life she'd missed during the past 10 years. She didn't attend the ceremony on Michigan State's sweltering football field in June of 1976 when I tossed my green graduation cap in the air. She didn't celebrate with me when my Ph.D. in Human Development and Family Studies was conferred at Penn State six years later, when I started my first professional job at the Miami Jewish Home and Hospital for the Aged in the fall of 1982, or when one of the world's prominent gerontologists recruited me to join the Philadelphia Geriatric Center in 1984. So too did she miss witnessing Ben become a doctor and Brian an engineer.

My mother was one of the 27,063 people in the United States who committed suicide in 1975.[1] As a psychologist, I knew that suicide leaves in its wake millions of family members, many of whom experience grief, rage, and pain for decades. I was well aware that rates of exhaustion, migraines, colitis, alcoholism, sleep problems, anxieties, crying spells, heart trouble, and fear of being alone are significantly higher among survivors of a family member's suicide than in the general population. And I knew that many surviving family members experience suicide as the ultimate rejection, that they see someone they loved choosing to leave them – not in an ordinary, reversible fashion by walking out or filing for divorce, but by death.[2]

But, I never felt that my mother had rejected me. Although I wept at her gravesite, sat *shiva,* and endured the sadness of missed first anniversaries – Passover, Mother's Day, her birthday, my birthday, and Thanksgiving – I knew she had not abandoned me. Rather, her illness filled her with such inescapable pain that she had no option but to end her life. It was the only exit she had from what she viewed as an impossible situation. And so, I felt neither guilt nor blame, and I was never angry with her. It's hard to be angry with someone whose life was so tortured.

Losing my mother as I neared the end of my college years had a tremendous influence on the course of my career. My interest in psychology, developed as an undergraduate at Michigan State, transformed into a lifelong passion to understand mental illness and mental health. My mother's experiences steered me far from the role of clinician, as I feared taking responsibility for protecting people with serious mental illness from harming themselves. And so I was drawn to the world of research. Certainly my mother influenced the ideas expressed in my first major paper, published the year before my wedding. In it, my colleagues and I introduced the term "life event webs" to express how events such as marriage, birth, illness, and death can alter the lives of multiple family members.[3]

Surprisingly, my mother's death also brought relief. It meant I no longer had to worry about her. I no longer closed my eyes and wondered whether this would be the day she would kill herself. I no longer was constantly on edge, waiting for that phone call to tell me she had taken an overdose of pills and was again in the hospital.

But I never could figure out how to explain my mother's death to my friends. There never seemed to be the right time to come out and say, "My mother suffered from manic depression and she killed herself." I couldn't tell this to someone I was beginning a relationship with. It was much too personal. As friendships blossomed and I shared concerns about boyfriends and worries about work situations, my silence about my mother persisted. I knew I was hiding. My stomach squirmed each time I told my made-up story of her death. Yet, when I imagined conversations in which I told the truth, I fell apart. I don't know whether I worried more about how difficult it would be for me to say the words or for others to hear them. I didn't want pity and I didn't want them to think poorly of my mother or me. I knew that, should the floodgates open, the pain would be intolerable. And so I hid the truth.

On our first date, I got lost in Josh's voice. By our second date, I knew I had a future with him and had to tell him about my mother's mental illness and her suicide. For days I worried about what to say and whether this would be a deal breaker.

My ten-year silence was broken as I sobbed, searching for the words to tell him. He held my hand and made it easy. Yet even this didn't free me to share my secret with friends, as I rationalized his response as a function of his being infatuated with me. I refused to consider the possibility that Josh's reaction might be typical.

Walking down the aisle, I gazed at one pair of eyes after another, feeling guilty that none of the people I'd met since my mother's death, so dear to me that they were attending my wedding, knew the truth.

Reaching the *chuppah*, I let go of my father's arm, gave him a kiss, and took hold of Josh Segal's hand.

CHAPTER 5

Tough Decisions

Spring 1991. I am thirty-seven years old.

"Do you think I could love an adopted child as much as I would love my own?"

I looked up from the book I was reading and smiled, thinking about the question my husband of nearly six years asked.

I'd thought a lot about that question. I believed that I could love an adopted child as much as I'd love my own. Josh was more cautious. And so, we debated the pros and cons of adoption for months.

We had suffered through countless rounds of fertility evaluations requiring close monitoring of my monthly cycles. Spontaneous sex had become history. Josh had learned to administer painful shots of the fertility drug Pergonal to my butt. It made my moods reel. Were these mood swings anything like what my mother had experienced? There'd been several inconveniently timed trips to the University of Pennsylvania Hospital for attempts at inseminations, even one on New Year's Day at nine in the morning. Yet I'd gladly ceded my body to the chemistry experiments of the physicians, their promise of success attested to by the photos of babies they'd helped create adorning their office walls. I'd gotten brave enough to have a laparoscopy that confirmed fibroids invading my uterus prevented me from getting pregnant. The doctor mentioned surgery as a possibility, but suggested this would leave a weakened uterus, unlikely able to sustain a pregnancy.

Each month that I didn't get pregnant brought tears, sadness, and frustration. Yet, there were moments when I found myself relieved not to be pregnant, consoled by knowing I wouldn't pass along the mental illness genes that claimed my mother's life. I didn't wish the illness and pain she'd suffered on anyone, and I knew I'd feel guilty if I passed on the genes that doomed her.

After lengthy heart-felt conversations, Josh and I stopped the fertility treatments. The question remaining on the table was to adopt or remain childless.

I kept trying to explain to Josh that I needed a baby. At age thirty-seven, I'd hit every milestone of my professional career. Working at the Philadelphia Geriatric Center, I had four major grant awards from the National Institutes of Health. I was well-published and respected by my peers. Yet my quest to become a mother remained unfulfilled. I was able to come to terms with my inability to get pregnant, but how could I go through life without loving and nurturing a child? Josh seemed none too sure about starting a family. The product of a strife-laden marriage that ended in divorce when he was nine, he delighted in our happy marriage and felt little need to add children to the mix.

When faced with a difficult situation, some people pray. Not me. I read. Even as I recovered from the laparoscopy, books about adoption lay sprawled across my bed as I devoured all the information I could get my hands on. I read about domestic adoptions and foreign adoptions, open adoptions and closed adoptions. I read about adoption law and adoption agencies. I learned that adoption is a complex process, involving legal, social, and family issues. I learned about the heartbreaking decision a birth mother makes when she must give up her child. One book said, "Adoption is a lifelong process." It would take me years to understand how profound that statement is.

Josh wanted no part of my books. Instead, he grappled on his own. Days had passed since our last adoption conversation.

Josh had asked me to give him time to think, a few days without listening to me rattle on about how wonderful adoption would be
and what a great father he would make. As difficult as this was for
me, I gave him his space, content to read and muse on my own.

But now, seeking to make me happy, Josh had initiated the
discussion. My heart jumped with joy. Adoption was back on the
table.

I had no doubt that Josh would love an adopted child as
much as a biological child. "Are you kidding?" I answered, kissing
him. "Just look at this menagerie."

Josh had come into our marriage with a dog and two cats,
all of whom he'd rescued. He found our dog Virgil, tied up and
frightened, facing the barrel of a rifle held by a crotchety sheriff in
the hills of the Roanoke Mountains of Virginia. Our cats were hours
old when Josh opened the lid of a dumpster to throw out an ice
cream wrapper and heard their meows. He fished them out of the
trash and took them home, building a cozy bed in a large shoebox.
Josh had nurtured this brood for years.

No, if there were any man who could love an adopted child
as his own, it was Josh.

CHAPTER 6

Late Night Phone Call

July 4, 1992. I am thirty-eight years old.

Plans to build our family were put on hold when Josh and I moved to Cleveland, Ohio, where I was recruited as the Director of Research at Menorah Park, a long-term care facility. Bolstered by funding from the National Institute of Child Health and Development for a study of mothers providing care to adult children with chronic disabilities, I launched a new program of research.

Within months, we turned our attention once again to adoption. We identified an adoption agency, filled out volumes of paperwork, and got fingerprinted. The application process generated difficult discussions as we struggled with questions about the babies we would and wouldn't consider adopting. We agreed that we would not adopt a baby with cerebral palsy, Down syndrome, spina bifida, cystic fibrosis, or fetal alcohol syndrome.

Recognizing that the genetics underlying mental illnesses are complex and the accuracy of diagnosed and reported conditions questionable, we didn't rule out a baby whose parents or grandparents suffered from mental illness. Turning my back on a baby that, given my mother's genes, I could have birthed felt wrong. But even more, part of me reveled at the thought of a second chance to fight – and conquer – the demons that had defeated my mother. Had familiarity bred acceptance? As a child I'd been powerless to save my mother, but I was sure that as an adult, especially one with a Ph.D. in human development, the playing field would be more level.

Josh and I developed a photo collage showing prospective birth mothers that we would make wonderful parents. The adoption agency suggested that they could do the work of finding the baby, or that they could support our efforts to do so. There was no question which route Josh and I preferred. We embraced the opportunity to take charge of what seemed like an out-of-control world. Josh, now a newly minted Ph.D. in marketing, developed our advertising plan. He wrote the text for our newspaper ad. It read: "Psychologist Mom and businessman Dad have lots of hugs and kisses to share with your newborn. Our friendly family neighborhood, gentle dog, and two sweet cats will welcome your precious baby with open arms. Please call Josh and Rachel collect at . . ." We targeted a dozen or so newspapers and arranged for our ad to start running on July 1.

Following the advice of the agency, we installed a separate phone line with a ring we could distinguish from our regular home phone. Testing the phone and hearing its chime for the first time startled me. I hoped the next time it rang I would hear the voice of our child's birth mother.

The agency counseled that I, not Josh, should answer the adoption phone, explaining that many birth mothers had been abandoned by the fathers of their babies and were angry with men.

Josh and I spent the Fourth of July lounging at my cousins' pool. We got home late and, as I drifted off to sleep listening to the fireworks exploding over downtown Cleveland, the adoption phone clanged.

I jumped. "I can't do it. I'm not awake. You answer it," I mumbled, panic-stricken.

Josh gave me one of those You-Have-Got-To-Be-Kidding-Me looks as he reached for the phone.

"Hello," Josh said. I nuzzled close to the phone's receiver, anxious to hear the voice of the woman I hoped would become our birth mother. I listened as Josh talked with Jamie for the next hour. She was about to turn nineteen and had been a student at Texas Christian University. Her baby was due August 14. Jamie was living at a hospitality house in Altoona, Pennsylvania, loved animals, and said that our ad's mention of pets caught her attention.

Jamie had three demands for Josh. He listened, addressing one after the next, all the while nibbling nervously on his thumb.

First, Jamie wanted a promise we would send her child to college. Without hesitating, Josh said, "I can't make that promise. I can, however, tell you my wife and I value education and we both have Ph.D.s, so it would be our hope not only to send the child to college, but also to graduate school. However, the child may decide she doesn't want to go to college. She might want to learn a trade, like carpentry, or to be a chef. If that's the case, we'd support that decision and help her be the best carpenter or chef she can be." Jamie thought for a moment and said, "Okay. That makes sense."

Second, Jamie asked if we were good Christian people. "No," Josh answered. "We're Jewish, and our plan is to raise the child we adopt in our faith. If that's an issue for you, we're probably not the right parents." Jamie assured him she wanted the child to be raised with religion, and she found nothing wrong with Judaism.

Then, Jamie requested ten letters of reference. Josh explained that we had provided the adoption agency with six references. He told her we could make these available to her immediately, and if she wanted more, we would send them to her. "No," she said. "Six will be fine."

As he hung up the phone, Josh's wide-eyed gaze met mine. Although we hadn't followed the agency's protocol for answering the phone and Josh hadn't agreed to any of Jamie's demands, we'd made substantial progress toward my goal of becoming a mother.

CHAPTER 7

She's Here!

August 1992. I am thirty-eight years old.

I awakened to the squawk of the phone. The clock read 4:38. Who could be calling this early? Josh fumbled for the receiver. "Hello?" he said.

"Wake up, Papa!" said Jamie's paternal grandfather Rusty. His voice booming from the phone's receiver frightened Virgil, who barked. "Wake up and come to Altoona, for gosh sakes. She's here and she's beautiful. You're a dad!"

This was it. The day we'd waited for was here. Only seven and a half weeks since Josh first spoke with Jamie, we were now hours from meeting our daughter. We raced around the house getting ready for our trip.

I retrieved the dress I'd bought to wear on this very special day from my closet. Weeks earlier, browsing at Wanamaker's, I'd been drawn to this blue gingham jumper because it was identical to one my mother had worn when I was a child. Trying it on in the store and modeling it later for Josh, I'd been convinced that it made me look like the perfect mother. Now, as I pulled it over my head, all the insecurities I had about my new role flooded over me like a tidal wave. Will the baby love me? Will I love her? Will I be a good mother? I wondered whether my mother had similar thoughts the day I was born.

The drive to Altoona seemed endless. As we pulled into the hospital's parking lot, we saw Rusty and his wife Edna. Jamie's paternal grandparents had raised her and continued to play a major role in her life. Weeks earlier, they'd helped Jamie choose us to be the baby's parents. Overjoyed to see us, Rusty and Edna bubbled happy baby details at us. They knew Jamie wasn't ready to be a mother. While they had considered raising the baby, their advanced age and declining health made this impractical. They knew Josh and I would be wonderful parents for their great granddaughter.

Two nurses chatted as they strolled down the hospital corridor. The wheels of a gurney being pushed by an aide squeaked. Farther down the hall, a patient tethered to a monitoring device crept toward me. For them, today was an ordinary day. Not for me. Ever since I played house as a little girl, I'd wanted to be a mother. Now I was steps away from becoming one. I searched each room we passed, longing to catch a first glimpse of my daughter. When we arrived at Jamie's room, the door was ajar. Tentatively, I knocked.

"Come on in!" bellowed Jamie. "It's about time y'all got here!"

I pushed the door open. Jamie sat propped up by pillows, holding the baby close to her chest. Strands of disheveled dirty blond hair fell in her face. "Here you go," she said, handing the baby to me. "She's all yours."

Tears filled my eyes.

As I took my daughter from Jamie, I wasn't the only one in the room who was crying. Tears streamed down Jamie's face. How must it have felt to carry this child for nine months and now surrender her?

Holding the baby completed me. Had my mother felt this way the first time she held me? I wanted this moment to last forever. My contentment faded as I reminded myself that Jamie's legal rights to the baby hadn't yet been severed. What if she changes her mind? What if she wants her baby back? I tried to stop myself from falling in love, but my affection for the baby was immediate and unconditional. Gazing at her, I studied each tiny feature. She looked back at me, her eyes seeming to search my face, although I knew they weren't yet able to focus. Weighing in at six pounds three ounces and measuring nineteen and a half inches long, she was without doubt the most beautiful baby I'd ever seen. Her wispy hair was dark brown. Her face, sporting a prominent dimple on her left cheek and a less noticeable one on her right, was almost perfectly round.

"My turn," clamored Josh, as eager to touch her as I had been.

As I handed our daughter to him, he intercepted her with the ease of a seasoned wide receiver completing a pass. I grabbed the camera and began snapping one photo of Proud Papa after the next. The baby fussed, then settled in, content in her father's arms. Within a few minutes her face reddened and her body writhed as she produced her first messy diaper.

"Mine," bragged Josh. "I get to change her first diaper." He masterfully diapered her and re-wrapped her in her swaddling blanket. She calmed down and fell asleep. As Josh cradled her, he looked at me and said, "Let's go with our first choice for her name."

Our deliberations about names had been extensive. Josh wanted to name her Sophie, honoring his mother who had succumbed to cancer when he was in his early twenties. His mother was artistic, opinionated, and loved to read – all qualities Josh and I hoped our daughter would have. When my father died about a year before Sophie was born, Josh suggested we use the name Alysen, honoring his name, Albert. We'd gone back and forth with Sophie Alysen and Alysen Sophie, agreeing to finalize the name after we met the baby. We wanted to be sure the name we gave her felt right. So it was that this newborn became Sophie Alysen.

Although Jamie and her grandparents had said it would be too painful for them to have continued contact with us after the baby were born, at the end of the afternoon, Edna asked whether Josh and I would consider having an ongoing relationship with them. Jamie added that, while she and her grandparents were comfortable with our plans to adopt Sophie, she hoped we'd be willing to make room for them in the baby's life.

Without hesitation, Josh and I welcomed them into our future. Although we'd known them for just weeks, they'd become family. And so, as simple as that, our open adoption began. Based on what I'd read about open adoption, I believed it would be good for all of us. There would be no secrecy. As Sophie grew, she'd have no insecurities about her birth parents, no reason to fantasize about them, and no need to search for them. As adoptive parents, Josh and I would have access to medical information that could only be provided by those who shared a genetic link. And Jamie would have the comfort that comes from knowing her baby was well cared for and loved.

Jamie was eager to check out of the hospital, and the staff planned to release her that afternoon. The hospital's protocol required that newborns remain for at least forty-eight hours and, absent the birth mother, adoptive parents were prohibited from having contact with the baby until discharge. I worried about the wisdom of abandoning a baby in the hospital, devoid of both birth and adoptive family. But the charge nurse dismissed my protests, assuring me the baby would be fine.

Josh and I spent the weekend preparing to bring Sophie home. Bowing to the superstition that buying clothes or toys for a baby before birth is bad luck, we now headed for the local Carter's outlet. With abandon, we tossed pink shirts, purple sleepers, pink socks, purple pants, and a purple sleeper with pink hearts into our cart. The woman at the cash register took one look at our over-flowing cart and smiled. "Let me guess? First-time parents?"

Josh and I talked about the insecurities we had about becoming parents. "How will we know when she's had enough to eat?" I asked.

"I don't know," Josh worried. "Are we supposed to put her in the crib on her back or her stomach?"

"I think it's her side," I guessed. "How many diapers do you think she'll go through in a day?"

"No clue," he answered. "What do we do if she gets the hic-cups?"

Feelings of ineptitude left us in a fit of giggles.

Weeks earlier, Josh and I had begun decorating the Disney-themed nursery. As he hung the larger-than-life paste-up images of Donald Duck, Daisy Duck, Pluto, and Goofy and put the finishing touches on the nursery, I opened containers of baby powder and lotions, inhaling each, my senses overwhelmed.

The weekend seemed to last forever. I read and knitted to pass the hours. Yet every time I looked at the clock, no more than five minutes had passed. Searching for something to occupy him-self, Josh studied the piece of paper Jamie had given us as we were leaving the hospital. There the attending obstetrician had written Sophie's vital statistics.

The paper indicated Sophie's head measured "twelve." There was neither detail nor metric, so Josh had no idea what it meant. Yet somehow, it caused him tremendous concern. He called his cousin, a pediatrician, and asked her what a head measurement of twelve meant. "Twelve what?" she asked. "I don't know," was his worried reply. Inconsolable, Josh spent a sleepless night, mumbling about the number twelve.

I also tossed and turned, but my thoughts revolved not around the size of Sophie's head, but around my mother. I was about to become a mother and my mother wasn't here to guide me. She wasn't here to hold my baby, or to tell me how to care for her. I sobbed into my pillow, wondering whether she had felt so alone when I was born and she'd become a mother for the first time. Like me, her mother had died long before she met and married my father, and so, like me, she'd been compelled to venture into her new role alone.

When Monday morning came, we met Sophie's doctor, who assured us she was perfect. There was no need to worry about the size of her head or anything else. After I dressed Sophie in a pink and white dress and gave her a bottle of formula, Josh carried her out of the hospital with a look that screamed both determination and fear.

Sophie slept for most of our ride home, waking only for a bottle and diaper change.

Exiting the Ohio Turnpike, the car whined. "That's a strange sound. What could it be?" I said. A few miles down the road Josh worried, "Every time I give the car gas, it hesitates." We went a few more miles when the "check engine" light came on, adding to my worry that we'd be stranded on the highway, clueless parents with a newborn baby. The frequency and magnitude of the clunking and clanging grew as we drove. At every red light, the car lumbered.

Josh and I breathed a collective sigh of relief as we turned the corner onto our street. Ten feet from our driveway, the car sputtered and died. Josh carried Sophie into the house and introduced her to Virgil. Our sweet, lovable dog smelled her, licked her face gently, and led us to her crib.

Who cares about the car? I'm a mother at last!

CHAPTER **8**

In the Beginning

September 1992 to June 1993.
Sophie is one month to nine months old.

E ach time Sophie, our little "Munchy," scrunched her face, hiccupped, sneezed, or yawned, Josh and I marveled. We enjoyed spending countless hours gazing at her, touching her little feet, delighted when she grabbed one of our fingers. So smitten were we that we even competed for the privilege of changing her dirty diapers. Watching her sleep, I was intrigued by the faces she made as she sucked contentedly, as though enjoying a tasty delight. Nothing was as intimate or as soothing to me as cuddling her and swaying back and forth in our white Bellini rocking chair.

But within a couple of weeks, I knew I needed to return to my career. I missed my research team. I missed my writing. And I needed to think about more than diapers and formula. The flexibility my boss gave me, Josh's ability to work from home, and my cousin's willingness to babysit for Sophie gave me the confidence to return to work knowing that Sophie would be well cared for.

Because I was as unsure about normal child development as my mother had been, I did what she told me she'd done when I was born – relied on Dr. Spock. Sophie met or exceeded each of the infant milestones described in Spock's sixth edition. Within a few weeks, she followed objects with her eyes. By four months, Sophie babbled to herself. When she gurgled and gave us "raspberries," Josh laughed with delight.

When Sophie was four months old, I took her to the annual meeting of the Gerontological Society of America in Washington, D.C. This year, my professional responsibilities took second place to tending to Sophie. Friends and colleagues took turns wearing out the hotel lobby's carpet with me as I pushed Sophie's stroller. They marveled at her cherubic cheeks and sweet disposition.

Her first tooth broke through at six months, at eight months she crawled several feet toward a toy and babbled "Da-Da," and by eleven months she let go of my hand and walked. The biggest surprise to me was that Sophie never exhibited the stranger anxiety that reduced many other babies to inconsolable sobbing.

We finalized Sophie's adoption shortly before she turned six months old. After waiting our turn at the Montgomery County Courthouse as "Family Number Five," we were summoned before the judge who asked whether we understood that, if he signed the adoption decree, we would be assuming care for Sophie as though she were our biological child. After our wholehearted agreement, the judge banged his gavel on the table and proclaimed, "The well-being of this child will be furthered by this couple's assuming legal responsibility for her. I hereby finalize this adoption." She was all ours.

The legalities of Sophie's adoption addressed, we turned our attention to the religious aspects. Following Jewish custom, we converted her to our faith by momentarily immersing her under water three times in a *mikvah*, a ritual bathing pool, while three rabbis bore witness. The final step of welcoming Sophie into our religion was the naming ceremony, where we presented her to the members of our synagogue community.

As the service concluded, I was holding Sophie and playing patty-cake with her. Ben leaned over and whispered, "How did she get Dad's eyes?"

I looked at him, tears streaming down my face. Months ago, I recognized that Sophie's bright hazel eyes were identical to my father's, but hadn't mentioned this even to Josh. I hoped that, in addition to his eyes, Sophie would inherit my father's lust for life, his sense of persistence, and the value he placed on family.

Baby Einstein

When Sophie was fifteen months old, I went to New Orleans for the annual meeting of the Gerontological Society, leaving Josh to care for her. With a vocabulary of about two hundred words, Sophie had started stringing two and three words together. That evening Josh made a tuna noodle casserole for dinner. Sophie ate heartily and wanted more. Josh, chatting on the phone and making dinner for Virgil and the cats, didn't hear her clamoring for attention.

"Daddy?"

No response.

"Daddy?" She smacked her plastic Mickey Mouse plate on the tray of her highchair.

Still there was no response.

Exasperated, she screamed, "Daddy!"

"Yes, Sophie?"

Sophie held out her plate. "Daddy, may I please have more tuna casserole. It's delicious."

Her first full sentence! Josh, stunned by what he was sure was pure genius, spooned another helping of the casserole onto her plate.

Six months later, as Sophie approached her second birthday, Josh opened the door to her room, greeting her as she awoke.

"Daddy, what's that?" She pointed to the ceiling.

"That's a fan."

"No, not that. The dark things on the ceiling. What are they?"

"They're shadows."

"What makes shadows?"

"The blades from the fan block the light and make shadows."

"What do you mean?"

Josh, who had enamored himself to me on our first date by explaining that there were billions and billions of stars in the universe, now embraced his first opportunity to regale Sophie with his love of science. He made duckies and bunnies with his hands for her and showed her how his hand blocked the light to produce shadows on the wall. He demonstrated how the shadows moved as fast as his hand, and explained that this happened because light was made of tiny particles called photons that move quickly in straight lines.

He drew her attention to the blurry edges of the shadows, explaining that they look blurry because the particles of light, though traveling in straight lines, move in a wave-like motion, much like the waves in the ocean. Josh concluded his treatise by fastening her diaper and saying, "And that, Sophie, is the wave-particle duality theory of light."

A week later, we were strolling in the parking lot of a petting zoo with the kids and their parents from our adoption group. As I chatted with one of the other mothers, Sophie grew wide-eyed.

"Daddy!" she yelled, tugging on Josh's arm.

"Yes, Sophie?"

"Look. The shadows!" Her voice bubbled.

"Yes, Sophie," Josh nodded.

"The people are making shadows!"

"Yes, Sophie."

"The shadows are moving as fast as the people."

"Yes, Sophie."

"And they're making shadows by blocking the light from the sun."

"Yes, Sophie."

"The shadows move as fast as the people."

"Yes, Sophie."

"And that's because light travels very, very fast and goes in straight lines."

"Yes, Sophie."

"And that's what the light from the sun does, Daddy. It goes very, very fast and lets the people make shadows."

The other parents stared at Sophie. They looked at me, dumbfounded. I was as amazed as they were.

Josh beamed with pride.

Aside from the smart generalization about the sun being a source of light, we might have thought Sophie was merely mimicking what Josh had told her. But six months later, it became clear to Josh that Sophie's intelligence was exceptional.

As he was driving Sophie to day care, she squawked, pointing to a colorful display on the car's white leather seat, "Daddy, look. A rainbow!"

"Yes, Sophie."

"Why is there a rainbow in the car, Daddy?"

Josh explained that the rainbow was a spectrum of light caused by the sun passing through the ice on the windshield. "Like light, ice and everything else in the world is made up of tiny particles too small to see. What's cool about light is that light particles have different colors and their colors depend on the size of the wave they move in," he said as he waved his hand back and forth in a slow undulating motion and then a quick flutter. Continuing his Bill Nye the Science Guy lecture, Josh said, "When light passes through ice, it gets bent because some of the colors go through faster than others. Different colors in the light bend by different amounts. This happens because the differences in the wave sizes allow some light particles to bounce into fewer ice particles as the light passes through the ice. The differences in bending make the colors in the light spread apart so you see a rainbow of colors. Do you understand, Sophie?"

Sophie thought for a minute, and then asked, "So the particles of light are bumping into the ice and the bumping slows down the particles of light?"

"Yes, Sophie."

"But light particles are different colors because they move in waves of different sizes?"

"Yes, Sophie."

"Daddy, is that another example of the wave-particle duality of light?"

"Yes, Sophie," Josh said shaking his head in astonishment.

Having barely survived my high school physics class, Josh's enthusiasm was lost on me.

"Rachel, don't you see? You don't need to understand the science. But surely you can recognize that Sophie's ability to remember what I told her last summer about the shadows from the fan and to generalize and connect these same scientific ideas to the light spectrum appearing on the car's upholstery is phenomenal."

Finally, I understood why Josh was so jazzed. We'd hoped to have an intelligent child who would grow into a talented and productive adult. But Sophie's language skills and her extraordinary focus, memory, and grasp of the scientific concepts bedazzled us.

Was I mother of the next Einstein?

CHAPTER 10

Racing Toward Fire

Fall 1994. Sophie is two years old.

I t was one of those lazy autumn afternoons that tricked me into believing that maybe winter wasn't just around the corner. The brilliant azure sky was cloudless. The fallen brown leaves crunched beneath our feet. Two-year-old Sophie wedged her way between Josh and me and clamored, "Swing me!"

"One, two, three, swwwiiinnng," Josh and I sang in unison as we lifted Sophie off the ground.

"Again!" she giggled. "That was fun!" Her flushed face beamed as her pigtails swung in the wind, one of the red ribbons loosening.

And so we accommodated her.

"More!" she shrilled.

"Once more, and that's it," I said.

Wandering through the crowded Amish crafts fair, we stopped to let Sophie watch the demonstrations. We watched a candle maker form elaborate twists and turns of wax around wicks to produce colored candles and then admired a cobbler turning leather into shoes.

"Ice cream!" chirped Sophie.

We strolled toward the ice cream vendor, Sophie's small hand in mine. I smiled at how good it felt and thought about how much I loved her.

In an instant, she dropped my hand and vanished. Straining through the crowd, I gasped as Sophie raced toward a cauldron suspended above an open blazing fire. Josh yelled, "Sophie, stop!" and bolted after her. But Sophie pushed on, her arms reaching out toward the fire.

Panting, Josh dove and grasped at the straps of her red and white striped overalls. He tackled her to the ground from behind, rescuing her only a split second before she would have darted into the blaze.

My heart didn't stop racing even as we reprimanded her, explaining the danger she had put herself in. She looked at me, cocked her head, smiled coyly, and said, "I know, Mommy."

CHAPTER **11**

First Flu Shot

November 1994. Sophie is two years old.

Sophie's pediatrician, Dr. Rome, recommended that she get her first flu shot at two years old. I prepared her for the shot, telling her it would hurt for a minute, and after that she'd be fine. As we walked to the car after day care, I listened to her processing what I'd said.

"So the flu shot is going to hurt for one little minute, right, Mommy?"

"That's right, Sophie. And then you'll be fine."

"And I won't get sick."

"That's right."

As I drove to the doctor's office, Sophie clutched Elmo, her favorite stuffed animal, and chatted with him. Listening to her explain the upcoming shot to Elmo, I smiled, recalling how Brian and I had tried to dodge a shot when we were young. We'd chased each other around the pediatrician's office, neither wanting to be the first recipient of the inevitable shot.

Getting out of the car, Sophie hesitated. "Mommy, can I bring Elmo with me?"

"Sure, Sophie."

Hers was the last appointment of the day. The office staff of five women stood around the appointment desk, talking quietly.

Sophie marched up to the desk holding Elmo and piped, "I'm here for my flu shot. It's going to hurt for a little minute and then it won't hurt anymore."

Trying hard not to laugh at this little urchin, a nurse with white hair said, "You can go and play with the toys. Dr. Rome will be with you in a minute."

Sophie was engrossed in play when the nurse called her name. She retrieved Elmo and marched into the exam room. Bringing up the rear, I watched the office staff watching us.

Within moments, Dr. Rome knocked on the door.

"Dr. Rome, do you have a flu shot for me?" she asked.

"I sure do," he replied with a smile.

Sophie watched Dr. Rome as he prepared the syringe, dabbed a cotton swab with alcohol, and cleaned a spot on her arm. From the outer office the staff watched.

"Are you ready?" he asked.

"Yup," she replied, squeezing Elmo.

Dr. Rome administered the flu shot. Sophie was silent. She didn't squirm or flinch. When he was done, Dr. Rome, a sparkle in his eye, said, "All done. You can say 'ouch' now."

"Ouch!" twittered Sophie, happy to cooperate.

The nursing staff gazed in amazement. Sophie had convinced herself the shot wasn't going to hurt and indeed, to all of us watching, there was no evidence that it had.

"Thank you, Dr. Rome," Sophie said as he put a Sesame Street Band-Aid on her arm.

"You're most welcome, my dear," he chuckled.

I wondered how Sophie could show such silent resolve and what other things she was capable of hiding.

CHAPTER 12

Trash Pick-up

December 1996. Sophie is four years old.

W hen Sophie was three, Josh was recruited to work for Caterpillar and we moved to Peoria, Illinois. Capitalizing on funding from a new grant from the National Institute on Aging focused on the mental health of grandparents raising grandchildren, I convinced Bradley University to establish a center on aging and appoint me as its first director.

I approached my forty-second birthday with more than a little angst. That was the age at which my mother first showed signs of mental illness and I was sure I would follow suit. For months, I awoke each morning wondering whether this would be the day I would be faced with crippling depression or uncontrolled mania. If something made me sad, I was sure the debilitating depression my mother experienced would be just around the corner. If I were happy, I knew the mania that had my mother waking long before the sun rose and spiraling like a whirlwind would be sure to follow. But it did not.

When Sophie was four, we enrolled her in a Pre-K program. Her teacher, Mrs. Taylor, was young and energetic and greeted her class each morning with a dazzling smile. Sophie took an instant liking to her teacher and shared stories with us each evening about whatever Mrs. Taylor had taught the class that day. Although she enjoyed school, Sophie proved to be a challenge for the new teacher. Faced for the first time with classroom rules that required her to sit in her seat, raise her hand, and ask permission to go to the bathroom, Sophie was not easily regimented.

The school encouraged teachers to redirect inappropriate behavior. If that failed, the child was put in time-out for a few minutes and a note was sent home alerting parents to the problem. Multiple stays in the time-out corner resulted in the child being sent to the principal's office. Parents were asked to reinforce the importance of behaving in the classroom.

By late fall, we were receiving notes from Mrs. Taylor two or three times a week. "Sophie keeps jumping out of her seat during the day," read one. "Sophie was singing in class while we were reading this morning," read another. Still another reported, "Sophie tripped a girl this afternoon." Despite this, Mrs. Taylor insisted Sophie was one of her favorite students. She said Sophie's spark and love of learning were infectious.

Josh and I were concerned. Why was Sophie so disruptive? Our household had changed that summer when we adopted Aaron. Sophie had enjoyed our trip to California, where we met Aaron's birth mother, and she reveled in holding her hours-old brother even before Josh or I did. Sophie enjoyed being a big sister to her newborn brother, taking delight in feeding and entertaining him. Hoping to convince Sophie that our love for her wasn't diminished by Aaron's arrival, both Josh and I often spent special time with Sophie and praised her for being a helpful big sister.

As directed by the school, we made it clear to Sophie that her disruptive behavior in the classroom was unacceptable. At Mrs. Taylor's suggestion, we set up a sticker sheet on our refrigerator and rewarded Sophie with a sticker for each day she followed the rules. After a month, there were fewer than ten stickers on the chart.

Although Sophie liked putting the stickers on the chart and receiving the doting praise Josh and I bestowed on her, there was no change in her classroom behavior. She talked out of turn, and her antics often caused her classmates to dissolve into fits of giggles. One afternoon, when Sophie insisted on calling out answers to questions without raising her hand, Mrs. Taylor sent her to the principal's office. The principal told her to sit quietly and think about what she'd done wrong. It didn't take Sophie long to realize she had a whole new audience to play to as she charmed the secretaries and serenaded them with her chatter.

By January, Sophie had created a well-worn path between the classroom and the principal's office. No longer relying on notes for communication between home and school, we now received frequent phone calls from the principal. Sophie exhausted everyone's patience one afternoon when she ripped the pages out of a library book and tossed them in the air.

That afternoon the principal called me. In a calm but stern voice she said, "Mrs. Segal, I'm afraid Sophie doesn't understand her behavior is unacceptable."

I worried she was going to kick Sophie out of school.

"We've talked with her about her behavior and tried everything you and Mrs. Taylor suggested," I said, hearing the frustration in my voice.

"I know you have," the principal encouraged. "We appreciate all you and your husband have done to help. We know you're trying and we know you don't condone her behavior any more than we do."

"So, what do we do now?"

"I've got a consequence I think will turn Sophie around. I want to make sure you're aware of it before we implement it."

"Of course. Her father and I are behind you all the way. What's the plan?"

"I'm going to give her gloves and trash bags and make her empty all of the trashcans in the school. That should convince her we're serious about her following the rules."

"Sounds like a great idea."

When Sophie came home from school I asked about her day.

"It was great, Mommy," she smiled, her eyes twinkling. "The principal gave me gloves and garbage bags and I got to empty all the trash in the whole school."

It didn't sound like the principal's plan had gone well. Later that afternoon, the principal called me. She described how Sophie had put on the gloves and merrily marched from one classroom to the next collecting the trash. By school dismissal, more than a half-dozen children approached her requesting they have the privilege of emptying the trash next.

Shaking my head, I smiled, recalling the antics of Tom Sawyer whitewashing the fence. Sophie had bested the principal, a veteran administrator.

Within minutes my smile vanished. Were Josh and I capable of rearing this child?

CHAPTER 13

Make Believe

Fall 1998. Sophie is six years old.

T he summer Sophie turned six, she broke her arm
swinging from the monkey bars at school, Josh's
grandmother was diagnosed with dementia, and we
moved to Boston. There, Josh secured a position at a financial cor-
poration and I pursued my career at Boston College.

As our frenzied summer gave way to fall, the first of
Sophie's baby teeth came loose. She'd anticipated the loss of her
first tooth, a sign that she was growing up, and longed for the day
that she could put her tooth under her pillow and wait for the
Tooth Fairy to bring her a shiny silver dollar. The tooth wriggled
and flopped. When it got so loose I worried she'd swallow it, Josh
offered to pull it out, but Sophie insisted that, to be official, the
tooth must come out on its own. One evening she bit into an apple
and out popped the tooth.

"Mommy, look," she exclaimed waving her bloody trophy.
"Now I can put my tooth under my pillow and the Tooth Fairy will
come. I wonder what she looks like. I'm going to stay awake all
night so I can see her."

"What a great idea," I agreed, knowing full well the minute
her head hit the pillow she'd be fast asleep.

That night, after Sophie took her bath, brushed her teeth,
and listened to me read a chapter of *Harry Potter and the Sorcerer's
Stone*, she put her tooth in the official tooth-holding treasure pouch

that Mrs. Pike, her first grade teacher, had given her, and placed it under her pillow. I kissed her goodnight and turned out the light.

An hour later, sure that Sophie had fallen into a deep slumber, Josh exchanged a polished silver dollar for the tooth.

The next morning Sophie raced into our bedroom.

"Mommy, Daddy," she squealed. "Look what the Tooth Fairy gave me!"

"Let me see it," Josh said, examining her sparkly prize.

"Daddy, did you ever see such a shiny coin?"

"No, Sophie, I don't think I ever have."

"And Daddy, the best part is I stayed awake all night and I saw the Tooth Fairy."

"Did you really?"

"I did. She was about this big," Sophie said, showing him with her fingers that the Tooth Fairy was about five inches tall. "She flew around my room. She landed on my bed and I almost caught her. Then she flew up to my ceiling fan and sat there watching me. When I turned my head for a little minute, she flew down, took my tooth, and left this coin under my pillow. She was wearing a purple tutu with glitters and sparkles on it. She had a little crown on her head. Her hair was brown, just like mine."

Sophie laughed and said, "Daddy, the Tooth Fairy was so funny. She had one pink sock and one purple sock!"

Josh and I were astounded by the detail of Sophie's report. We were tickled at her cleverness. Was this her imagination? Was it her memory of a lucid dream? Was it an elaboration of a fairy tale we'd read? I didn't know, but she told the story with such fervor that it seemed as if she believed every word. Of course I knew her story couldn't be true. Still, the earnestness and charm with which Sophie told her story had an unexpected effect on me: I wanted to believe her.

Josh and I weren't the only people awed by Sophie's imagination. One afternoon, a cancelled meeting left Josh free to pick Sophie up from school. Arriving at the classroom, he was greeted by Mrs. Pike. "Congratulations on the new baby. Sophie's been telling us all about her. How's your wife doing?"

Surprised, Josh said, "You must have me confused with someone else. I'm Sophie's father."

"Why, yes," she continued. "Sophie's very excited about having a new baby sister. She told us today at circle time about how she helps take care of her sister, how she picks out her clothes every morning, and how she loves to help give her a bath."

"Mrs. Pike," Josh began, "Sophie doesn't have a baby sister. She has a brother, Aaron, who's two years old. But there is no baby sister."

Mrs. Pike was taken aback. "At the beginning of the school year, Sophie told the class her mother was pregnant. Three weeks ago, she told us her baby sister Andrea had arrived. She was very excited and told us about how you took her to the hospital to visit the baby and your wife. She said she was the first person to hold the baby and that she picked out her name."

"Andrea is the name of one of our cats," Josh sighed. "We knew she had a great imagination, but this is over the top."

When Josh and Sophie returned home, he told me about his conversation with Mrs. Pike.

"Sophie, why did you tell Mrs. Pike you have a baby sister?" I asked.

"I wanted to have a new baby sister like my bestest friend, Abby."

"But Sophie, you know you don't have a baby sister, right?" asked Josh.

"Of course not, Daddy. But I want a baby sister. I was pretending." She batted her eyes. She was so damn cute that I wanted to burst out laughing.

"Sophie, Mrs. Pike thinks you really have a baby sister. It's not nice to trick your teacher," I added.

"But Abby got to be the line leader and it wasn't even her turn. I wanted to be the line leader so I told them we had a new baby, too."

"Sophie, you need to apologize to Mrs. Pike tomorrow and tell her you made up the story about a new baby," Josh rebuked.

"Okay, Daddy, I will." Her eyes twinkled as she gave him a hug.

A couple of months later Josh, Sophie, Aaron, and I ran into Mrs. Pike and her family at a McDonald's PlayPlace. I waved to her and went to say hello.

"So," I asked, "have I had any more children in the past few weeks?"

She laughed. "Sophie has an amazing imagination. She had me fooled. I thought about how she kept building on the story. She told us you were pregnant and that she visited you and the baby at the hospital. The details were far more than I'd expect from a six-year-old."

"Sophie loves to make up stories and engage in fantasy play," I explained. "Her imagination is so vivid, it sometimes seems like she's having trouble distinguishing what's real from what's not."

CHAPTER 14

Halloween

October 2000. Sophie is eight years old.

"Mommy, I'm going to be a very scary ghost," four-year-old Aaron announced from the backseat of the car as I drove him home from day care.

"I'm sure you will," I answered, preoccupied by thoughts of the two phone calls I'd received that afternoon. The first call brought news that my five-year study of end-of-life decision making by patients with end-stage renal failure and their spouses would be funded. This was cause for celebration. The second, from Sophie's third grade teacher, Mrs. Linick, was cause for alarm.

"I'm going to scare all the little kids," Aaron chortled with confidence. "I might even scare the grown-ups."

I always knew trouble was brewing when a teacher called me in the middle of the afternoon. "Mrs. Segal," she had said, "this is Mrs. Linick, Sophie's teacher. She's fine, but I need to tell you about a little problem we've been having." I had steeled myself as I waited for details about The Little Problem.

"Sophie hasn't turned in math homework for the past five days. Each day she's said she completed it, but she forgot it at home. She's falling behind in her work and I'm worried about her ability to keep up with the class."

Heat crept into my cheeks as I listened. As a child, I'd always done my homework; no teacher ever had cause to have such a conversation with my mother. If she had, I expect my mother's disappointment in me would have made me change my behavior instantly. Just the previous evening, I had told Sophie that it was surprising she hadn't had much math homework lately. She'd looked me in the eyes and explained that, because she was one of the few kids in her class who knew the multiplication tables, she didn't have homework. Then, she'd gone to her room to practice applying the makeup she intended to wear as part of her Halloween costume.

I told Mrs. Linick that Sophie hadn't done the homework. Together, we figured out Sophie had been playing us against one another, telling me she had no homework while telling the teacher she'd done the work but forgot to bring it to school. I assured Mrs. Linick that Sophie would complete the work that evening, and promised that Josh and I would discipline Sophie for lying. Now I pondered the appropriate consequence. How would my mother have handled this? How had she always managed to make parenting look so easy?

"Mommy, can I put my ghost costume on when we get home?" Aaron's question transported me back to the present.

"You sure can. Do you remember what you're going to say when someone comes to the door?"

"Can I please have some candy?" he answered proudly.

"How about trick or treat?" I reminded him.

"Oh yeah. Trick or treat – smell my stinky feet!" he piped, parroting the phrase he'd heard Sophie sing countless times over the past several days. He worshipped his big sister.

As I pulled into the driveway, I steeled myself for the confrontation I was about to have with Sophie. She met us at the door, dressed in her witch costume, her makeup perfectly applied.

"Aaron, go put your costume on," I said as he dashed into the house. "Sophie, you and I need to talk."

"What's wrong, Mom?" she asked innocently.

"Mrs. Linick called me this afternoon. She told me you haven't done your math homework for a week. On top of that, you told me last night you didn't have any math homework. What's going on?"

"I didn't understand the homework, so I didn't do it."

"Sophie, you know better. If you don't understand something, what are you supposed to do?"

"Ask the teacher?"

"Right, and you can also ask Dad or me. You've lied to your teacher, you've lied to me, and you haven't done your math homework for a week."

"I'm sorry, Mom."

"Sorry doesn't cut it. Take off that costume right now and finish those math assignments. No trick-or-treating until it's done."

"But, Mom, it's almost time to go," she whined. "I don't have time to do my homework now."

"Sophie, no trick-or-treating until that math homework is done and Dad or I have checked it."

"Why are you always so mean to me?" she asked stomping up the stairs.

For the next hour, Sophie sat on her bed pouting, her costume wrinkled, her makeup smearing. The more she refused to cooperate with me, the more frustrated I got. By the time Josh came home, Sophie hadn't even taken her math book out of her backpack.

I told Josh about my conversations with Mrs. Linick and with Sophie. He, too, was concerned about Sophie's deception and surprised that she'd shown neither shame nor remorse at getting caught in the lie. Her failure to make any attempt to rectify the situation by doing the homework baffled us. We agreed these behaviors were unacceptable and that the consequence we imposed needed to be meaningful.

"No trick-or-treating tonight," Josh declared.

"Don't you think that's excessive?" I questioned, knowing Sophie had been counting the days to Halloween for months.

"No. She needs to understand that lying is not acceptable."

"You're right. In fact, instead of going trick-or-treating, she can stand at the door and give out the candy."

When we told Sophie she couldn't go trick-or-treating, she said, "That's okay. I didn't want to go anyway."

Her failure to beg us to reconsider the punishment, to cry, or to show any outward sign of anger or regret left me dumbfounded. How had she mustered the resolve to hide her disappointment?

I thought back to the Halloween when I was eight. It was 1962, long before Detroit's Devil's Night became an orgy of arson and Halloween candy was x-rayed for razor blades. That year, my mother transformed me from a pudgy girl into an exotic gypsy. She whipped up my costume using tan material with green, red, and black swirly designs and gold foil pieces hanging from delicate threads that she'd bought at a garage sale and stored in the coffin-sized red sewing box in the basement. She carefully applied foundation and pink rouge to my cheeks, blue eye shadow to my eyelids, and ruby red lipstick to my lips. As my pirate brothers and I ran from house to house that damp evening, swinging our orange bags, yelling "trick or treat" and collecting candy, Mom walked a few paces behind us to ensure our safety. Exhausted, our bags brimming with candy, we returned home to begin the annual candy trade before storing our bags of candy in the back closet. Butterfingers were my favorite. I begged Ben and Brian to give me theirs. Mom let us have one or two pieces of candy each evening before bed. My brothers snuck into the closet daily, so their candy disappeared in a few weeks. I still had candy in March.

Given my fond childhood memoires of Halloween, I was certain that, had my parents caught me in a lie and said I couldn't go trick-or-treating, I would have cried, been contrite, and done my homework. But Sophie was strangely unmoved. If this were an act she was putting on for Josh and me, she deserved a standing ovation. It left me feeling impotent, incapable of disciplining her, a huge failure as a mother.

Josh took Aaron trick-or-treating. Sophie stood at the front door all evening, by all appearances content to dole out candy. Toward the end of the evening, one of the neighborhood fathers greeted Sophie, "What are you doing here? Why aren't you out trick-or-treating?" Without missing a beat, she said, "Oh, this is so much more fun. I love giving out the candy."

We'd landed in foreign territory. By the age of eight, Sophie didn't seem to care about any of the natural consequences we imposed.

When she did complete the missed math assignments, it was clear that she understood the work. Even the explanation she had provided for not doing her homework had been a lie.

This episode was part of a growing pattern in which Sophie would remain unfazed by the normal consequences we devised in hopes of teaching her right from wrong. My frustration mounted.

What would it take to reach her? How could she not have been disappointed? How could she hide her feelings so well?

Was this evidence of a resilient personality or a disturbed one? I tried to convince myself it was the former, but my suspicions that it was the latter mounted.

CHAPTER 15

"Please Put On Your Shoes"

November 2001. Sophie is nine years old.

Sophie's lies and deceit grew. As frustrating as they were, nothing compared with the obstinate and defiant attitude Sophie developed. Even the most innocuous requests Josh or I made of her were refused. House rules were ignored. She began arguing when she woke up and didn't stop until she was asleep.

We tried a host of strategies to cope with Sophie's behavior. We tried negotiating, choosing our battles, threatening, and screaming. We tried ignoring her. We tried giving her extra attention. We put her in time-out. We offered rewards for good behavior. We pointed out the natural consequences of her behavior. We even tried the time-honored strategy of making her write her crimes one hundred times. When we tasked Sophie with writing "I will not be rude to my father" or "I will not hit my brother," rather than completing the task, she would sit at the kitchen table for hours humming, tapping her foot, or daydreaming. Each attempt to correct her inappropriate behavior brought a more outrageous response from her. Tempers flared, voices were raised, and fights ensued as Josh and I tried one ineffective consequence after the next. Nothing worked.

The inability to parent Sophie exhausted me. All I could think about were my mother's laments about not being a good mother. In reality, she'd contended with all the challenges my brothers and I sent her way very competently. Yet here I was, living in a war zone where my nine-year-old had seized control of the whole family. I felt totally incompetent.

Hoping to understand and more effectively manage Sophie's behavior, I read an endless parade of parenting books. Defiance, I learned, is a normal part of child development, a sign that the child is testing rules and learning limits. Yet I remained unconvinced that our daily power struggles could be anything close to normal.

It was amidst this pandemonium that we joined my brothers and their families in Phoenix for Thanksgiving. Sophie was delighted to see her cousins, Sara and Allen, and enjoyed playing in the hotel pool, shopping, and sightseeing with them.

Our weekend was to conclude at the Cheesecake Factory with a celebration of Allen's seventh birthday. At five o'clock, I said, "Sophie, it's time to get ready for Allen's birthday dinner. Please put your shoes on."

No response.

"Sophie," I tried again. "Time to put your shoes on."

"I don't want to wear shoes," she replied.

"Sophie, your mother told you to put your shoes on. Let's go," said Josh.

"Why do I have to wear shoes?" Sophie whined.

"Sophie, do you want to have dinner with your cousins?" I asked.

"Yes," she said.

"Then put your shoes on."

"I don't want to," she challenged.

Josh and I looked at each other, dumbstruck. The last thing we needed was one of Sophie's I-Can-Be-More-Obstinate-Than-A-Lazy-Mule-On-A-Hot-Summer-Afternoon routines. We agreed that a logical consequence of refusing to heed our request to put her shoes on – and one likely to capture her attention – was to present her with the prospect of being excluded from the dinner.

"Sophie, you have to the count of three to put your shoes on. If you don't, you can stay in the hotel room with Dad while Aaron and I go to Allen's birthday dinner." I delivered this ultimatum with all the calm I could muster.

She made no movement to put on her shoes.

"One," I counted and then paused. "Two," I said with deliberation, hoping she'd take me seriously. But she sat on the bed, staring at me. "I mean it, Sophie." I heard the pleading in my voice as I worried about how I would explain to my brothers and their families why she wasn't at Allen's party. I didn't want Josh to be stuck in the hotel room for the night. "Three. Okay, that's it, Sophie. You lose. No dinner with your cousins," I said with as much control as I could muster. "Aaron, let's go."

"Mom, why wouldn't Sophie put her shoes on?" Aaron asked as we crossed the restaurant's parking lot.

"I wish I knew, Aaron," I sighed. Sophie and Aaron had a close sibling bond. Much like the relationship I had with my brothers when we were young, Sophie and Aaron played together, tussled, and competed for Josh's and my attention.

Learning that Sophie wouldn't be at his birthday dinner, Allen cried. Sara joined in. Despite my best attempts to explain, they didn't understand. Their distress made my sister-in-law Rebecca furious.

"How can you do that to the kids?" she seethed. "They were looking forward to playing with Sophie on our last night together. You've ruined Allen's birthday. There are times and places for disciplining your kids and this isn't one of them."

My face burned. I wished I could tell Rebecca what Josh and I had been dealing with for the past several months. I wanted to tell her how impossible it had become to discipline Sophie. Sophie's behaviors weren't normal, but I feared that telling Rebecca – telling anyone – would confirm the ugly reality that Sophie was not a normal child. I didn't want anyone to think ill of Sophie. So, I took the heat. I was a bad mother in Rebecca's eyes. I didn't know when or how to discipline my child. Rebecca never would have thought that if I had told her the truth. But I could not.

This secret, meant to protect Sophie, cost me dearly. It was close to a year before Rebecca forgave me.

What were we dealing with? How could one small child cause so much pain?

CHAPTER 16

Camping

July 2002. Sophie is nearly ten years old.

T he chaos characterizing Sophie's thinking was evident for as long as I can remember. Whether it was cleaning the playroom as a toddler or organizing her backpack as a young child, Sophie always did things differently than I expected. Her room was forever in a state of utter clutter – the nightstand piled high with books, socks, and pencils and draped with yesterday's dirty clothing. Heaps of random belongings, including her toothbrush, hairclips, and jewelry tangled together, were often strewn on the floor.

From the time Sophie was in first grade, I worked hard to find ways to help her keep her backpack and school papers organized. When I expressed concern to the teachers about Sophie's disorganization, they always reassured me that Sophie was young and would grow out of it. We tried color-coding notebooks and files. We tried expanding accordion files. We tried putting everything in a single binder. We tried putting everything in separate binders. I hoped each new idea would be the magic elixir, yet she remained frighteningly disorganized. Homework, even if completed, was often lost before she could turn it in.

Although I was aware that Sophie's organizational abilities were flawed, I didn't recognize the severity of her difficulties until the summer she turned ten, when she insisted she was old enough to go to sleep-away camp and we obliged her.

Her excitement mounted as the day came for her to leave for the girls-only camp nestled in the Berkshire Mountains. She would be there for four weeks and looked forward to learning horsemanship and tennis skills. Together, Sophie and I packed her footlocker, putting her clothes, bedding, and toiletries in places where she would find them.

We loaded the car and drove two and a half hours to the camp. Excited, Sophie chattered non-stop. After meeting her counselors and helping her make her bed, we bid her adieu. Sophie was anxious for us to leave so she could make friends with the girls in her bunk. The few letters Sophie wrote to us that summer made it clear she was having fun and enjoying her bunkmates. Letters from her counselors corroborated that a playful camaraderie existed among the girls in the bunk.

The camp's tradition was to host a Mom's Weekend at the end of the third week, during which mothers were invited to spend the weekend at camp with their daughters. I approached Mom's Weekend with more than a little trepidation. While I looked forward to spending time with Sophie, I didn't look forward to camping. Having grown up in the concrete jungle of Brooklyn, camping was as foreign to my mother as a vacation on the moon. As a child, memories of more than three hundred mosquito bites, a rodent-infested cabin, and cold showers marked my sole camping experience.

But my daughter wanted me to camp with her and I was bound and determined not to disappoint. My friend Carla lent me her tent and air mattress and taught me how each worked. Under her tutelage, it looked simple, and I was convinced that, despite my limited engineering talents, I could master this.

However, when I took the tent home and tried to erect it, that miserable contraption was far less cooperative than it had been under Carla's direction. Josh snickered at me. Aaron, who had mastered Lego, K'nex, and Transformers by the time he was four, looked at the apparatus, rolled his eyes, and scoffed, "Mom, it's not that hard. Even you can do it." With that, my just-turned-six-year-old picked up the stakes I'd been staring at, and slipped them into place in the loops attached to the tent's shell. Within minutes, the tent was standing.

Aaron and I practiced setting up the tent and taking it down until I convinced myself I could do it.

Driving to camp, I thought about Sophie. Three weeks was longer than I'd ever been away from her, and I couldn't wait to hear about her adventures. My friends had told me about dramatic growth spurts in maturity they'd witnessed in their daughters after a few short weeks at camp. How had Sophie changed? Had she become more organized? Had she figured out how to take responsibility for herself and her belongings? I couldn't wait to find out.

As I got closer to the camp, the skies darkened. The windshield wipers tapped back and forth in time to the rhythm of the tunes playing on the radio. This wasn't a promising start to my camping weekend. I'd steeled myself for denial of the basic creature comforts, but the idea of sleeping in a cold tent with a damp floor and rain dripping in at the seams was more than I'd bargained for.

When I arrived, dozens of tents had already been set up and campers were reuniting with their mothers. For the moment, at least, the rain had stopped. Maybe it won't rain, maybe I'll be able to get the tent to stand, and maybe this won't be as bad as I thought.

I parked the car and looked around. Suddenly, there was Sophie. She made a beeline for me, threw her arms around me, and shrieked, "Oh, Mom, I'm so glad you're here." After hugging and kissing, she helped me carry the camping equipment to a spot she'd selected on the lawn near her bunkmates and their mothers. She looked taller and lankier than when we dropped her at camp. Taking a closer look, I saw that Sophie was filthy. The gritty dirt encrusted on her face and knees surprised me. I looked at her feet. They were black. Her tussled hair hadn't been brushed for days. Not wanting to hurt her feelings, I didn't comment on her lack of hygiene, but I wondered whether the counselors had noticed and tried to do anything about it.

We inflated the air mattress and started setting up the tent. As I pulled the stakes out of their sheath, it began to drizzle, and by the time all the stakes were in position, it was pouring. Our camping neighbors headed for the shelter of their tents while Sophie and I hurried to finish setting up ours.

Twenty minutes later, we were still trying to raise the tent. Despite all the coaching Carla and Aaron had given me, I had no idea what I was doing. Sophie tried to help, but we made little progress. Seeing our struggle, two of the mothers came to our rescue, and within a few minutes our tent was standing. Sophie and I darted inside, laughing.

When the rain ended, the regular afternoon activities began. I tagged along with Sophie, first to tennis and then to horseback riding. She was proud of the progress she had made riding horses.

Walking back to her bunk, she began scratching her arms furiously. I watched as angry red blotches appeared on her face and arms. I winced as her eyes reddened.

"Are your eyes itching?" I asked.

"Yeah, that happens every time after I ride horses. It usually goes away in a couple of hours."

"I think you may be allergic to the horses. Let's stop at the infirmary and talk to the nurse."

Hearing the story, the nurse confirmed Sophie's worst fears: most likely, she was allergic to the horses. The nurse advised Sophie to take a soapy shower in order to remove the horse toxins from her body. While I was saddened to see Sophie's disappointment when she realized horseback riding would no longer be part of her camp activities, I was delighted to have a medical reason to clean her up.

Back at her bunk, I waited outside while Sophie collected her toiletries, towel, and a clean change of clothes. When she hadn't emerged after fifteen minutes, I went in search of her. I found her rummaging through her belongings.

"What are you doing?" I asked.

"Looking for my soap," she answered with annoyance.

"When did you see it last?"

"I don't remember," she answered, a growing agitation to her voice.

"Isn't it in your toiletries bucket?"

"Mom, I don't know where that is either." The frustration in her voice mounted.

She dumped her footlocker upside down and screamed, "Why can't I ever find my dumb old things?"

I hugged her. "Sophie, calm down. It's not easy being on your own for the first time. You'll figure this out."

Sobbing, she said, "I haven't seen my soap and toothbrush for days. One day I went to the shower and forgot to take my towel. Another day I forgot to take a clean change of clothes. Another day, I forgot my shampoo. I don't think there was even one day when I brought everything I needed with me to the shower."

I cleaned Sophie up as best I could with the few toiletries we could find. Then we joined the rest of the campers and their mothers for dinner. We sang one endless camp song after the next, and the girls put on a talent show for the mothers. Among the brief announcements prior to the performance of the final skit was a request that no opened foods be left in the tents, as a bear had been sighted on the campground that week.

"Bear?" I asked, looking at Sophie and the other girls.

The girls giggled. "Yeah, Mom. Last week when Anna and I were coming back from arts and crafts, we saw a mama bear and her baby. They were walking down the path. They were so cute. We stopped and watched them," Sophie explained with glee.

Great, so not only am I sleeping in a tent, but it's drizzly and damp, and I get to share the campground with a family of bears. On top of it all, my daughter can't figure out how to take a shower and she hasn't brushed her teeth in weeks.

Seeing the concerned look on my face, Sophie assured me, "Don't worry, Mom. They won't hurt you."

Exhausted and somewhat giddy, we stumbled toward our tents, yodeling yet one more refrain of *That's What Hippos Do*.

Nestling in for the night, Sophie and I chattered about how much we'd missed one another and what an enjoyable evening it had been. As she snuggled into her sleeping bag and relaxed, she initiated the game we'd played since she was two years old.

"Hey, Mom?"

"Love you," we said simultaneously. The game was seeing who could utter this response first.

Within minutes, the rhythmic cadence of her breathing let me know she'd fallen asleep. I, on the other hand, tossed and turned for what seemed like an eternity. When I closed my eyes, I imagined dozens of worms wriggling in the wet ground under our tent. A mosquito buzzed in my ear. The tent smelled like rotting apples. I counted sheep, tried to convince myself I was cuddled in my comfy bed in my air-conditioned house, and then I counted more sheep.

I thought about all I'd learned that afternoon. The disorganization that had been evident for years compromised more than Sophie's room and her backpack; it pervaded every aspect of her life. I wracked my brain, trying to identify strategies to help her. How ironic that organization, one of my mother's and my strengths, should be so difficult for Sophie. I would work hard. I would find a way to help her.

The next morning, I went to a drugstore and bought soap, shampoo, a toothbrush, and toothpaste. Though I hadn't yet devised my grand plan for addressing Sophie's organizational issues, cleaning her up would be my first course of action.

That afternoon, Sophie screeched with delight as she scrubbed herself clean with soap and hot water. I helped her wash her hair, made difficult by countless tangles. After she brushed her teeth, she marveled, "Wow, my teeth feel great!"

Strolling toward the dining hall, Sophie gushed, "I'm all tingly and clean, Mommy."

We ran into a girl who looked to be a year or so younger than Sophie. "Hi, Sammi," Sophie called.

"Hi, Sophie," she responded.

"Is she a friend of yours?" I asked as Sammi skipped toward her cabin.

"No, not really. One day I was at the camp store buying a Popsicle and she was there. When she found out she didn't have any money left in her camp account, she started crying. I had money so I bought her a Popsicle."

"Sophie, that was so sweet of you," I praised.

"Yeah, I didn't want to see her so sad."

I admired Sophie's kindness.

The rest of our weekend together was bittersweet. I enjoyed our time together, but was saddened knowing that, by the time Josh and I came to pick Sophie up from camp the following weekend, she would probably have lost her new soap and toothbrush and returned to the state of grunginess in which I'd found her.

CHAPTER **17**

An Unexplained Welt

August 2003. Sophie is nearly eleven years old.

S
ophie went back to the sleep-away camp in the Berk-
shires at the beginning of the next summer and,
although she was no more organized, she enjoyed her
stay. She spent the last four weeks of the summer at the Jewish day
camp she'd attended in years past. Each morning, either Josh or I
drove Sophie and Aaron to the Shaw Supermarket's parking lot,
minutes from our home, where a camp bus picked them up. From
there, they were off for a day of activities.

One afternoon, as Sophie got off the bus, a sizable red welt
on her right cheek caught my attention. While helping her and
Aaron load their backpacks, towels, and art projects into the trunk
of my car, I asked how she'd gotten the bruise. She said, "Oh, I
don't know. It's nothing."

When Josh came home from work, he too noticed the blotch
on Sophie's face. "What happened to her?" he asked me.

"No clue. She told me it was nothing."

Sitting down for dinner, Josh questioned Sophie, "What
happened to your face?"

"What do you mean?" she asked innocently.

"You have a big red mark on your check. Does it hurt?"

"No, not really."

"How'd you get it?"

"I don't remember."

"Did you play any sports today?"

"Wiffle ball," she answered. "I was the catcher."

"Did you get hit by the ball?"

"Yeah, maybe."

"I like Wiffle ball," Aaron chimed. "I played it yesterday and my team won."

"I do too, Aaron. It's a lot of fun," Josh concurred. "I'm glad your team won and I'll bet you helped a lot."

After dinner, Josh examined Sophie's cheek. He shook his head, glanced over to me, and then turned back to Sophie.

"So you got hit by a Wiffle ball, Sophie?"

"I guess I must have, Daddy."

"When you were catching, is that right?"

"Yes, I think so."

Something was bothering Josh. "When they throw a pitch to the batter, Sophie, is it tossed underhanded or do they throw it real hard and fast like Pedro Martinez does when the Red Sox play the Yankees?"

"It's underhand, Daddy."

"It seems pretty unlikely a Wiffle ball tossed underhanded could leave such a welt on your face."

Sophie was silent. Josh waited for an explanation.

"Sophie, how about telling me what really happened?" I knew the tone in Josh's voice. He was frustrated, on the way to angry.

Sophie said nothing. Josh tried a softer approach.

"Sophie, I'm not angry with you. I don't like to see you get hurt. I'm concerned because I love you. That's a pretty painful looking mark. You must remember how it got there. Why won't you tell me?"

"I told you. I was playing Wiffle ball," she insisted, tears welling in her eyes.

Where was Josh going with this? Why was he so suspicious? The camp had come highly recommended by friends. It was the one all the Jewish kids in the neighborhood had gone to for years. We knew the director and had met many of the counselors. There wasn't a safer place on Earth.

"Josh, stop," I pleaded. "You're upsetting her. Why can't you believe her and drop it? She was playing Wiffle ball. Kids sometimes get cuts and bruises at camp. It happens. Why all the questions?"

"The story she's telling doesn't make sense, Rachel. She got hurt and I want to know what happened." Turning back to Sophie, Josh asked, "So did this really happen when you were playing Wiffle ball?"

Sophie was silent. She looked at me, her eyes begging me to make him stop.

But Josh continued. "Come on, Sophie. There's no way this welt was caused by a Wiffle ball."

"Why do you always have to make such a federal case out of everything? Leave her alone," I said.

When the first tear rolled down Sophie's cheek, Josh melted. Not wanting to upset her further and trying to placate me, the tenor of his questions softened.

"You said you were playing catcher? Is it possible that the batter fouled the ball back into your face? Is that what happened?"

"Yes, Daddy," Sophie sighed with relief. "That's what happened."

Josh gave her a hug. "I'm glad you're okay," he said. "You shouldn't ever be afraid to tell me about anything that happens to you, even if it's something bad. You're my baby girl and I'll always love you."

"I love you too, Daddy."

Years later I would be haunted by my insistence that Josh let Sophie have her way.

CHAPTER 18

The Initial Diagnosis

Summer 2003. Sophie is eleven years old.

F ifth grade was a difficult year for Sophie. It often took her hours to complete homework the teacher said should take no more than twenty minutes, making me angry and Sophie frustrated. Frequently, she didn't do her homework and sometimes, even when she did it, she didn't turn it in. In response to the flurry of notes I received from her teacher informing me that Sophie was not working up to her potential, I struggled to keep her on track.

That spring, the students worked on developing their writing skills by crafting autobiographies. Each week brought a new assignment, as Sophie's teacher Ms. Wyser had the class draft several paragraphs, each describing a different time in their lives. These smaller projects were threaded together to develop the autobiography.

Despite the structured process and the teacher's clear expectations, Sophie fell behind. She turned in only two of the ten assignments on time; the others were late or not done. The Friday before the final assignment was due, Ms. Wyser sent reminder notes home. When I asked Sophie about her progress on the project, she assured me she'd completed the work in school and already turned it in.

When Ms. Wyser asked for the autobiographies, Sophie told her she'd finished the work, but had forgotten it at home. The next day when Ms. Wyser asked for the project, Sophie said she'd brought it to school, but couldn't find it. Sophie and Ms. Wyser searched through her backpack, locker, and desk. After school, they scoured the classroom yet again, but the work was nowhere to be found. Sophie insisted she'd done the work, and mustered tears that convinced both Ms. Wyser and me that she was telling the truth. But the work was never found.

Several weeks into the summer, Sophie and I were driving to a dentist appointment when she said, "Mom, I have something important to tell you."

"Yes, Sophie."

"Remember that autobiography?"

I nodded.

"I started mine, and then I lost parts of it. I didn't want to tell you or Ms. Wyser because I'd get into trouble, and I didn't want to turn in part of it because I'd get a bad grade, so I tossed it behind a bookcase in the classroom."

A dozen grey hairs popped out of my scalp. The ease with which Sophie told the initial lie and then bamboozled both her teacher and me by embellishing it with an Oscar-winning teary-eyed performance astounded me. I took a deep breath. This behavior wasn't normal. Something was very wrong with her. I needed to find out what it was and fix it.

"Sophie," I said in the calmest voice I could muster, "it seems to me you're having trouble organizing and keeping track of things. How about if, the next time we see Dr. Gilloway, we mention it to her and see what she thinks?"

"Yeah, Mom," she sighed. "That's a good idea."

Her willingness to seek help from her pediatrician surprised me.

Before we even had a chance to meet with Dr. Gilloway, I started trying to figure out what was wrong. As a member of Boston College's Education faculty, I had easy access to experts knowledgeable about children and their learning problems. Each person with whom I consulted came to the same conclusion – Sophie probably had Attention Deficit/Hyperactivity Disorder, better known as ADHD.

One evening, I found a checklist of behaviors describing ADHD on the NIMH website.[1] Intrigued, I read aloud to Josh. It began with descriptions of the inability to stay focused and pay attention:

a. Easily distracted, misses details, forgets things, and frequently switches from one activity to another

b. Has difficulty focusing on one thing

c. Becomes bored with a task after only a few minutes, unless they are doing something enjoyable

d. Has difficulty focusing attention on organizing and completing a task or learning something new

e. Has trouble completing or turning in homework assignments, often losing things (e.g., pencils, toys, assignments) needed to complete tasks or activities

f. Doesn't seem to listen when spoken to

g. Daydreams, becomes easily confused

h. Has difficulty processing information as quickly and accurately as others

i. Struggles to follow instructions

"Yes, yes, yes, that's her," we said in unison. Continuing, we read about evidence for hyperactivity:

a. Fidgets and squirms in their seats

b. Talks nonstop

c. Dashes around, touching or playing with anything and everything in sight

d. Has trouble sitting still during dinner, school, and story time

e. Constantly in motion

f. Has difficulty doing quiet tasks or activities

"Amazing," I said, expecting Sophie's picture to appear on screen. We continued reading about symptoms of impulsivity:

a. Very impatient

b. Blurts out inappropriate comments, shows emotions without restraint, and acts without regard for consequences

c. Has difficulty waiting for things they want or waiting their turns in games

d. Often interrupts conversations or others' activities

It was as though someone had studied Sophie and built a diagnosis around her. The only missing pieces were the lying and the stubbornness, evident almost from the time she could talk. Yet, the diagnosis explained so much: her inability to sit through a movie without creating a running commentary; difficulty paying attention in school; constant motion; tendency to take four hours to do homework her teachers said should take fifteen minutes; and inability to organize.

I was relieved to learn that the behaviors that drove me wild weren't unique, that they were part of a diagnosable problem for which treatments existed. It didn't take long, however, until guilt overwhelmed me. Had I understood that Sophie's behaviors were part of a disability, I would have been more sympathetic, patient, and tolerant.

As I read about ADHD, I learned that scientific evidence suggests that genes played a major role. Wondering about Sophie's genetic background, I called her birth mother, Jamie.

Over the years, our open adoption had expanded our family in ways that enriched us all. Jamie and her grandparents sent holiday and birthday presents to both Sophie and Aaron, and we sent letters and photos updating them on developmental milestones. We had visited them at key family turning points – shortly after Aaron was born and just before Jamie's grandfather and father died. When I realized that Jamie's grandmother would be alone for the first Christmas after her husband died, I spearheaded an impromptu surprise visit to her. Learning of our plans, Jamie added to the festivities by joining us.

In response to my queries, Jamie said that Sophie's birth father, Gary, was easily distracted, had trouble concentrating, and was fidgety, yet to her knowledge he hadn't been diagnosed with ADHD. Although I didn't realize it then, years later I came to understand that, for most people, getting an accurate mental health diagnosis requires significant financial resources and perseverance.

When we brought our observations of Sophie's behavior to Dr. Gilloway, she listened. Although she agreed the symptoms I described were consistent with ADHD, she gave me the Connors Rating Scale, a set of questions about specific behaviors, and asked me to complete it. She also gave me a version of the scale for Sophie to complete and yet another version for a teacher to complete.

Reviewing the information a few weeks later, Dr. Gilloway agreed that Sophie probably had ADHD. She told us about a host of treatments, including medication, talk therapy, and education. Though Dr. Gilloway was quick to acknowledge that many parents hesitate to medicate their children for ADHD symptoms, she assured us that medications were the most effective treatment. She explained that the most common medications used to treat ADHD were stimulants such as Ritalin, Adderall, Concerta, Dexadrine, and Vyvanse. In response to my questions about the wisdom of giving a stimulant to a hyperactive child, she said these medications have a calming effect on children with ADHD. Baffled, I wondered how Sophie's brain was wired.

Dr. Gilloway said that, while these stimulants were often effective, she believed that Strattera, a non-stimulant medication recently approved by the Food & Drug Administration, might be even more beneficial. A selective norepinephrine reuptake inhibitor, Strattera increases levels of norepinephrine, a natural substance in the brain that regulates behavior. Dr. Gilloway was resolute in her belief that this medication would be effective for increasing Sophie's ability to pay attention and stay organized while reducing her impulsiveness and hyperactivity.

Josh and I agreed that medication should be an important part of the treatment plan. At the same time, we worried about the long-term effects of Strattera, especially since it was a newly approved medicine. After reading some of the scientific literature about Strattera and consulting with my brother Ben and sister-in-law Rebecca, both physicians, we concluded that the benefits of Strattera far outweighed the risks. It was worth a try.

Reading about ADHD, I learned the importance of using a system of rewards and consequences to help manage Sophie's behavior. Responses on our part needed to be immediate and positive for behaviors we wanted to encourage, while behaviors we hoped to discourage should be ignored or redirected. Time-outs would be effective when Sophie's behavior escalated out of control. Josh and I identified pleasurable activities to share with Sophie, and we rewarded her when she did well. As we implemented these new strategies, we consulted with Dr. Gilloway.

Sophie started taking Strattera a couple of weeks before sixth grade began, allowing it to be as effective as possible before the challenges of the school year started and giving us the chance to monitor her reaction to it.

Strattera proved to be nothing short of miraculous. Sophie said it helped her pay attention. She completed homework quickly. Her grades improved, and she took greater responsibility for organizing her schoolwork. Not only did Sophie's teachers find her more attentive in class, even her classmates commented about how much calmer Sophie had become. We were convinced we had identified the problem and solved it.

However, although Strattera calmed Sophie down and enabled her to focus on her schoolwork, Josh and I noticed several subtle, undesirable changes in her behavior. Sophie became more combative and sullen, and less jovial. When we brought these behaviors to Dr. Gilloway's attention, she assured us they were not known side effects of Strattera. With a smile, she suggested they probably were indicative of surging pre-adolescent hormones. Of course, I thought, amazed by how little I, as a gerontologist, knew about child development.

Equally surprising to me was Sophie's sudden fear of being alone. If I sent her up to her room to retrieve a book or to the basement for a board game, she dawdled or begged Aaron to accompany her. If he resisted, she tempted our dog Deirdre with the promise of a treat.

At bedtime, Sophie begged Josh or me to stay in her room with her until she fell asleep. It became commonplace for her to come looking for me in the middle of the night. Although Josh and I were befuddled by her behavior, we attributed it to a phase Sophie was going through, agreed to keep her company, and conceded to her numerous requests for a second dog, Dunkin, whose most charming trait was that he faithfully followed her everywhere.

CHAPTER 19

A Star is Born?

Fall 2003 to Spring 2004. Sophie is eleven years old.

That summer, Sophie found a best friend. For years, I'd hoped she would experience the close connection I first had at age four when I met Thea. The secrets that made us giggle, the knowing looks that only we understood, and the late-night stories we told one another taught me I wasn't alone in the world.

In all the years I knew her, my mother never had a best friend. She never spoke of it. Had she ever known the joy and grounding of being connected with a girlfriend?

When Sophie was young, I arranged play dates with girls I thought she might like. When she got older, I encouraged her to invite friends to come to our home to play. I tried to impress upon her the importance of having close friends and of being a good friend. Yet, as with so many other issues, Sophie either didn't believe me or didn't value the life lessons I had to offer.

An end-of-the-year homework assignment brought Sophie and Kate together. They were inseparable for months. They spent hours on the phone, visited one another's homes, shared secrets, and had sleepovers.

One fall afternoon, Sophie came home from school and said, "Mom, Kate's going to try out for *The Miracle Worker*. Can I do it too?"

"Sure. As long as you get your homework done first."

Josh took Sophie to the audition. When they got home he said, "You're not going to believe it. Sophie was amazing."

"Yeah right," I teased. "Like you're not biased."

"No. She did a great job. Maybe she'll grow up to be a professional actress. She showed a lot of talent tonight."

"We'll see," I said. Although Sophie was skilled at convincing her teachers and me time and time again that her wild stories were true, I'd never considered that those talents might lead her to the stage.

I was delighted when Sophie got a callback. However, when the director suggested he was considering casting her for the role of Helen Keller, both Josh and I panicked. Sophie had never been on stage. She had never taken direction well from anyone, and we knew she had a mind of her own.

As luck had it, a young girl who'd already made a name for herself as a professional actress tried out and was cast as Helen. Sophie won the role of Sarah, the youngest girl attending the Perkins School for the Blind. Kate also was cast as one of the blind girls, further cementing their relationship.

Paradise ended over Christmas break, as Kate and Sophie became enmeshed in a vicious conflict. Sophie was vague about its cause and so it remained a mystery to me. I was privy to much of the fall-out, however. Kate called all the girls in the play, convinced them Sophie was a horrible person, and organized a Do-Not-Talk-To-Sophie club. So powerful was Kate's influence on the girls that, no matter what strategies Sophie tried in an effort to befriend them, she was rebuffed by one and all. Sophie was devastated, but she made me promise not to call Kate's mother, claiming it would make things worse. She worried about going back to school after the break, and she talked about dropping out of the play.

Fortunately Josh was able to dissuade her from doing that. Although Sophie was on stage for five minutes, her performance as a blind child was convincing, poignant, and engaging. She stole the scene.

By the time *The Miracle Worker* run ended, the acting bug had bitten Sophie. She begged us to find another acting opportunity for her. Josh identified a local community theatre group casting for *The Innocents*, a play set in Victorian England. The play tells the story of a wealthy businessman who hires a new governess to raise his young nephew Miles and niece Flora. Soon after her arrival, the new governess learns that the former valet, with the complicit knowledge of the previous governess, molested the children, and she helps the children confront the ghosts of their deceased caretakers.

Although Josh and I were concerned about allowing Sophie to be in a play with such dark content, we agreed to let her try out and to maintain high vigilance should she be cast as Flora.

Sophie was one of more than twenty girls who auditioned to be Flora. Just as she'd done in her audition for *The Miracle Worker*, Sophie gave what Josh described as a "breathtaking and eerily haunting" performance. By the time they returned home, Josh knew Sophie would be the director's first choice to play Flora. And he was right.

Preparing to play Flora was a major undertaking. Sophie was one of six actors. She appeared in all but one scene, and she had many lines to learn. But she worked hard, practiced her lines daily, and attended rehearsals evenings and weekends for nearly three months. As she had promised, she kept up with her schoolwork.

On opening night, as the play began, a lone spotlight shined on Sophie. She wore a simple white dress with a bow tied in the back. Braided pigtails hung to her shoulders. She stared into the distance, her eyes wide, as though seeing a ghost. I was mesmerized. Although I'd schlepped her to countless rehearsals and knew her lines almost as well as she did, I had not seen this coming. During the first act, she didn't miss a single line; her delivery was perfect. I could barely move.

At intermission, Sophie's rendering of a disturbed and haunted child had the audience's attention. "How could such a young girl deliver such an amazing performance?" "She must be an up-and-coming professional actress." "Where did they find this kid?" The audience buzzed. Josh and I glowed with pride.

During *The Miracle Worker*, Sophie had stolen a five-minute scene. This time she stole the entire show. Was she headed for a life on stage?

It wasn't until almost five years later that we understood why Sophie had the capacity to deliver such a bewitching performance.

CHAPTER **20**

Transitions

Fall 2004. Sophie is twelve years old.

D uring the summer of 1966, as I completed sixth grade, my family joined the flight from Detroit to its suburbs. Racial tensions were increasing, the school system was in decline, and my father's hard work was rewarded with a promotion. My parents decided the time was right to move. The move took me away from the neighborhood where I'd spent all twelve years of my life, robbed me of my closest friends, and deposited me in a world where I knew no one.

This experience made me vow never to put my children in the position of having to relocate during early adolescence – until the University of Medicine and Dentistry of New Jersey's School of Osteopathic Medicine recruited me to become the first Director of Research at the New Jersey Institute for Successful Aging. Sophie had just completed sixth grade. The NIH's decision to fund my study of the effects of work-family conflicts on older women made the timing for a career move optimal. After a great deal of discussion and much anguish, Josh and I agreed that accepting the job and moving was in our family's best interests.

That summer, my mother would have turned eighty. While twenty-nine August 30ths had passed since her death in 1975, the annual approach of her birthday still saddened me. With each passing year, I thought about what she would have been like and about the relationship she and I might have had.

When she would have been sixty-one, I envisioned her with graying hair walking me down the aisle at my wedding. When she would have been sixty-eight, I smiled, thinking how delighted she would have been to hold my newborn baby and give me advice about how to care for her. When she would have been seventy-four, what would she have counseled me to do when I was miserable living in Peoria with a husband who loved the job that had brought us there? But these events would never be, because my mother died when she was fifty-one. On the other hand, I didn't have to watch her age and become infirm. As a gerontologist who'd spent years studying the stresses of family caregiving in late life, I knew how heartbreaking it is for adult children to watch a parent age and die. Still, if I'd had my druthers, I would have happily cared for her in her old age.

When I told Sophie we were moving to New Jersey, she screamed, "No, Mom, how can you do that to me?" It tore my heart out. She ran to her room and slammed the door. But then, within an hour, as though a switch had been thrown, she told me she was looking forward to the move. She explained that it would give her a chance to reinvent herself. I was stunned at her ability to grieve and then adjust so quickly.

That fall, Sophie engineered a transition that was nothing short of amazing. Entering seventh grade, she created a new image for herself, vowing to do well in school and to make new friends. Whereas I'd remained hidden in the shadows for most of my middle school years, Sophie was determined to shine. Within a few months of the move, Sophie was invited to one Bar or Bat Mitzvah after the next. The girls she introduced me to were polite, serious about their schoolwork, and happy to include Sophie in their circle of friends.

In the late fall, Sophie was cast in the school's musical theatre production of *Guys and Dolls*. She enjoyed her experience as part of the award-winning drama club. Yes, it looked like the move to New Jersey was working out well for Sophie.

CHAPTER 21

Laundry Wars

Fall 2004. Sophie is twelve years old.

T o say Sophie was headstrong and wanted to do things her way is like saying Albert Einstein had a few interesting ideas. Her pigheadedness could make me laugh and cry, sometimes at the same time.

Before Sophie was twelve and Aaron was eight, our nanny or housekeeper did the family laundry. When we moved to New Jersey, I took over the task and Sundays became Laundry Day. I outfitted each child's room with a clothes hamper and told them it was their responsibility to deliver their dirty clothes to the laundry room by eight thirty on Sunday mornings. I washed, folded, and delivered their clean clothes to their bedroom doors. Sophie and Aaron were responsible for putting their clothes back in their drawers. It seemed like a straightforward division of labor to me.

Aaron had no problem fulfilling his responsibility. Each Sunday morning, he dragged his dirty clothes out of his hamper and deposited them on the laundry room floor. That evening, he put the folded clothes away. As I suspected, this was a manageable task.

But not for Sophie. She rarely roused from bed on time, and bitterly bellyached about being saddled with having to bring her clothes downstairs. Invariably, she and I exchanged loud words before the task was completed.

Returning her clothes to their drawers was an even greater battle. Some weeks, Sophie shoved the pile of clean laundry under her bed. Other weeks, she buried it in her closet – hidden beneath shoes, papers, and art projects – or stuck it under the sink in the vanity cabinet of her bathroom. Still other weeks, I found the clean, folded laundry tossed back into the hamper, sometimes mixed in with dirty clothes. I don't believe her clean laundry was ever put away without incident. I would have laughed at her antics if they hadn't made me so furious.

After months of begging and pleading for Sophie's cooperation, I decided that her unwillingness to take responsibility for such a small task provided an opportunity to teach her how easy her life really was. I told her I would no longer wash her clothes and taught her how the washing machine and dryer worked. It was now her responsibility to wash, dry, fold, and put her clothes back in her dresser drawers.

Two weeks passed without Sophie doing her laundry. A month went by. Still she didn't do her laundry. Figuring sooner or later she would run out of underwear and have to cave, I waited, taking bets with friends about how long it would take.

After six weeks, with no evidence Sophie had done even a single load of wash, I dropped some not-so-subtle hints. "Sophie, do you remember how to use the washing machine?" or "I'm going to use the washing machine this morning. If you'd like, it'll be available this afternoon."

When three months had passed and Sophie still hadn't done a single load of laundry, I upped the ante and told her she was grounded until all her laundry was done. She responded with her usual dismissive, "Okay," not seeming to care about the consequences. What was she using for underwear?

Finally, the opportunity I'd waited for presented itself.

"Mom," she said, one Saturday morning, "A bunch of the kids are going to Friendly's tonight. Can I go with them?"

"Sure. Just make sure your laundry's done first."

"But, Mom," she wailed, "there's so much of it. I can't possibly get it done by tonight."

"Too bad. You probably should have thought about that weeks ago."

She spent four hours washing laundry, folding it, and putting it away, confirming that taking responsibility for the tasks I expected of her was well within her capabilities.

And then she went to Friendly's.

CHAPTER 22

Close Call

March 2005. Sophie is twelve and a half years old.

J osh stumbled up the stairs to our bedroom, his hands shaking, voice quaking. "You won't believe what happened."

"What?" I asked. "Are you alright?"

He'd been working in his basement office when the phone rang. Simultaneously, he and Sophie, who'd been doing homework in the first-floor study, picked up the phone. Josh heard the cracking of an adolescent boy's voice say, "Hello." Realizing the call wasn't for him, Josh was about to hang up when intuition halted him. Several times during the past few weeks, when either Josh or I answered the phone, the caller had hung up. Josh pressed down on the phone's receiver switch and released it, remaining silent as he continued listening.

What he heard next made his blood run cold.

"Whew, that was close," replied the boy-man, his voice suddenly dropping an octave.

"Yeah," whispered Sophie. "That was smart of you to change your voice for my Dad."

"I miss you," he sighed.

"I miss you, too," said Sophie.

"When am I going to get to see you?"

"I can never get out of here. My parents are mean."

"They don't know how much I love you – how special our love really is."

For nearly ten minutes Josh sat in his office, his hand over the phone's mouthpiece, listening to the conversation between Sophie and a man he soon realized she'd met on the Internet.

After Josh calmed down, we asked Sophie to join us in the kitchen.

"Sophie, who called earlier tonight?" I asked.

"I don't know. I wasn't on the phone, Mom. I was doing my homework."

"The phone rang about twenty minutes ago. You were talking for ten minutes or so and hung up a few minutes ago."

"Oh, that was just Jimmy, my friend from math class."

"What did he want?" I asked.

"Just to talk. Can I go back to studying? I have a math quiz tomorrow."

"Sophie," Josh seethed. "You're lying. I heard everything that man said to you. Who is he?"

Sophie raced up the stairs to her bedroom and slammed the door. I followed quickly on her heels.

"Sophie," I pleaded, "Please open the door. We need to talk."

She opened the door and stood there, her face red, tears streaming down. "Mom, you don't understand. I love him and he loves me."

Could these words really be coming out of the mouth of my twelve-year-old? "Sophie, who is he? Where did you meet him?"

"He's a really nice guy I met on the Internet," she answered. "We've been talking every day for weeks."

So that explained the hang-up phone calls. What on earth made her seek him out or respond to his overtures? Had she forgotten Barney the Dinosaur's lessons about not talking to strangers? Wasn't she paying attention in school when they talked about Internet safety? Did she think the rules Josh and I had given her and Aaron about using the Internet didn't pertain to her? As my blood pressure returned to normal, I asked her why she was talking with this man. She sobbed, "I don't know, Mom." I reminded Sophie about how easy it is for people to disguise themselves on the Internet, and about how dangerous that could be.

My words fell on deaf ears.

Frustrated and concerned, I called the police, both to alert them to the incident and to let Sophie know how worried I was. The sergeant said nothing could be done, given that no crime had been committed, but he offered to send an officer to our home to speak with Sophie about the perils of Internet chatting. I accepted his offer.

The young policeman spent more than an hour talking with Sophie, explaining how unsafe talking with strangers on the Internet can be and how easy it is for people to hide behind its anonymity. Sophie listened politely and asked appropriate questions. However, watching her nonverbal behavior, I knew she didn't give credence to a single word he said. Like our message, the policeman's words went unheeded, dismissed as the alarmist reflex of yet another clueless adult. Attempts on the part of the police to trace the calls failed, but the hang-up calls stopped. Was this because Sophie was intercepting his calls? Had he moved on? Or had they found a secret way to communicate?

CHAPTER **23**

Tics, Cutting, and Theft

Spring 2005. Sophie is twelve and a half years old.

Sophie was constantly in motion. Had she been a car, I would have taken her to a mechanic to have her idle adjusted. She gnawed her fingernails until they bled. She twirled her hair around her finger or pulled it out strand by strand until she had a bald spot the size of a quarter on the back of her head. Her knees bounced up and down vigorously, and she fiddled constantly with her jewelry. My attempts to make her to stop these behaviors were met with annoyance. The constant motion, which Sophie claimed calmed her down, drove me nuts. When I brought my concerns to the pediatrician, she increased Sophie's dosage of Strattera, explaining that during adolescence, as the hormones were surging, the need for medication adjustments was common.

Around this time, Sophie complained that her left eyelid had more of a droop to it than her right. In reality, this slight imperfection had always existed. She worried about how it made her look and asked whether she could have cosmetic surgery. Within weeks, Sophie convinced herself that her left eye was so horrifyingly ugly that it was all anyone noticed when looking at her. Just to appease Sophie, we asked the pediatrician's opinion. The doctor said it was minor and told Sophie not to worry about it. But Sophie couldn't be convinced. She tried compensating for this minor imperfection with makeup, applying rings of black eyeliner around each eye, making her look like a raccoon. When she tired of her camouflaging strategy, she let her bangs grow until they concealed the objectionable eye. Her hairdresser suggested she looked like Veronica Lake; I wasn't as kind, likening her to Cousin It from the *Addams Family*. When Josh's cousin, a neurosurgeon, explained that depriving her eye of light could result in loss of balance, an ongoing sense of disorientation, and long-term adverse neurological consequences, she laughed. It didn't matter what anyone said. Sophie ignored all pleas, counsel, and advice.

Equally troubling was the change in Sophie's relationship with Aaron. She teased him mercilessly, stopping only after he cried. She lashed out at him physically as well as verbally, and scoffed at the punishments Josh and I delivered in response. Was this change part of Sophie's adolescent rebellion? Thinking about my relationships with my brothers when I was Sophie's age, I didn't think adolescent rebellion explained her behavior.

I didn't know the cause of these behaviors, but they all suggested Sophie was desperately unhappy about something. The combination of not knowing what caused her anxiety and not being able to soothe her pain left me frustrated. I was hounded by the feeling that I was an incompetent mother. I thought about my mother. Now, at fifty-one, I was the same age she was when she had killed herself. I remembered how her distress had centered on her feelings of not being a good enough mother, how frustrated she had been about not doing the laundry right, how worried she had been about what to cook for dinner each night. What would she have made of the challenges Sophie presented to me?

A family vacation to the Dominican Republic made me realize that Sophie's problems were even more serious than I'd thought. Forced to exchange the long-sleeved shirts and sweatpants she'd hidden under during the winter for a bathing suit, she revealed angry crimson scratch marks covering her arms and legs. A scarlet burn on her upper left arm glared at me. Initially, Sophie shrugged off questions I asked about the cause of these marks, but before the vacation's end, she confessed that she had cut herself with razor blades or burned herself with a cigarette lighter when she was alone and feeling sad. She insisted that hurting herself made her feel better, but she assured me that she hadn't cut herself for several months. I couldn't look at her self-inflicted scars without cringing. What pain could have made her do this?

The day after we returned home, Sophie and I met with her pediatrician. The doctor's exam corroborated Sophie's report. The cutting and burn scars were not new. They were, however, taken very seriously by the doctor. Sophie reiterated her claim that she'd hurt herself when she'd felt sad, but she very quickly added, "It was a dumb thing to do. I haven't done it for months, and I won't ever do it again." Sophie agreed with the doctor's plan that, if she felt sad or felt like she wanted to hurt herself, she would tell Josh or me.

Sophie's interest in boys continued to develop. One, a neighbor named Rick, who was nearly two years older than she, took to knocking on our front door frequently. Each time he did, Sophie hid and refused to talk with him. When Sophie started leaving for school earlier and earlier, Josh and I wondered what she was up to. One morning Josh followed her. Watching from his car, Josh saw Sophie and Rick snaking their way to school, holding hands, stopping every few moments to grope one another. That evening, Josh confronted Sophie, but she claimed not to know what he was talking about. Then she shrugged her shoulders, and said, "It's no big deal, Dad. Besides, today he told me he likes another girl better than me."

A few weeks later, we visited Ben and his family in Omaha to celebrate Passover. Our journey home included a two-hour stop in Chicago before flying to Philadelphia. We arrived home late in the afternoon. By evening, Josh and I were exhausted. We'd just crawled into bed when the phone rang.

Josh said, "You know your sister. She's almost asleep. Can I have her call you tomorrow?"

Apparently, whatever my brother wanted couldn't wait.

"It's Ben. Seems important." Josh handed me the phone.

"Rachel," Ben began, halting as he spoke. "I don't know how to tell you this, but, … um, … I think Sophie took Allen's cell phone."

"What?" I asked, suddenly wide-awake.

"After you left, Allen couldn't find his phone. He said Sophie was playing with the phone all weekend. We looked all over the house and called the cell phone company. They traced calls made from the phone, first to Chicago and then to Philadelphia."

This was no mistake. The calls Ben described were along the route we'd taken that afternoon.

"I think Sophie has it," Ben continued, "and has been using it. I'm so sorry to be telling you this."

"Oh my God. I can't believe she would do that to Allen."

"There's more," Ben added. "Sara's wallet, her new shirt, and her favorite eye shadow are missing." Ben paused, allowing me to digest the information. "I'm wondering if Sophie has them."

"How could she take her cousin's things?" I wailed. "I'm so sorry. I'll talk with her and call you back."

Sophie had pinched makeup from my vanity, video games and toys from Aaron's room, and tools from Josh's workbench. Each time we'd discovered her thefts we made her return the items and imposed an appropriate consequence. Still, this hadn't stopped her from taking our things. But would she steal from her cousins?

I called Sophie into my bedroom and told her about the call from Ben. She insisted she hadn't taken her cousins' things.

Josh and I looked at one another. Is it possible she's not responsible for these missing items? Is there some other explanation that fits the facts?

Sophie barreled out of our room and slammed her bedroom door.

Now wide-awake, I took the suitcases downstairs to put them away. Hoisting Sophie's suitcase to put it on the shelf, the weight of its contents shifted. Something was inside. Opening its zippered pocket, my heart sank. There they were – Sara's wallet, shirt, and makeup.

I bolted up the stairs and pounded on Sophie's door. "How could you?" I screamed. "How could you steal from your cousin?" I flung open the door and barged into her room.

As Sophie sat up, Allen's cell phone fell to the floor. She looked at me and calmly said, "I wanted a phone like that and you wouldn't get me one."

CHAPTER 24

Help!

Spring 2005. Sophie is twelve and a half years old.

Sophie's angry and impulsive behaviors frightened Josh and me. Something wasn't right with her, but I didn't know what. Each attempt we made to talk with her in hopes of learning what was wrong was rebuffed. Hearing my concerns, her pediatrician suggested I take Sophie to a psychiatrist and gave me the names and phone numbers of five doctors.

Working my way through the list, I learned the first three weren't taking new patients. One receptionist offered to put Sophie's name on her waiting list, but told me it wasn't likely an appointment would be available for at least six months. I had better luck with psychiatrist number four, who had an opening two weeks later, albeit during school hours.

On the way to the appointment, Sophie insisted I was blowing things out of proportion and that she was fine, but offered no explanation for her aberrant behaviors. The psychiatrist met us at the door of his office. He was in his sixties, wore a rumpled shirt, and had long hair pulled back in a ponytail. He took a brief history, talking only to me, and then asked to meet alone with Sophie. She looked at me nervously as she followed him into his inner office. I signaled back with my eyes that it would be okay.

Fifteen minutes later they emerged. Sophie rolled her eyes and handed me the prescription he'd written for Concerta, a stimulant used to treat ADHD. The psychiatrist said he believed that Strattera and Concerta together would control the impulsive behaviors Sophie had been exhibiting.

Slamming the car door, Sophie balked, "I'm never going back there. He was creepy."

When we got home, I called psychiatrist number five, Dr. Kane. The receptionist described her as kind and engaging. Fortunately, she had an appointment available later that week.

I breathed a sigh of relief when Sophie and I met Dr. Kane. Her warm Spanish accent was soothing. While the questions she asked were similar to those the previous psychiatrist had asked, Dr. Kane talked to both Sophie and me, and she quickly put Sophie at ease. I read a magazine while Dr. Kane met with Sophie. She also recommended adding Concerta to the Strattera that Sophie was taking.

Little did I realize this first visit to Dr. Kane was the beginning of what would become an infuriating pattern in which, as Sophie's behavior became increasingly difficult and more bizarre, the response would be to add another medication.

As we were leaving her office, Dr. Kane suggested Sophie would benefit from talking with a therapist – either a psychologist or a clinical social worker. She was quick to explain that, as a psychiatrist, she would see Sophie once a month to manage her medications. With the therapist, Sophie would be able to discuss her insecurities and develop strategies to gain control over her impulsive behaviors.

The model whereby it was a psychiatrist's job to tinker with the chemicals and the therapist's responsibility to counsel the patient dumbfounded me. I didn't understand how separating these intertwined functions could benefit the patient and how it could result in appropriate treatment. At best, it seemed an inefficient process. I was even more skeptical when I asked Dr. Kane for the names of the therapists she'd worked with and she could give me no names. I had hoped, at least, that the doctors would communicate with one another. Dr. Kane made it clear that I was on my own to find a therapist and that there would be little if any communication between her and the therapist. I would have looked for another psychiatrist, but I already knew enough about the system to realize I was lucky to have found someone with appointments available whom Sophie liked.

That afternoon, I set out to find a therapist for Sophie. I networked among my friends for recommendations. Armed with a list of names, I phoned one office after another, only to be told by the frosty gatekeepers that either the doctor wasn't accepting new patients or that the doctor didn't accept insurance. I would be responsible for paying for treatment and filing paperwork with insurance companies for reimbursement, even though my employer provided excellent health insurance. While this arrangement was the exception when it came to physical heath care, it looked to be the norm for mental health care. It boggled my mind. Why should there be such differences depending on whether it were your brain or your leg that was ailing? Clearly, I had a lot to learn about the mental health system in the United States.

I mobilized my resources and capitalized on my position within a medical school by calling a well-known child and adolescent psychiatrist on the school's faculty. He confirmed that therapists specializing in adolescents were few and far between, that many of them are not adequately trained, and that the good ones had long waiting lists. He referred me to three therapists, promising to call their offices and pave the way for my call.

My calls to these offices were somewhat more productive than my initial attempts. However, none of the therapists accepted insurance. All payments were out-of-pocket; reimbursement from my insurance company would be my headache, not theirs. Initial fees for a one-hour consultation ranged from four hundred to seven hundred dollars; subsequent visits ranged from one hundred fifty to two hundred fifty dollars for each fifty-minute hour of therapy. Apologizing, each therapist reported they wouldn't be able to see Sophie for at least four months, but offered to put her name on a waiting list. I made tentative appointments with all three, and asked that they call me should an earlier appointment become available.

Two weeks later, to my delight, I received a call from Dr. Coyne's office. She had a cancellation that afternoon and offered to see Sophie. The suddenly available appointment meant I had to reschedule a meeting with my research staff and have Sophie excused early from school, but I seized the opportunity. Never had I been so ecstatic about the prospect of spending five hundred dollars.

On the way to our appointment, Sophie grumbled, "So, why are we doing this?"

"Remember how Dr. Kane said it would be good for you to talk with a therapist about why you're cutting yourself and stealing?"

"Right," she scowled. "What if I can't think of anything to tell her?"

"I think she'll help you talk. Just be honest with her. We need to figure out why you're doing these things and make them stop."

When we arrived at Dr. Coyne's office, I was given a stack of paperwork to complete. As I worked through the usual checklists inquiring whether the patient had been diagnosed with various medical conditions, I noted questions I'd never seen before. "Has the patient ever . . . Attempted suicide? Harmed an animal? Lashed out for what seemed like no reason?" Sophie was always lashing out at Aaron, she'd cut herself, but she'd never attempted suicide and there wasn't an animal or insect on the planet that she wouldn't protect. Her compassion for strangers often astounded me. As I pondered the gravity of these behaviors, Sophie thumbed through a *Seventeen* magazine, idly commenting on the dress Madonna was wearing, the article about dieting, and a picture of the Back Street Boys.

"The doctor will see you now," came a voice from behind a glass window. Sophie was ushered inside. I was stopped. To my questioning look, the receptionist said I'd be invited to join the session toward its end.

I crossed the waiting room and reclaimed my chair. I completed the forms, paid the receptionist, and flipped through pages of the *Good Housekeeping* and *Parenting* magazines lying on the coffee table. Forty minutes later, the receptionist said, "The doctor will see you now."

Dr. Coyne's office was filled with Barbie dolls, blocks, stuffed animals, and a host of art supplies. It looked more like a kindergarten classroom than a doctor's office. Dr. Coyne, a slight woman in her late thirties, had long hair, freckles, and an infectious smile. My initial thought was that Sophie would like and easily relate to her. My next thought was that it would be easy for Sophie to bewitch Dr. Coyne with her shenanigans.

"Thank you for seeing Sophie today," I said.

"We've been having a great talk," she said. Sophie's body language told me she too enjoyed her talk with Dr. Coyne.

"Wonderful."

"I wanted to spend a few minutes with you and Sophie together so we can make sure you understand what therapy is and how we're going to proceed here. Generally, I'll meet with Sophie alone. Our sessions will be private and I won't share anything with you that Sophie doesn't want me to share. For therapy to be effective, Sophie and I need to establish a rapport where she feels safe to talk to me about anything. There is, of course, one exception to this. If I believe Sophie is likely to hurt herself or anyone else, I'll let you know. For some sessions, if Sophie and I agree that it would be beneficial to include you, we'll invite you to join us. At some point, we might want to have a session with you and your husband. Most likely, however, the sessions won't include you. If you think there are things I should know about or address with Sophie, please put them in an e-mail message to me. If I have questions, I'll let you know. Do you have any questions, Mrs. Segal?"

I winced. What a mistake it had been not to use my hard-earned credentials. When Josh and I married, I faced the dilemma many professional women face. Would I be Dr. Pruchno, Dr. Segal, Dr. Pruchno-Segal, or Mrs. Segal? After much debate with my father and with Josh, I'd decided to use Dr. Pruchno professionally. I was well-published and known by that name in my field. In my personal life, I'd be Mrs. Segal, making my connections with Josh and our future children clear. But doing so had created the situation where Dr. Coyne could have no idea that my academic credentials were just like hers. I'm sure she would have spoken to me differently had she known I was a psychologist.

Here was more evidence of the difference between the mental and physical health systems. Sophie would have a relationship with Dr. Coyne that excluded me. I was the outsider, there to transport Sophie to appointments and pay the bills. This hadn't been the case with the pediatrician or the orthodontist. They'd spoken with me at each visit and consulted with me about treatments. While I wasn't at all comfortable with Dr. Coyne's arrangement, I nodded my head with resignation. If this is what it would take to fix Sophie's problems, then this is what I would do.

CHAPTER 25

Letters

June to August 2005. Sophie is thirteen years old.

A couple of months on the new medication regimen controlled many of Sophie's impulsive and agitated behaviors. Though Sophie complained of feeling dizzy and nauseous, Dr. Kane assured her that these side effects would dissipate over time. I had my own worries about Concerta. It was a federally controlled substance that is highly addictive. When I read Robert Whitaker's article[1] contending that all major classes of psychiatric drugs, including stimulants such as Concerta, can trigger new and more severe psychiatric symptoms in some patients, I panicked. But, Dr. Kane convinced me that there were no alternative treatments that would alleviate Sophie's symptoms.

Sophie seemed to enjoy her therapy sessions with Dr. Coyne, yet she shared little about them.

At the beginning of that summer, Jamie told us that her father Craig was dying. At Sophie's insistence, Josh took her to visit Craig. I was touched that Sophie understood the severity of Craig's illness and appreciated how important the visit would be to him.

When she returned, Sophie spent two months at a sleep-away arts camp about an hour's drive from our home. With the others, we waited our turn in line to check in with the camp nurse. Each child carried a gallon-sized plastic bag filled with medications. Sophie freely compared diagnoses and treatment regimens with the other campers. Was it the camp? Did it attract kids with behavioral problems? Or was this phenomenon of medicated kids more common than I realized?

Although Sophie wasn't home for much of the summer, she made her presence known — in all the wrong ways. We, her clueless parents, had made but a single request of her while she was at camp – that she write at least two letters home each week. The first week passed without even one letter. So did the second week. Josh and I wrote to her several times, and reminded her about her responsibility to write back. After two weeks, Josh told Sophie that, unless we received a letter that week, we wouldn't participate in family visiting day. Still, no letter arrived.

When I spoke with her by phone, Sophie was apologetic. She said she'd written several letters, but kept forgetting to mail them. I believed her, convinced that her explanation was credible. She told me she didn't like several of the girls in her bunk, and that the role in the play for which she'd hoped to be cast hadn't materialized. It didn't sound like the summer was going well for her. When I hung up, I told Josh I was worried about Sophie and thought that, despite her failure to write to us, we needed to visit.

During our visit, we learned that Sophie was in a bunk with five other girls who all had been to the camp in previous years. They weren't interested in befriending Sophie, the new kid in the cabin. Even worse, the minor acting role for which she'd been cast was of little interest to her. Had I been in this situation at her age, I would have sought my parents' help, switched bunks, changed plays, or some combination thereof. Sophie, however, made the best of a bad situation. In fact, at the end of the summer, she surprised me when she asked to go back to camp the following year.

I marveled at Sophie's ability to cope. Her incredible inner strength and perseverance awed me. I reckoned this ability to make lemonade out of lemons was a characteristic that would serve her well in life, as I envisioned Sophie meeting the challenges of a difficult boss or a frustrating assignment with this same knack for making the best of a bad situation – and not only overcoming it, but thriving despite it. Yet I wondered whether pathology explained her behavior. How could she not be angry?

The camp counselors took note of Sophie's ability to cope with the difficult situation. One of them wrote a note saying, "Sophie's a joy to live with. She's helped stabilize the bunk." Reading the note made me happy for Sophie and proud of her for being able to live with difficult people and be part of a team. But it also made me sad, as I contrasted the counselor's experience with my own. Sophie wasn't an easy person for Josh, Aaron, and me to live with.

Our visit with Sophie was fraught with tension. She'd enjoyed her independence from us and reacted poorly to our expectation that she treat us with respect. She was surly, and not at all happy to see us.

Hoping to make the best of our time together, Josh and I placated her, inviting her to set the agenda for the afternoon. She wanted to come home and see her dogs, so we let her. She wanted to get a haircut and buy shampoo and hair products, so she did. She wanted to have some quiet time in her room, and so we left her alone.

My relationship with Sophie was great, provided she always got her way and I asked nothing of her. The moment I disagreed with something she said or wanted to do she became defensive, abusive, or silent. Once conflict was evident, Sophie would become obstinate. Under no circumstances would she give up the fight. In fact, it was only in rare instances that she ever admitted she was wrong, and then only after days had passed and she wanted something from me. She had a similar relationship with Josh.

Was my relationship with Sophie normal? I thought not. From the adolescent psychology courses I'd taken in college, I remembered G. Stanley Hall's proclamation of early adolescence as a period of "sturm and drang" – storm and stress. I knew about the hormonal changes underlying the emotional turmoil and rebellion. Yet my own experiences as an adolescent were very different from Sophie's. From the time I was twelve, my mother's illness made me careful of anything I said or did. Fearing even the slightest misstep on my part would upset her, I'd made it my goal to be the perfect daughter. I did my homework, got good grades in school, practiced the piano, and helped out at home. I didn't even listen to loud music. How ironic that, as a teen-aged girl, I didn't have a normal relationship with my mother and now, as a mother, I didn't have a normal relationship with my teen-aged daughter. Yet my not-normal experiences were two extremes that couldn't have been more different.

Sophie was adept at picking fights with Josh, Aaron, and me. She could quibble over anything, from Aaron killing a bug in her presence to Josh expressing a political view to my asking her to help in the kitchen. She delighted in inciting tumult and did so at every opportunity.

During the ride back to camp, Sophie taunted, "Mom, I have something to tell you that you're not going to be happy about."

"Okay." I braced myself, "What is it?"

"I let the girls in my bunk draw all over the new jeans you bought me."

"Why did you do that?" I asked with annoyance.

"Just for fun."

"You're right, Sophie, I'm not happy about that. In fact, I should have had my head examined for buying you new jeans to take to camp."

"I told you that you wouldn't like it," she taunted.

"So why did you let them ruin your pants? They were pretty pricey jeans too, not the inexpensive ones from Target." I cringed, remembering how awful I'd felt after a fight I'd had with my mother over clothes, when my adolescent sense of style collided with her grown-up frugality.

"It's no big deal. They're just pants," she argued.

Exasperated, I exclaimed, "Sophie, you're acting like a spoiled brat. You don't recognize the value of anything and your sense of entitlement is amazing. Don't come to me when you need new clothes for school."

"Fine, I won't," she huffed. Her snarky comments angered me. I fumed silently. She always had to have the last word.

When we had arrived back at camp and were saying goodbye, I said, "Sophie, would you get the letters you wrote? I'd like to read them."

"Mom, I don't want to walk all the way back to my cabin and then back here again. I'll put them in the mail tonight."

"We can walk you back to the cabin and get them."

"No, I'll put them in the mail," she insisted.

She'd never written the letters. "Sophie, did you write the letters?" I asked.

"Yeah," she answered.

"Then I'd like to have them."

"Mom, I've got to go. I promise I'll mail them tonight." She kissed me and scampered off.

What made me even sadder than the realization that Sophie hadn't written the letters was that, even when I caught her trying to dupe me, she refused to admit she'd done wrong. And even now, when most kids would have quickly written and mailed letters to cover their lie, Sophie did not.

CHAPTER **26**

Cutting

Spring 2006. Sophie is thirteen and a half years old.

"Mrs. Segal, this is Mr. Cromwell from the middle school. Sophie's all right, but there's a situation we need to talk about."

Calls from Sophie's guidance counselor in the middle of the day never brought good news.

"Could you please come to my office?" Mr. Cromwell asked. "We'll talk more when you get here."

"I'll be there in fifteen minutes," I answered.

I flew out of my office, explaining my unplanned departure to my colleagues by mumbling something to the effect that I wasn't feeling well. As I drove, my thoughts raced. Why am I being summoned? What has she done now? I tried to calm myself with a few unlikely explanations. Maybe she has a headache. Maybe her stomach is upset. But these couldn't be the reason for the call. Neither is "a situation" and neither would involve a guidance counselor.

When I arrived at the guidance office, I found Mr. Cromwell pacing in the reception area, a worried look on his face. He escorted me into his private office, where Sophie sat staring into space.

"Sophie," Mr. Cromwell began, "Would you like to tell your mother what happened?"

"No," she said.

"I think you should be the one to tell her. But if you won't, I'll have to," he said.

"You can tell her," she said diverting her eyes from my gaze.

I looked at Mr. Cromwell, the suspense eating at me. What drama was about to unfold now?

"This afternoon, a couple of Sophie's friends came to my office and told me Sophie was planning on hurting herself tonight. The reports from the girls varied. One girl said Sophie told her she was thinking about killing herself."

Thoughts of my mother flooded through me. I paused to gain my composure. "Sophie," I asked, "What's going on?"

"I don't know," she said, her eyes filling with tears.

The previous year, when Josh and I had realized Sophie was cutting herself, we'd told her it was important for her to come to us, or to a teacher or a friend, if she ever felt like she wanted to hurt herself again. Though we'd ended her therapy sessions with Dr. Coyne once it became clear that Sophie spent the expensive therapy sessions talking about her desire for a nose job and breast implants, she'd continued seeing her psychiatrist, Dr. Kane. Recently, Sophie had started seeing a new, more experienced therapist, Dr. Grey. Although he'd tried to get Sophie to tackle the demons that made her want to harm herself, she refused to talk to him. I explained this to Mr. Cromwell.

"Sophie, can you show your mother your arm?" Mr. Cromwell asked.

Sophie pushed up the sleeve of her navy blue hoodie, revealing angry red scratch marks that read *I HATE ME.*

My knees turned liquid. I leaned on his desk to balance myself.

"Sophie, when did you do that?" I asked.

"Last night. I was doing my homework and broke off a piece of the spiral from one of my notebooks."

"Why, Sophie? What made you scratch those words into your arm?"

"I don't know."

"Remember how we talked about the importance of your telling someone about these feelings, rather than hurting yourself?" I heard my voice shaking.

"I did. I told my friends," she retorted.

"Sophie, what you told your friends frightened them. That's why they came to me. If you ever feel that way again, would you please come and talk to me?" asked Mr. Cromwell.

"Sure," Sophie sulked.

When I reported the cutting behavior to Dr. Kane, she added Zoloft, an antidepressant, to Sophie's regimen of Strattera and Concerta. In response to my concern about adding an antidepressant, since Sophie didn't seem to have what I thought were characteristic symptoms of depression – the crying and sadness that had all but paralyzed my mother – Dr. Kane explained that adolescent depression typically manifests itself as anger. She added that cutting is an expression of self-directed anger and, thus, indicative of depression.

We brought this situation to the attention of her therapist, Dr. Grey, who talked with Sophie about the importance of telling an adult should she have these feelings again. Josh reminded Sophie that it would always be safe for her to tell us if she felt likely to hurt herself.

I found it impossible to sleep at night, worrying that Sophie, like my mother, was destined to kill herself.

CHAPTER 27

Nose Piercing

July 2006. Sophie is fourteen years old.

T he summer between eighth and ninth grades, Sophie looked forward to returning to the arts camp. I left the responsibility for packing to her. She procrastinated and didn't begin packing until the morning that camp began.

"Sophie," I called, "Ready to go?" She was anxious to arrive at camp early so she could secure one of the prime pieces of real estate in her bunk – a lower bunk bed near a window – and I wanted to respect her wishes to get an early start.

"Almost," she hollered back.

I froze at the door to her bedroom where I'd gone to grab one of her suitcases and help her lug it downstairs. I watched her fling clothes, both dirty and clean, into her suitcases.

"Sophie, that's not how you pack." I took a deep breath, fearing I would explode.

"Whatever," she retorted. "It doesn't matter."

"Yes, it does. Why are you packing dirty clothes?"

"'Cuz I want to have them with me."

"Then you should have either washed them last night or asked me to do it for you."

"Mom, it's fine. Let's go," she threw her toothbrush and a book into the open suitcase.

"I don't think so."

"Mom, we have to go," she whined. "It's late and you know I wanted to get to camp early."

Reaching into her open suitcase, I picked up a pair of soiled panties and a bedraggled tee-shirt. "You've got to be kidding! No way are you going anywhere with these filthy clothes."

Sophie snatched the clothes from my hand and tossed them back in the suitcase. I flipped the suitcase upside down. Sophie slammed her fist into my arm with a force that sent me reeling backward.

"You fucking bitch," she screamed, hurling a book at me. "I hate you."

Hoping to teach her a lesson, part of me wanted to forbid her from going to camp. The other part of me couldn't bear the thought of having her home all summer. I told her that if she wanted to go to camp, she needed to apologize for her outburst, do a load of laundry, and pack clean clothes. Her fury continued, but she realized she had no choice but to cooperate. After she did her laundry and packed, I drove her to camp.

For five weeks, peace reigned. One afternoon, cuddled in Josh's embrace as our afternoon tryst ended, my cell phone clamored. It was the camp director.

"Mrs. Segal? Sophie's fine, but we've had a little incident I think you should know about."

I hate these calls with their sugarcoated overtures. What did she do now?

"The kids were in their bunk during rest hour this afternoon." So? "Sophie and Dakota were reading a magazine." Sounds harmless. Why is she calling me? "The magazine featured an article about facial piercings and they got to talking about how that was something they'd always wanted to do. Dakota had a safety pin that they dipped in hydrogen peroxide. Sophie pierced her nose and then Dakota pierced her lip."

I winced. "They did what?" I sputtered. "Where were the counselors?" Josh rolled his eyes.

"In the cabin taking a nap. The girls were quiet, so the counselors had no idea about their activities until after rest hour when they showed off their new piercings. The nurse removed the rings and cleaned the wounds. Sophie's fine but I wanted to let you know what happened."

During the past several months, Sophie's fascination with facial piercings had grown. She'd told us countless times that she wanted to get her nose and other parts of her face pierced. Each time, Josh and I made it clear to her that anything beyond a single piercing in each ear lobe, which she already had, would not be tolerated. I recalled the camp's *Code of Conduct*, which forbade campers from cutting their hair or defacing their bodies with piercings or tattoos, and the conversation Josh and I had with Sophie before she signed the form acknowledging she understood it. This was no innocent impulsive move on Sophie's part. While doubtlessly Sophie and Dakota had egged one other on, Sophie knew our rules and the camp's rules.

"Please ask Sophie to pack up her things. We'll be there this evening to pick her up. She's done with camp," I sighed.

Although it pained me to lose nearly three Sophie-free weeks, I had to bring her home. Her defiant behavior demanded a severe consequence. Sophie valued camp and her independence. I hoped depriving her of them would make her reconsider engaging in future actions she knew were wrong.

Sophie knew it was I, not the camp director, who'd decided she had to leave. Her lip-piercing comrade wasn't exiled. She smoldered. She whined. She insisted it was "not fair." She called me every spiteful name she could muster. Then she refused to talk to me for twenty-four hours.

While Sophie gave me the silent treatment, I turned my attention to what she was going to do for the four weeks remaining until school started. What she was not going to do was wallow in self-pity or sit at home and watch television.

I told Sophie she needed to do volunteer work, and suggested she consider working with children, old people, or animals. We made a list of local organizations that might offer such opportunities and she called each one, inquiring whether they could use her help. We visited a handful of agencies that expressed interest in her and, within a few hours, Sophie had a volunteer job at an assisted living facility.

She started work the next day. One afternoon a few days later, Sophie said, "There's this resident who emigrated from Germany. He was a member of the Hitler Youth when he was a teenager. He told me he hates Jews."

"I'll bet you don't like being around him," I said.

"It doesn't bother me," Sophie shrugged.

"It would be understandable if you wanted to steer clear of him. Have you told the activities director you'd rather not work with him?"

"No. In fact, I've been going out of my way to be nice to him. This afternoon, I pushed him around the halls in his wheel-chair. I'm trying hard to help him."

"Why would you do that?"

"My job is to help people. He needs to learn that Jewish people are just people like everybody else. I figure if I'm nice to him, and since he knows I'm Jewish, maybe he'll see he's wrong about Jews."

I was in awe. What a mature response. I hadn't had such sensitivity and courageous determination when I was her age. But then again, I wouldn't have gotten over the disappointment of hav-ing to leave camp as quickly as she had.

By the end of the summer, Sophie had befriended dozens of residents and was the official Bingo-caller. While part of me was glad she'd had this experience, this was yet another time when Sophie took my attempt to impose consequences for bad behavior and turned sour lemons into a pitcher of sweet lemonade.

As school was about to begin, she admitted that piercing her nose wasn't the wisest of decisions. Maybe my consequences had been effective after all.

CHAPTER **28**

Working the System

W hen Sophie was motivated to succeed, she soared, no matter how difficult the challenge. Her Bat Mitzvah required that she chant long, difficult Hebrew passages and explain the lesson to be gleaned from what she'd read. Wearing a turquoise jacket, black pencil skirt, and high-heeled pumps, she could have passed for a young professional woman with her perfectly coiffed long brown hair and impeccably applied makeup. When she faltered over a difficult passage, a slight nod of my head or smile was all she needed to gain the confidence to get back on track. I couldn't have felt more connected to her.

My quest to motivate Sophie to succeed in school, however, was met by her unremitting resistance. Each time we agreed I would hover less and she would take greater responsibility for her work, she reveled in the newfound freedom. Then she refused to do the work. While she said she was college-bound, her behavior indicated otherwise.

I learned the importance of vigilant communication with Sophie's teachers when she was in elementary school. Whenever there was an opportunity for Sophie to fall through the cracks, she took it and tumbled. Her modus operandi was simple: "If Mom doesn't know I have homework, I don't have homework." So I became "That Mother," the one who was on a first-name basis with each of Sophie's teachers. At the beginning of each school year, I made several new friends among the teachers; by June, I was sorry to lose them.

Sophie's good-natured personality, her quick wit, and her keen intelligence made her well-liked by her teachers. Because they liked her, they worked hard, often going far beyond the call of duty, to help Sophie succeed. But Sophie rarely rose to the occasion. She didn't write assignments in her agenda and usually didn't study for exams. It was the exceptional project that she completed and turned in on time.

Rather than do the work expected of her, Sophie concocted one fib after the next, telling me she had no homework and telling the teachers she'd done it and forgotten it at home. Each time Josh or I caught Sophie lying about schoolwork, we imposed a consequence. We took away her cell phone, suspended her allowance, and forbade her from attending parties. Yet rather than reigning Sophie in and convincing her to take responsibility, these consequences angered her and drove a wedge between us as she insisted that going to parties and spending time with her classmates were her inalienable rights. Josh had even less patience for this than I.

By the end of ninth grade, Sophie's grades in math and history were so poor that her guidance counselor suggested she would benefit from taking online summer classes. Although Sophie was disheartened about spending her summer doing homework, she understood this was the consequence for failing to work during the school year. Told that until she completed the courses she had no privileges, Sophie moped around the house for two weeks, but ultimately buckled down and, within a month, earned A's in both classes.

Sophie's success with the online program validated my belief that she was intelligent and capable of mastering the work. At the same time, Josh and I realized we needed help identifying what kept Sophie from taking responsibility for her work and being a successful student.

To that end, we enlisted the guidance of Dr. Kline, an educational consultant. After extensive – and expensive – testing, Dr. Kline concluded that Sophie lied to compensate for her poor organizational skills. How I wanted to believe that this was why Sophie lied. Dr. Kline explained that, because disorganization was characteristic of ADHD, Sophie had a right to academic accommodations to compensate for the injustices rendered by her disability.

We petitioned the school several days before the start of her sophomore year to institute a 504 Plan. It included having a second set of textbooks to be kept at home, extra time to complete tests, timely communication between her teachers and me, highly structured assignments and organized teachers, and preferred seating in the front row of her classrooms. With Dr. Kline's prompting, Sophie convinced the committee she wanted to succeed, but that her ADHD got in her way. The committee granted all of our requests.

The start of the school year brought even more communication between the teachers and me. Now, rather than talking with someone every week, I was talking with someone nightly. Yet Sophie continued to circumvent the system. She lied to the teachers and she lied to Josh and me. We'd embraced Dr. Kline's explanation that Sophie told lies not out of willfulness or evil intent, but because she lacked the supports she needed to succeed. Dr. Kline had been wrong. We'd implemented the prescribed supports and the faculty was doing a yeoman's job of complying with the plan. But Sophie's deceit continued.

CHAPTER **29**

The Double Rainbow

November 2007. Sophie is fifteen years old.

T he bedraggled young woman caught my attention the moment she slinked into the ice cream parlor. Her thick brown hair, hanging limply past her shoulders, looked as though it hadn't seen a brush in months. Her clothes were tattered and dirty, her tight blue jeans ripped at the knee. I doubted the baggy plaid wool shirt she wore over a skin-tight tee-shirt proclaiming *Save the Whales* had ever fit her slender shoulders. Her feet, protected from the ground by flip-flops, were black; her toenails were long and bore the remnants of chipped blue polish.

She ogled the vats of ice cream, inching her way across the length of the store, pausing several times to touch the glass separating her from the ice cream. Her green eyes were blank, her face expressionless.

"Can I help you?" asked the pimply teenage boy. He wore a Double Rainbow Ice Cream Shop apron and wielded an ice cream scoop.

She glared at him, saying nothing.

"Can I help you?" he repeated.

Still there was no response. It was hard to tell her age. Her waif-like appearance made me think she could be as young as fourteen, yet the way she carried herself made me believe she was older.

"Miss, can I help you?" he asked, the frustration growing in his voice.

"Fuck you!" she screamed and bolted out of the store.

She leaned against the building, trying to steady herself, closed her eyes, and mumbled. She wandered toward a nearby garbage can and started rummaging through the refuse. Dirty napkins, spoons, and cups were strewn on the ground as she excavated her way through the garbage can. It looked like she was searching for buried treasure. Suddenly she stopped digging and stood upright, grinning as she held a child-sized ice cream cup filled with melted chocolate ice cream. She sat down on the ground, crossed her legs, picked up one of the spoons she'd tossed to the ground, and began eating the melted mess.

Josh and I sat in the ice cream store, watching her. We'd flown to San Francisco earlier in the day to attend the annual meeting of the Gerontological Society, leaving Sophie and Aaron with our next-door neighbors. Now, hoping to forestall sleep for at least a few hours, we'd gone for a walk.

"You know," Josh said, "I worry so much about Sophie. She has no interest in anything and doesn't take anything seriously. That could be her in a couple of years – someone who's reduced to rummaging through the garbage for food."

I nodded.

"Where are the girl's parents? How could they leave her out on the street like that?" I asked.

She probably suffered from a mental illness, but how could her parents let her sink into this depraved lifestyle? What had she done to be banished from their lives? What kind of heartless, low-life people were they?

CHAPTER **30**

A Visit to the Promised Land

December 2007. Sophie is fifteen years old.

Attending Hebrew School until age thirteen was non-negotiable in my family. My parents had insisted on it, as had Josh's. We figured what had been good enough for us was good enough for our kids.

Once Sophie's Bat Mitzvah was over, we made continuing religious education an option. Our synagogue upped the ante with a strategy that kept the kids engaged in Judaic studies. Part of the curriculum included a two-week trip to Israel – paid for by parents, of course. Sophie quickly decided to continue attending Hebrew School in exchange for the opportunity to travel to Israel with her class.

I was delighted with Sophie's decision, both because she made it with no input from Josh or me and because I believed it was the right one. I hoped the trip would cement the values Josh and I had worked hard to teach her. I was concerned about Sophie's lack of commitment to anything and hoped she would develop a connection with and dedication to Israel. I also hoped the trip would help her bond with some of the kids from our synagogue whom she'd known for years, yet with whom she hadn't developed any meaningful friendships.

Sophie's teachers and school administrators supported the trip even though it extended the year-end break by several days, but they expected the kids to take responsibility for missed work.

The synagogue provided a letter describing the trip as an educational experience, and asked that travelers share the letter with their teachers. Sophie lost the letter twice and, when I checked with her teachers the week before the scheduled departure, I learned she hadn't mentioned the trip to at least half of them. When I reminded her that it was her responsibility to complete the work, Sophie nodded, smiled, and said, "I know, Mom." My suggestion that Sophie complete the work before the trip fell on deaf ears, as she insisted she'd have plenty of time to do it on the plane.

The day Sophie left for Israel was cold and snowy. Josh, Aaron, and I drove her to our synagogue where she and the other travelers boarded a bus bound for Newark International Airport. Before we left the house, I asked, "Sophie, are you sure you have everything?"

"Yes, Mom."

"Did you pack your toiletries?"

"Yeah."

"What about your hiking boots?"

"Got 'em."

"Do you have your homework?"

"It's in my backpack," she said with annoyance. "Let's go. I can't wait!"

Excitement filled the air as parents and kids hugged and said tearful goodbyes. Sophie kissed us and dismissed us, impatient to join the other travelers.

Returning home, I picked up some clothes Sophie had left on the floor of her room. While making her bed, I stepped on something. Kneeling down, I found the homework she'd stuffed under her bed. She'd hoodwinked me yet again. Annoyed, I turned off the light in her room.

For the next two weeks, I enjoyed the trip vicariously, reading the daily updates sent from the staff. I viewed each photo, hoping to catch a glimpse of Sophie. In one picture, she sat in the middle of the desert with one of the other girls. In another, she rode on the back of a camel, a wide smile on her face. I charted their movements on a map, fondly remembering my own trip to Israel nearly thirty years earlier. One of the notes I received from the staff said, "Sophie is a joy to be with. Her love for Israel is apparent."

Another said, "Last night, Sophie and several of the girls danced at the Western Wall. She's having a blast."

On the morning of Sophie's return, Josh, Aaron, and I waited in the parking lot of the synagogue along with the other parents. My excitement mounted as the bus pulled into the parking lot. I couldn't wait to hug Sophie and hear about the trip. Getting off the bus, Sophie made a beeline towards us, saying "Mom! Dad! Aaron! Thank you so much. That was the best trip of my life!"

Wow. The first thing out her mouth is a thank you.

Eager to hear about her trip, we headed to IHOP for breakfast. Savoring pancakes and omelets, we listened as Sophie talked non-stop. She described her visit to the Western Wall on a Friday afternoon, amazed to see hundreds of people from all over the world congregating, singing, and dancing as they greeted the Sabbath. She talked excitedly about swimming in the Dead Sea, exploring the tunnels under the Western Wall, climbing Masada, picking oranges at a kibbutz, and playing with Israeli children.

As we finished breakfast, I said, "Sophie, I'm so glad you enjoyed the trip. Did you get your homework done?"

"Yeah, Mom. I finished it on the plane."

So many times I didn't know Sophie was lying to me until long after the fact. Now I watched the lie effortlessly roll off her tongue. Wanting to end the charade, I said, "Okay, Sophie. It's time to tell the truth. What happened with the homework?"

"I finished it," she insisted in a convincing tone. She looked me straight in the eye.

I stopped and stared at her, silent for what seemed an eternity.

"What's wrong, Mom?" she asked with an air of innocence.

"Sophie," I said thoughtfully, "You left the homework under your bed. I found it the day you left. What were you thinking? What are you thinking now?"

"I don't know," Sophie pouted, her joy dissolving into anger. "I didn't want to do it."

"Sophie, you've created this problem. You're going to have to fix it. I'm glad you enjoyed the trip, but your teachers and I expect you to do the work you missed."

"I know, Mom," she sighed, the buoyancy of moments ago deflating as quickly as a collapsing soufflé.

The homework she'd left under her bed was never done. She told her teachers she took it with her, did it, and lost it in Israel. Even when given a second and third chance to complete the work, Sophie came up with one lame excuse after another until, one by one, each teacher entered a failing grade.

CHAPTER 31

Sneaking Out

March 2008. Sophie is fifteen and a half years old.

The piercing ring of the phone startled me. It was 4:07 A.M.

I reached over Josh and grabbed the phone.

"Hey, Mom, it's me," Sophie's voice was hoarse. "I'm at the front door. Can you let me in?"

I flew downstairs and turned off the security system.

Opening the door, I looked into her vacant eyes. She hobbled inside, a pinkish-grey slipper on her right foot. Her left foot was bare. She wore a thin hoodie. Her jeans were ripped. She held her right hand to the back of her head. Her hair was disheveled.

"What happened?" I cried.

"I got scared and needed to get out of my room. I couldn't breathe."

"How long have you been gone?"

"Since 11:30. I went for a walk to the pond."

Her hand was covered with partially dry blood.

"Sophie, your hand is all bloody. What happened?"

"I slipped on some mud, fell, and hit my head on a rock."

I guided her to the bathroom and gently moved her damp hair so I could examine her scalp. There was a two-inch gash across the back of her head. I was overcome by a wave of wooziness.

"Josh, Sophie's hurt," I said, in a voice loud enough for him to hear but not loud enough to wake Aaron.

Josh scrambled down the steps. As he cleaned the wound, I tried to catch my breath.

"How did you get out of the house without my hearing you?" We'd set the house alarm that night, as we did every night.

"I tied a bunch of sheets and belts together and slid down them from one of my windows," she said.

This can't be happening. I raced to her second floor bedroom. The small window on the side of the house was wide open. The sheets she'd tied to her bedpost and thrown over the sill dangled out the window, billowing in the wind. The rest of the room looked like a tornado had hit. Clothes were strewn about. The evening's math homework lay abandoned on the floor.

Josh took Sophie to the emergency room where five staples and gobs of surgical glue closed the laceration. Hours later, despite our pleas that she rest, Sophie insisted on not missing her first period English class.

I was shocked. To climb out a second story window in the middle of the night! To walk to a park in the dark! Never in my wildest imagination would I have done such things. But then I was the high school senior whose legs had quivered as, for two weeks, I'd stood at the end of the low diving board during gym class. Each period, I stared at the pool, finally jumping in only because not doing so would have meant failing gym. Even as a child, I would climb the dozen steps of a slide, only to freeze at the top, gaze down at the silvery surface, and then cautiously turn around and descend the steps.

Many of Sophie's untoward behaviors – the lying, homework avoidance, and laziness – were characteristic of normal kids. Her cutting and insistence on talking to strangers on the Internet may not have been normal, but they were not uncommon. With her escape in the middle of the night, she'd crossed into foreign territory.

When I reported this to Dr. Kane, she added Lamictal, an antipsychotic medication that she described as a "mood stabilizer," to the medicinal cocktail of Strattera, Concerta, and Zoloft that Sophie was already taking. Dr. Kane said Sophie's behavior suggested she was deeply troubled and she reminded me that her role was to make sure Sophie was properly medicated, and that it was critical that Sophie have a therapist with whom she could discuss her feelings and problems. I reminded her of our two failed therapeutic relationships and asked whether there was someone she could recommend. Just like the last time I'd asked, she had no one to recommend.

Sophie's long history of lying and the bizarre tale she told after sneaking out of the house convinced me there was more to the story than the panic attack she had described. What could have caused her to tie sheets together and shimmy out her second story window in the middle of the night? Short of nailing shut her windows and locking her bedroom door, how could we keep her safe? Josh and I spent countless hours talking about what could have happened. We tried desperately to get Sophie to explain why she'd snuck out of the house, but each time, no matter how we asked the question, she stuck to the story she had told us early that morning.

CHAPTER 32

First Love

Spring 2008. Sophie is fifteen and a half years old.

From the time Sophie was in preschool, she always had a boyfriend. In pre-kindergarten, she was smitten with Michael; in first grade, she wanted to marry Ryan. Her preference for boys as playmates was different from my own experiences as a child, but I never discouraged her from having friends who were boys.

During her sophomore year of high school, Sophie announced she and Max were "going out." This puzzled me since I'd never been introduced to Max nor had he ever come to the house. In fact, as far as I knew, they'd never gone anywhere together. Clearly, the phrase "going out" had evolved from what it meant when I was in high school.

That spring, when the high school announced the date for its Sophomore Cotillion, Sophie and Max made plans to attend. Concerned that their friends Ashley and Rick didn't have dates, Sophie and Max played matchmaker. Sophie told Ashley that Rick thought she was "hot;" Max told Rick that Ashley thought he was cute. Their efforts succeeded, and the four friends went to the dance together.

Shortly after the cotillion, Ashley and Rick decided they were ill-suited. Sophie and Max broke up and, within a few days, Sophie told me Rick was "adorable."

Unlike with Max, Sophie couldn't wait to introduce us to Rick. Josh and I liked him immediately. He was a clean-cut kid, his widowed mother paid attention to his comings and goings, and he was college-bound. I was struck by Rick's concern for Sophie. He called her in the morning to make sure she was awake and on her way to school, and often reminded her to finish her English homework. What was there not to like about him?

Proof that Sophie's feelings for Rick differed from those she had for other boys was her willingness to complete her homework and keep her room clean in exchange for the privilege of seeing him. One afternoon Sophie asked, "Mom, can Rick come over this evening and watch a movie with me?"

"Sure. Just as long as your homework is done and your room is clean."

"My homework's almost done. I have to finish a few math problems. It shouldn't take me more than ten minutes. But my room's a mess. I don't have time to clean it before he comes over."

"I guess you'll have to make plans with him for some other time."

"But Mom," she whined. "I really, really want to see him."

"Then finish your math and clean your room."

Not thirty minutes later, Sophie called from the second floor banister, "Mom, my room's clean. Come check it."

"On my way," I called dashing up the stairs.

Entering her room, I was amazed to see she had, in fact, picked up all the dirty laundry from the floor and put it in her hamper. Her desk was clutter-free, as were her nightstands. How'd she do it so fast? Certain she'd stuffed everything under her bed – a trick she frequently resorted to – I bent down to look. I moved the dust ruffle and, to my astonishment, there was but a lone sock.

"Sophie, this is amazing. How about the bathroom vanity and your closet?" I asked, knowing these were her favorite squirrel zones.

"Clean as a whistle," she proclaimed proudly. "See for yourself."

Cautiously I opened the door to the vanity under her sink that so often held a hodgepodge of trash, candy bars, and makeup. I found only her hairdryer and curling iron with their cords neatly wrapped, a couple of rolls of toilet paper, and a bottle of bubble bath.

"Sophie, this is mind-boggling!"

Opening the door to her closet, I was sure the fifty pounds of junk she'd stuffed in there would topple on my head. But it didn't. She had hung up her shirts and pants; even her hoodies were on hangers. Matched pairs of shoes were lined up along the bottom of the closet, and her purses were organized on the shelves.

"Looks great, Sophie. Go ahead with your plans to see Rick tonight."

Yes, for me, Sophie's relationship with Rick was a useful one. It confirmed that she was capable of fulfilling her responsibilities, despite her protests to the contrary. I encouraged Sophie to invite Rick to join us for dinner, and enjoyed getting to know him.

It wasn't long, however, before Josh and I suspected Rick had some significant emotional problems of his own. At dinner one evening, Rick said, "My mom is such a pain in the butt. Last weekend, she pissed me off so much that I ripped the oven door off its hinges and threw it at her."

I was struck not only by his intense anger and callousness, but also by his decision to share the story with us. As Rick spoke, even Sophie wriggled in her chair.

That evening after Rick left, I shared my concerns about Rick's temper with Sophie. She brushed off my worries, defending Rick as she lambasted his mother.

It was clear to me that Rick was bad news, but I knew that if I insisted Sophie stop seeing him, it would only draw them closer.

One afternoon Sophie called me in a panic. "Mom, I'm worried about Rick."

"What's the problem?"

"He's angry with his mother. She told him that he's not allowed to see me anymore because he didn't do his chores. He has a knife, and he says he's going to kill himself. I have him on the other line. What should I do?"

"Sophie, do you believe he's telling you the truth?"

"I do, Mom," she answered anxiously. "He's hurt himself before."

What is it with these kids and harming themselves?

"I want you to keep talking to Rick. Try to calm him down.

While you're doing that, I'm going to call 9-1-1 and get someone over there to help him. Do you understand what I'm telling you?"

"Yes, Mom. I'll talk to him. Thanks for helping me."

I hung up the phone and dialed 9-1-1. A rescue squad was dispatched to Rick's house and, within a half hour, he was admitted to Tri-county Hospital's crisis center. When he was released to his mother's care later that evening, he called Sophie to thank her.

A couple of weeks later, I awoke at two o'clock in the morning and noticed the hall light was on. As I reached to turn it off, Sophie's cough, coming from the first floor, startled me. "Sophie?" I whispered tiptoeing downstairs. "Is that you?"

"Yeah, Mom, it's me." She stood in the dining room, wearing shorts and a blue hoodie, the hood wrapped around her head.

"What are you doing?"

"I got thirsty. I was going to the drugstore for a Coke."

"What? At two o'clock in the morning? Upstairs now. Goodnight. I'll see you in the morning." She plodded up the stairs, her plans quashed, head hung in disappointment.

I climbed into bed in utter disbelief. What was that about? Walking a mile and a half to the drugstore for a Coke in the middle of the night when she has a refrigerator full of food and drinks? About an hour later, the phone rang. It was Rick. "Mrs. Segal?" he asked, his voice shaking.

"Yes."

"Uh, do you know where Sophie is?"

"In her room asleep," I said groggily.

"Are you sure?"

"Yes, Rick. I'm sure."

"Oh, okay. I wanted to make sure she was okay."

"She's fine," I reassured him. "We'll talk about this tomorrow." I hung up the phone.

"What was that about?" asked Josh rousing from sleep.

"Crazy kids. I'll tell you in the morning."

Over breakfast, Sophie confessed this wasn't the first time she'd snuck out of the house to meet Rick in the middle of the night. She explained she would say goodnight to us, feign retiring to her room for the evening, and then creep downstairs and sneak out the basement door before we set the house alarm. Our home was three miles from Rick's, so she'd meet him at a mid-point.

There they would talk and kiss until the skies lightened. She would return home and sneak back in after I turned off the alarm and let the dogs out.

How could she leave the house during the night without Josh, Aaron, or me knowing? It never occurred to me to check her bed before retiring for the night. Would a good mother have checked?

Did this explain her tying the sheets together and leaving the house in the middle of the night months ago? No, I thought. Sophie and Rick weren't dating then.

I attributed this behavior to teenagers with too much time on their hands. But I would soon learn that Sophie's sneaking out of the house in the middle of the night to meet her boyfriend was mere child's play.

CHAPTER 33

Sex in My Father's House

Summer 2008. Sophie is nearly sixteen years old.

Nothing on my résumé qualified me to be Sophie's mother. As a child, I was reserved, obedient, and shy. I never got into trouble. The most egregious challenge I presented to my parents was when I fell in love with a boy who wasn't Jewish – and that was when I was a freshman in college.

I first had "The Talk" with Sophie when she was in fifth grade. I'd given her the thirty-second where-babies-come-from explanation, to which she'd responded with an air of sophistication, "I know, Mom. They made us watch the movie in school." Following the elementary school curriculum, we talked about periods, sanitary napkins, and tampons. She couldn't wait for her first period.

When her best friend Kate got her period, Sophie worried it would never be her turn. I reassured her time and time again it would happen, counseling her to be patient. I also told her that having a period, like growing up, wasn't all she thought it was cracked up to be.

One day, shortly after her eleventh birthday, Sophie came home from school with a wide grin and said, "Mom, it finally happened."

I looked at her quizzically. "What happened?"

"My period. I got my period," she jumped up and down.

"Congratulations," I said, giving her a hug and handing her a bag of sanitary napkins. "Want to do something special to celebrate? How about getting your nails done?"

"Yes!" she squealed.

We'd engaged in other versions of "The Talk" over the years – talks in which she asked about sex, wondering what it would feel like, worrying whether it would be painful. Like the talk my mother had given me at that age, I assured Sophie that sex with the right person at the right time was a very loving experience, but sex with the wrong person could be heartbreaking.

Sophie's dangerous behaviors – sneaking out of the house in the middle of the night, cutting herself, rages when she didn't get her way – and now her growing infatuation with Rick, made it clear that Josh and I needed help parenting Sophie. All the love we had for her wasn't enough. Her previous experiences with the two therapists hadn't been productive, largely because Sophie went to the sessions begrudgingly. Once there, she either set the agenda or humored the therapist, avoiding a meaningful discussion by telling lies, much as she so skillfully did with Josh and me.

Heeding Dr. Kane's advice, I searched again for a therapist Sophie would trust enough to work through some of the issues that troubled her. This time, I used the recommendation of a colleague to find a seasoned therapist, Dr. Shuman. Even though we'd have to wait two months for Dr. Shuman's first available appointment *and* she didn't accept insurance *and* her rates were considerable, Josh and I agreed that, if she could help Sophie, it was worth the wait and the expense.

Sophie took an immediate liking to Dr. Shuman and, after each of their weekly sessions, she looked forward to the next. Within a few weeks, Dr. Shuman expressed concern about the medications Sophie was taking. She questioned why Sophie needed an antidepressant, especially with the other medications she was taking, and she suggested we get a second opinion. I was impressed with Dr. Shuman's recommendation, but I felt guilty questioning Dr. Kane's expertise, so I did not follow through on her advice.

Dr. Shuman told me about a summer program for kids with ADHD held at Wellspring College in Vermont. One of her former patients had attended the program, and Dr. Shuman suggested that the three-week program might strengthen Sophie's organizational skills.

Scouring the Wellspring website, I learned the program offered kids the opportunity to discover and practice academic skills as well as the chance to experience college life first-hand. Most impressive was that many of the faculty had overcome learning and organizational problems of their own. I figured these teachers would provide Sophie with positive role models.

Sophie's guidance counselor, Ms. Blanche, loudly sang the praises of the Wellspring program. She said that two boys from the high school who'd attended the program had seen marked improvement in their grades and had been accepted to first-rate colleges.

This was a program tailor-made for Sophie. Now my problem was pitching this incredible opportunity to her. While I didn't like the idea, Sophie had been looking forward to spending the summer with Rick. Should I, her clueless mother, suggest the Wellspring program to her, there was no way she would go. I needed to develop a plan that would have Sophie begging to go and so I enlisted the help of her guidance counselor. I asked Ms. Blanche to call Sophie down to her office, tell her about Wellspring, inform her it was a very select and prestigious program, and ask Sophie's permission to nominate her for the competitive program. I knew Sophie would respond positively to such an opportunity.

A couple days later, Sophie met me at the door, bursting with excitement. "Mom, you'll never believe what happened today."

"What, Sophie?"

"Ms. Blanche called me down to her office and told me about the most amazing program. It's just for kids with ADHD. It teaches you how to get organized. Even the teachers have ADHD!"

"Wow," I admitted, "that sounds great." Careful not to let her see my enthusiasm, I asked, "Do you know how much the program costs?"

"Yeah, it's expensive," she said, an edge to her voice. "Ms. Blanche told me it costs about five thousand dollars. She's going to nominate me for the program. The only way to get into the program is for your guidance counselor to recommend you." Her voice rose in excitement. "Ms. Blanche could only nominate one person from our whole school, and she chose me! Can you believe it?"

"Five thousand dollars for three weeks? That's even more expensive than Aaron's camp. I'm afraid that's probably not within our budget this summer, but let's talk to Dad tonight and see what he thinks."

I was ready to nominate myself for "Devious Mother of The Year" for coming up with the plan and an Oscar for the stellar performance I'd just delivered. Perhaps I had learned something about acting from watching Sophie through the years.

Aaron's camp and Sophie's summer program started on the same day. We packed the car early that morning and headed for Aaron's camp. From there we would drive to Wellspring and get Sophie settled.

Lulled as always by the car's rhythmic motion, Sophie snoozed for the first two hours of the trip. When she awoke, she read, and then, as though just realizing Aaron would be starting middle school that fall, said, "Oh my gosh, Aaron, I can't believe you're going to be in middle school! Those were some of the best years of my life. There was no pressure. People weren't dating. Life was great back then."

Aaron grunted. Josh continued driving, attending to the road rather than to the conversation in the back seat. I listened, my antennae up. Had I heard what I thought I'd heard? My mind raced. Pressure? Dating? What had I missed? Not wanting to get the answers to these questions while Aaron was within earshot, I said nothing until we stopped for gas.

"Sophie, come with me to the bathroom and then we'll get some munchies for the trip."

Approaching the convenience store, I asked, "Where did that comment you made about no pressure in middle school come from? Is Rick pressuring you about sex?"

"No, but we've talked about it," she said.

And then, as she tried to decide whether she wanted potato chips, corn chips, or Doritos, she said, "Mom, I think I should go on The Pill."

I'm sure there's a right time for a conversation like this, but standing in the snack aisle at a highway convenience store wasn't it. Although Sophie would be sixteen on her next birthday, and half of all high school kids have had at least one sexual relationship by that age, her emotional maturity fell far short of her chronological age. Caught unaware, I said, "Sophie, this conversation needs more time than we have now. Let's talk about it when I pick you up from Wellspring."

"Okay, Mom. Let's get something to drink, too. I'm thirsty," she said nonchalantly, as if we had been discussing the weather.

I spent the next three weeks figuring out what parental wisdom I could come up with that might dissuade my headstrong daughter from having sex. Knowing Josh would become distraught over the idea that his baby girl wanted to have sex, I didn't discuss it with him. I did talk with some of my girlfriends and learned that many of those with teenage daughters had already agreed to let their daughters go on The Pill. Their rationales were pragmatic. As one friend said, "She's going to have sex no matter what I say, but at least I can help avoid the nightmare of an unwanted teenage pregnancy." A reasonable perspective, I thought. Still, I couldn't help but think Sophie just wasn't ready.

The week before Sophie's program ended, I met my friend and colleague Maureen in Amherst where we attended a three-day statistics seminar at the University of Massachusetts. I knew Maureen's levelheaded approach would serve as a great sounding board for my dilemma. Between power walks across the campus and quiet dinners, we analyzed and strategized. We agreed that my telling Sophie to abstain from sex would be as effective as telling a young child not to eat an unwrapped lollypop placed in her hand. Rather, I needed to let Sophie know my opinion and give her practical things to think about so she could make an informed decision. She faced an adult choice, and I needed to treat her like an adult.

Our seminar over, I headed north on I-91 toward Vermont where I spent two glorious nights and a day by myself before retrieving Sophie. I meandered through the shops, learned about the marvels of maple syrup, and enjoyed the nearby Marlboro Music Festival.

Pleasant memories of my respite centering me, I steeled myself for the conversation I promised Sophie we would have on our way home. For the first half-hour of our trip, she regaled me with stories of her most amazing roommate, Mindy, and their friend Steve. The trio of Mindy, Steve, and Sophie had been insep-arable for the three weeks, and there had been tears all around when we left.

Academically, Sophie performed well at Wellspring. She completed her coursework and won accolades from her instructors. She set thoughtful goals for her next academic year that included completing assignments in a timely manner, using active reading skills, taking thorough notes, earning at least three A's, and effec-tively managing her time. Socially, she had the time of her life. She was jazzed about college life. Five thousand dollars well spent.

With fifty miles behind us, Sophie, said, "So Mom, about that conversation. I've been thinking a lot about it, and I really want to go on The Pill."

I took a deep breath, thinking I'd try the practical tactic first. "Do you realize you have to take The Pill at the same time every day, and that you can't miss any days?"

"Yes," she nodded.

"Do you think you can be responsible enough to do that?"

"Yeah," she shrugged.

"You haven't expressed interest in taking your ADHD meds by yourself. I can't see myself doling out your birth control pill every morning."

"I'd take it myself."

Next tactic.

"Sophie, you and Rick have been dating for just a few months. Why not wait awhile before you think about having sex? Give the relationship a chance. You're still getting to know each other."

"Mom, I really love Rick. I've never felt this way about any-one before."

"I understand, but sex is a huge commitment. So many things can go wrong. You have to be in the right relationship before you have sex or you can get badly hurt." What I wanted to tell her was that any boy who would throw an oven door at his mother was bad news but, I knew if I said that, there would be no chance she'd listen to me.

"He is the right guy for me. I really love him," she whined. Ah, the whining – further proof that she was so not ready for sex. It was like talking to a three-year-old.

"You know, Sophie, at barely sixteen, you're awfully young to be engaged in a sexual relationship. I was in college when I first had sex."

"Mom, things were different then. You worry too much about me."

"Of course I do. I'm worried you're rushing into something that has the potential to hurt you. Birth control pills, if used correctly, can keep you from getting pregnant, but you also need to worry about sexually transmitted diseases. When you have sex with someone, you're also having sex with all their previous partners."

"Mom, Rick's never had sex. That's not a problem."

She'd been thinking about this and had reasonable answers to my questions. I had one chance left.

"So Sophie, if you and Rick were going to have sex, where would you go to have it?"

She thought about it for ten seconds. "My room?"

"You've got to be kidding! Do you think Dad would stand by, knowing you were having sex in our house?"

"But, Mom," she moaned. "Where else could we go?"

"Precisely, Sophie. That's just one of the many reasons why teenagers aren't ready to have sex."

For the rest of the ride home, she gave me the silent treatment. But that was nothing compared to the agony she was about to put me through.

CHAPTER 34

Wrinkled Paper

September 2008. Sophie is sixteen years old.

T here were seven hundred twenty days of high school. On almost half those days, Sophie left her curling iron or hair straightener plugged in when she left for school. On two-thirds of the days, when we had the heat or air conditioning on, she left a window open. More often than not, she left the remnants of a midnight snack in her room – a melted half-gallon of chocolate ice cream seeping onto the bathroom floor, an open package of Oreo cookies, or a partially eaten bag of chips.

And so breezing through Sophie's room each morning became part of my daily routine. Sometimes there'd be evidence that she'd been developing a new homemade beauty treatment, and I'd find pieces of sliced cucumbers mixed with yogurt congealing in a container in her bathtub. Other days I'd find yarn, crayons, sewing material, and paper cut-outs strewn about. Some days I would find single-edged industrial razor blades, cigarette lighters, or a utility knife lying on the sink of her vanity. On those days my blood turned to ice. What was she was doing with them? I always threw them out, yet mysteriously replacements always reappeared within days.

On the day Josh turned fifty-three, I stopped when I reached her bathroom. A cardboard package on her vanity had caught my eye. A wrinkled piece of paper lay in the sink. Picking it up, horror set in. I was looking at instructions for administering a home pregnancy test. My hands shaking, I read its user-friendly instructions about urinating on a stick, waiting five minutes, and then reading the results.

I raced for the trashcan. A small white stick with a Plus symbol in its center greeted me. *She's pregnant!* I threw open the toilet seat lid and heaved.

Of course, I thought, my heart pounding. Being pregnant explains her lack of appetite, her complaints of nausea, and her mysterious trips to the bathroom. Although she'd tried to convince me that she had a stomach bug and that the Strawberry Special K I had bought by mistake was making her sick, it was now clear what the problem was.

Josh paled when I told him about my discovery. We decided that, since this was a problem Sophie had created, it was one that she, not we, should solve. We agreed if she wanted to keep the baby, she'd have to drop out of high school and get a job; we weren't going to allow her to abdicate responsibility by foisting the care, feeding, and support of a baby on us. We also agreed that, if she wanted to have an abortion, we'd support that decision. Josh spent the day researching her options.

Leaving the chaos of the morning behind, I drove to the office. There I reveled in my other life, the fulfilling career that was mine. I put the final touches on a paper and submitted it to a journal, reviewed a grant proposal for an upcoming meeting, and laughed with my research assistant about the latest antics of her six-year-old son. How sane this part of my life was!

When Sophie came home from school, Josh and I confronted her with my morning discovery. She seemed relieved that we knew. She confided she didn't know how long it had been since her last period, but she thought it was between six and eight weeks. When we asked what she intended to do, she said she was leaning toward terminating the pregnancy. She had shared her plans with Rick, and he was helping her get money together to pay for the procedure. But she hadn't yet found a doctor or a clinic.

Searching the Internet, Sophie believed the Morning After Pill made the most sense. "I mean, all I have to do is take a pill and it will take care of everything. And it's a lot less expensive than an abortion." Her child-like approach to what I expected should be a gut-wrenching decision to terminate a pregnancy was a cold slap in my face, all the more poignant given the efforts I'd made to get pregnant years ago.

Josh explained, "The Morning After Pill might not be the wisest choice. I did some reading about it and learned that the timing of the miscarriage it induces isn't predictable. You can't take the pill when you get home from school in the afternoon and expect by nightfall everything will be done. It could take several days and you might miscarry in the middle of a class at school."

Sophie didn't seem convinced. So Josh continued. "More importantly, you don't know how far along you are. You think six to eight weeks. If you're right, then it's too late. After a couple weeks, the Morning After Pill isn't reliable. If you want to terminate this pregnancy, I'm afraid you're going to need an abortion."

As Josh handed Sophie the information he'd amassed, his face was etched with sadness. It had been a long and stressful day for him. I shared in his pain. What a lovely way for a father to spend his birthday. Happy birthday from your sweet and innocent little girl.

Within hours, Sophie understood Josh's point and decided to have an abortion. She called the clinic he'd found and scheduled the procedure for the following day.

I called in sick, drove Sophie to the appointment, held her hand during the intake process, and sat in the waiting room for five hours while she underwent the procedure and recovered. Tests indicated she'd been between ten and twelve weeks pregnant. Counting the weeks backward, I realized that, when Sophie first mentioned the idea of going on The Pill at the convenience store, she already was pregnant. And, more likely than not, when we had our heart-felt conversation on the way home from Vermont, she'd already missed a period and suspected she was pregnant. These realizations were yet two more hard-hitting punches delivered right to my gut.

CHAPTER 35

The Aftermath of Love

Fall 2008. Sophie is sixteen years old.

A
lthough Rick was supportive of Sophie before and immediately after the abortion, he broke up with her during the first week of school. She cried non-stop, talked about him, and tried countless attempts to win him back. He only spurned her. Unfortunately for Sophie, Rick was in her history class. I doubt she heard more than half the words the history teacher said as she pined over Rick.

Sophie flailed in all directions. As always, when her emotions spun out of control, Sophie's mean behaviors toward Aaron increased. Now age twelve, the same age I was when my mother's illness became evident and my world exploded, Aaron was aware of at least some of Sophie's problems. I worried about what he must think of his sister and what, if anything, he'd told his friends. Harkening back to the secrets kept when my mother was ill, I struggled with finding a balance between wanting Aaron to be honest and wanting to protect him. More than once, fearing he'd be ostracized if others knew of Sophie's strange behaviors, I warned him not to tell anyone the truth.

Although Josh and I had made it clear to Sophie that lashing out at Aaron was unacceptable, her behavior continued unabated. One afternoon, after Sophie punched Aaron, I said to him, "I know you know hitting is wrong, and you'd never hurt

Sophie, but she's not getting it. The next time she hits you, you have my permission to haul off and slug her right back."

"Really, Mom?"

"Really, Aaron. We've tried everything else – talking to her, punishing her – and she just doesn't get it. Maybe if she gets a taste of her own medicine, she'll figure out hitting is wrong."

Minutes later, Sophie walked by Aaron, pushed him, and said, "What's up, Shrimpo?"

He looked at me. "Go for it," I said. Aaron slammed his fist into her arm, and stared at her.

"What the fuck?" Sophie screamed.

"Payback, Sophie," I explained, "How dare you push your brother."

She launched a full attack, hitting Aaron, screaming as she grabbed and pulled his hair. He looked at me, tears in his eyes, and said, "Guess that didn't work too well, Mom."

I wanted to crawl into a hole. What a horrible mistake I'd made.

Dr. Shuman tried to help Sophie work through her sadness and sense of loss. Josh and I shared with her our stories of our own unrequited loves – of how they hurt and of how we eventually got over them. While I wasn't sorry to see the relationship with Rick end, as I recognized that his problems only exacerbated Sophie's, it broke my heart to witness her pain. She was inconsolable. I felt as ineffective as I had years ago when I'd watched my mother's pain overwhelm her. I worried Sophie might harm herself.

Toward the end of October, my cell phone rang. "Mrs. Segal, this is Mrs. Leland, Vice Principal at Northern High School. Sophie's not hurt, but I need you to come to the school as soon as possible."

Now what? I drove to the school, my stomach oozing. It was just my luck that Josh had started his new job that morning and was on a plane to Peoria. I was on my own.

Arriving at the school, I found my way to Mrs. Leland's office. Sophie sat in a chair, staring out the window. She didn't even look up when I entered the room.

"Sophie and Lorna got into a scuffle during lunch period," Mrs. Leland began. "There was pushing, hitting, and hair pulling involved. One of the teachers witnessed the fight begin, warned the girls, and tried to stop the fight, but they wouldn't listen to him."

My ears roared. "What?" I asked. While Sophie had hit her brother, I was astonished that she would resort to a physical tussle with a peer. A rush of heat overcame me.

"It seems Sophie was trying to buy marijuana from Lorna's boyfriend," Mrs. Leland continued.

"I was not," Sophie bridled. "That's not what happened. She's lying."

"What did happen?" I asked, hoping even now that Sophie, the consummate liar, was telling the truth and there was a reasonable explanation for this bizarre accusation.

"A couple weeks ago, I asked Connor to get me some marijuana because I was so sad about Rick. He said he would, but then he got suspended for having drugs in school. This morning, I told him I didn't want the marijuana anymore. Lorna heard me talking to Connor. She thought I was flirting and encouraging him to smoke. But I wasn't. Lorna got mad at me and sent me nasty texts all morning. When we were standing in the lunch line, Lorna called me a bitch and told me to stay away from Connor. I tried to tell her what happened. The more I talked, the angrier Lorna got. She hit me and grabbed my hair. Then I hit her and grabbed her hair. Before I knew it, we were on the ground fighting."

The left side of my brain had me positing how such a situation could escalate into a fight while the right side of my brain wanted to kill Sophie for stooping so low. As I labored to maintain my composure, Mrs. Leland said Sophie and Lorna were being suspended from school for four days and that, because drugs were suspected, Sophie needed to pass a drug test before returning to school.

Four days?! Not only would this undermine Sophie's schoolwork, but it also meant I would miss four days of work – and with a major grant proposal due at the end of the month. Juggling my career and the challenges Sophie presented had never been easy, but this looked insurmountable, especially with Josh out of town. I tried negotiating with Mrs. Leland to lessen the sentence, but she wouldn't budge.

Dejected, Sophie and I left the school. As Sophie had insisted, the drug test supported her claim that she had not smoked marijuana. We spent our four days together, Sophie doing the schoolwork she was missing, while I wrote the grant proposal. This wasn't the first time I appreciated the flexibility that academic life provided. What would have happened to my career had I been a lawyer, a salesperson, or a high school teacher?

About a month later, Sophie left her cell phone in Josh's car. Turning it on, Josh saw Sophie was exchanging dark text messages and pornographic pictures with several high school boys. We suspected she was often high and deduced from notes she left around the house that she was engaging in sexual behavior with multiple partners. My daughter had become the school whore. I wanted to die.

I brought Sophie's behavior to the attention of Dr. Kane, who changed Sophie's medications yet again. This time she discontinued the Concerta and Strattera and started Sophie on Vyvance, keeping her on Lamictal and Zoloft. Dr. Shuman continued to help Sophie understand that her behaviors were counterproductive to her goal of gaining independence. I answered note after note from concerned teachers.

While Sophie struck out in all directions, she also became clingy. One night, when Josh was out of town, Sophie knocked on my bedroom door and said, "I'm feeling sad. I've been in my room, thinking about how much I miss Rick. Can we have a sleep-over?"

"Of course, Sophie. Grab your pillow and blanket, and come on in." Truth of the matter was I'd spent countless nights worrying about her. I knew she slept poorly, understood how distraught she was about Rick, and feared she might do something to harm herself. This fear was much too reminiscent of my experiences as a teenager when I had worried about whether my mother would kill herself. As Sophie flopped into bed, she said, "I love Dad, but I'm glad he's not here tonight."

Within minutes, the melodic rhythm of her breathing indicated she was sleeping. The stress of the day was over and she was, I hoped, dreaming of a more pleasant time.

I lay there thinking I would have done anything to make her pain go away – just like when I was twelve and wished I could make my mother's pain stop.

CHAPTER 36

The Kindness of Strangers

January 2009. Sophie is sixteen and a half years old.

Josh and I took our responsibility for educating Sophie and Aaron about culture seriously. We took frequent trips to New York City where we visited the Metropolitan Museum of Art, the Guggenheim, and The Museum of Modern Art. A Broadway show was always a must. We maintained a membership at the Philadelphia Museum of Art and frequently went to concerts at the Wang and Kimmel Centers. We were season ticket holders to the Sunday afternoon Phillies baseball games and had center stage tickets for Saturday evening performances at the Walnut Street Theatre.

Not surprisingly, Aaron much preferred the baseball games to the arts, although he spent more time sampling the ballpark's cuisine than actually watching the games. A cheesesteak dripping in onions, mushrooms, and hot sauce was a staple. French fries slathered in ketchup with a hot dog were favorites. A chocolate ice cream cone during the seventh inning stretch had become tradition.

While Sophie tolerated the baseball games, she lived for the theatre. This season we had chuckled our way through *Hairspray* and looked forward to Tennessee Williams' *A Streetcar Named Desire*. Sophie was excited about seeing the show since she recently had read the play in her English class.

As we made our way from the Thai restaurant to the theatre, I pulled my scarf tight against the wind.

"Oh good," Sophie squealed. "He's here." Despite the chilly evening, the homeless man who often sat outside the theatre was cuddled on the ground with his small dog. Both shivered beneath their tattered blanket. "I'll catch up with you guys in a minute, Mom."

I watched the ease with which Sophie greeted the man. Her comfort around strangers and casual acquaintances always surprised me, mostly because it was so different from my own behavior. As Sophie reached into her pocket to add money to the cup resting at his feet, I thought about how she would do almost anything to help people going through a difficult time. I remembered the campaign she spearheaded prior to her Bat Mitzvah, collecting and donating hundreds of stuffed animals for kids at the Camden Women's Shelter. She seemed to feel the pain of people less fortunate than she. I thought back to when Sophie was at camp and had given a crying child her last dollar, enabling the girl to buy a Popsicle. What made Sophie want to help strangers even when it meant she would go without? As she turned to leave, she reached into her other pocket and handed the man a baggie she'd filled with Milk-Bone biscuits for his dog.

Settling into our seats, Sophie's excitement grew. From the moment the curtain rose and the bluesy notes of the piano played, Sophie was captivated. My joy in seeing a play with Sophie always had as much to do with observing her reactions as it did with watching the actors. When Stanley beat Stella, Sophie cringed. When Stella forgave Stanley and passionately embraced him, Sophie smiled. When Blanche gave the paperboy a lustful kiss, Sophie rolled her eyes. When Stanley raped Blanche, a tear rolled down Sophie's face. When Blanche said, "I have always depended on the kindness of strangers" and the doctor led her from Stella's house to the psychiatric hospital, Sophie sobbed.

She was still crying when the curtain fell and the lights went up.

"What's wrong with you?" Aaron scoffed.

"The play," she answered. "It was amazing."

"Why would you cry over a dumb old play?"

She kicked him.

"Sophie, knock it off," I said. As we left the theatre, a blast of frigid air hit us.

On the way home, Aaron started again. "That was a stupid play."

"You're such a dumb fuck," Sophie said, smacking his arm.

"Sophie, don't hit him and lose the gutter talk," Josh said.

"He's such an asshole," she cried. "The play was amazing."

"Sophie, I'm glad you enjoyed the play, but Aaron has a right to dislike it and you have no right to hit him," I said.

"That's bullshit," Sophie snarled. "I hate all of you."

I looked at Sophie. Where had her venom come from? How could she have been so compassionate toward the homeless man just a few hours ago, so sensitive to the characters in the play minutes ago, and so callous toward us now?

CHAPTER **37**

Whack-A-Mole

Spring 2009. Sophie is sixteen and a half years old.

B y February, Sophie's grades plummeted and the number of Sophie-Isn't-Doing-Her-Homework notes grew exponentially. One of the teachers wrote, "Sophie seems very distracted. She's not at all interested in her schoolwork. Is she involved in some extracurricular activity I should know about?"

Occasionally, her clothes reeked of marijuana and she was giddy. Josh patiently explained that, aside from it being illegal to smoke marijuana and its potential to get her in serious trouble at school, it was a depressant that interfered with the medications Dr. Kane had prescribed. Sophie didn't care. We removed her privileges. She wasn't fazed.

As I toiled to keep Sophie organized, insisting she complete her homework and helping her study for quizzes and tests, her disdain grew. Although we'd become accustomed to her throwing candy wrappers under the sofa pillows, leaving apple cores on the coffee table, and tossing grape stems on the floor, we now found more serious evidence of her scorn. When she waxed her legs, she smeared wax on the walls of her bathtub and on the floor of her bathroom. When she dyed her hair red, the towels, the white carpet on her bedroom floor, and her robe were stained with red blotches. She glued a penny to her bathroom vanity.

One afternoon, Josh waited for Sophie after play practice. When she didn't meet him as planned, he went looking for her. The director told Josh that Sophie hadn't been at practice and volunteered that this wasn't the first practice she'd missed. In a panic, Josh called me to see whether Sophie had come home. She had not. While Josh looked for her, I called Sophie's cell phone.

She answered after a few rings. "Hi, Sophie. Where are you?"

"Play practice," she lied.

"How's it going?" I asked, playing along.

"Good. I'm between scenes right now, but we'll be running my scene next."

"How much longer do you think you'll be? I'll let Dad know when to pick you up."

"I don't know. I'll probably be done in fifteen or twenty minutes. Tell Dad a half-hour."

"Okay."

I hung up and called Josh. Clear that we'd caught her in a lie, he waited for Sophie to arrive and planned to confront her. About twenty minutes later, a car pulled into the school's parking lot and stopped two hundred yards from the theatre door. Sophie swung open the door and jumped out. As the car peeled out of the parking lot, Josh saw that its driver was Max, Sophie's former boyfriend.

Josh pulled up to the theatre entrance.

"Hi, Dad," Sophie began. "Mom said you were coming, but play practice ran late. Did you have to wait long?"

"Jig's up, Sophie. You can save your performance for the stage. I saw you get out of Max's car a minute ago and I know you skipped practice."

"No I didn't. I was at practice," she insisted.

"I don't think so, Sophie. I've been here for a half hour. The director said you weren't at practice, and I saw you get out of Max's car. You're busted. How about telling the truth now?"

"I want to talk to Mom."

"Be my guest. Call her."

"I want to talk to Mom in private."

"Fine. I'm going to talk to the director. He has a right to know where you've been. Meet me in the theatre when you're done talking to Mom."

Sophie burst into tears when I answered the phone. She admitted that she and Max had been at his house having sex. I was shocked that she would admit engaging in such promiscuous behavior, yet I wondered whether I had the right to be shocked at anything she did. "Okay, Sophie," I said hearing the resignation in my voice. "Go find Dad. We'll talk about it when you get home."

I called Josh and told him about my conversation with Sophie. He was furious. But, unlike me, he didn't want to wait until he got home to analyze the situation. "That's it. She's out of the play. I'm taking her into the theatre where she can explain where she's been to the director. Then we're going to the emergency room. I don't know when we'll be home."

"Why are you going to the emergency room?"

"She's just had unprotected sex. I'm sure this isn't the first time. Between this and all the pornographic texts I found on her phone, it's clear something's seriously wrong with her. She needs help. I'm taking her to the emergency room. I don't know where else to go." He was close to tears; my heart went out to him. What a horrible situation for a father to face.

At the emergency room, Josh told the intake worker he believed Sophie was very troubled, and pleaded with him to try and figure out what was wrong with her. Hearing only that Sophie recently had unprotected sex, the resident gave her a cursory test for sexually transmitted diseases and sent her home.

I was playing a real-life version of Whack-A-Mole, the popular arcade game where a player uses a mallet to whack a mole popping up from one hole, only to be rewarded with two moles popping up. Solve one problem and two more arise. Get good at the game and the moles come fast and furious. Like the moles, Sophie popped up with one challenge after another for Josh and me. We whacked down one problem after another by meting out consequences, but new problems kept popping up. The consequences were doled out so fast and furiously that Josh pinned a list to the refrigerator so we could remember what she'd done, what consequences we'd imposed, and when each penalty would be satisfied.

And then another problem popped up.

CHAPTER 38

Secret Life

Spring 2009. Sophie is sixteen and a half years old.

"Are you and Josh able to meet with me this week?"

This e-mail from Dr. Shuman shook me to the core. When she'd started treating Sophie almost ten months earlier, Dr. Shuman explained to us how important it was for Sophie to feel safe talking about anything. She had said she wouldn't break the confidentiality of their relationship unless she felt Sophie was a menace to herself or others. Now Dr. Shuman had requested a meeting. What had Sophie done?

Our appointment scheduled, Josh and I spent three days agonizing about what Dr. Shuman would tell us. The morning of our appointment – a drab, chilly day in March – began with snow. I drove to Dr. Shuman's office where Josh waited for me. We sat in the waiting room. He chewed nervously on his fingers while I played idly with my cell phone. The ten-minute wait seemed like an eternity.

"Thank you so much for coming in," Dr. Shuman said in a hushed voice as she ushered us into her office. Once we were settled, she asked, "Have you noticed anything different about Sophie lately?"

You mean other than her wanton sexual behavior and her flagrant disregard for us? What was Dr. Shuman getting at?

I looked at her big gold wristwatch and waited for her to explain why we'd been summoned to her office.

"Has she been spending more time on the computer than usual?" she probed.

In fact, Sophie had been spending an inordinate amount of time on the computer. I suspected she did more than communicate with friends on Facebook and play the mindless computer games she enjoyed, but each time I poked my head into the study, she would look up from the computer and innocently ask if I wanted to join her for a game of *Bejeweled Blitz*, *Zombie Lane*, or *Sorority Life*. Hoping to learn what she were up to, I'd sneak up on her in stocking feet, but I'd never caught her doing anything but playing harmless computer games.

"Yes, she has," I said.

"I think it might be a good idea for you to put surveillance software on your computer so you can monitor what she's up to," Dr. Shuman urged.

Josh and I looked at each other, surprised.

"I believe Sophie's planning on sneaking out of the house to meet up with someone she's met on the Internet," Dr. Shuman explained.

"No way," I said.

"Do you really think she'd do that?" asked Josh.

"I believe she's done it before, maybe more than once," said Dr. Shuman.

Sophie had snuck out of the house the previous year to meet her boyfriend, but Dr. Shuman's claim that Sophie was planning on meeting up with someone she'd met on the Internet took things to a different level.

"Are you sure she's not telling you stories?" Josh questioned. "She's a master of lies and deception, and can make up the most elaborate stories and convince you they're true."

"I don't think so. Do you think you'd be here if I had any doubt?" she asked, looking at Josh and then at me. The crinkles on her forehead deepened.

"How can that be? We have an alarm on the house that we turn on every night," I said.

"Rachel, remember last summer when Sophie was sneaking out to meet Rick – how she told us she'd pretend to go up to bed and then leave through the basement door before we set the alarm?" Josh said.

Lights and warning signs flashed in my head. "Josh, do you remember the night she snuck out the window and hurt her head? When she said she couldn't sleep and needed to get out of the house? How she said she went down to the pond to clear her head?" I paused, as memories of that unexplained night flooded me.

"There was another night when the alarm went off at about eleven o'clock. I checked the house and didn't find anything wrong. Remember, the next morning you found a screen from one of the basement windows outside. She might have gotten out that night," Josh said.

"Right, and there was one Saturday morning when I let the dogs out, went to wake Sophie for play practice, and found she wasn't in her room. I searched the house, calling her as I went from room to room. I couldn't find her. Then, as I was letting the dogs back in, I ran into her in the basement. She must have snuck in through the basement door after I turned off the alarm and let the dogs out."

The implications of this flood of recollections sank in. Dr. Shuman was right.

"Do you have any idea when she's planning this rendezvous?" Josh asked.

She looked at her big wristwatch. Our fifty minutes must have been over. "No, I don't. But I suggest you get the surveillance software on the computer sooner rather than later."

Josh installed surveillance software on our home computer that evening. After a few days passed without observing anything out of the ordinary on the tracking logs, we reproached ourselves for believing this could have been a good idea. We were good parents. We were paying attention. Sure Sophie was a master of deception. She'd hidden a pregnancy from us and had snuck out of the house to meet her boyfriend. But sneaking out to meet someone she'd met on the Internet? This is the nightmare that lands on the front page of the newspaper. Nothing like this could be happening in our home – could it?

CHAPTER 39

But He's a Really Nice Guy

Two weeks later.

T wo weeks after our meeting with Dr. Shuman, Josh and I were invited to join Sophie's therapy session. Thinking Dr. Shuman wanted to discuss Sophie's plans to sneak out of the house, we convinced ourselves that Sophie couldn't seriously be planning to meet up with someone she'd met on the Internet.

After some small talk, Dr. Shuman said, "Sophie has been working very hard in our sessions lately, and she has something important she wants you to know about."

There are some memories so clear that I can describe where I was, what I was wearing, and how I felt when they happened.

Learning about my daughter's rape is not one of them.

I heard the words. I remember that my initial reaction was a combination of disbelief and shock. Could it be true? For years, Sophie had lied to Josh and me, to her teachers, and to her therapists. Was this yet another story designed to shock us? Most unbelievable was that Sophie told us the rape happened when she was eleven years old. How could she have hidden this for five years?

Sophie explained that a sixteen-year-old camp counselor from the day camp she'd attended in Massachusetts began flirting with her. His interest made her feel special. One afternoon, he lured her into the woods during free swim session, initially kissing her and then forcing her to touch his penis and perform oral sex. He coerced her to have sex with him several times and threatened to hurt her if she told anyone.

I could not believe what I was hearing. What pain she must have suffered, then and for five years since. How had she gone all this time without telling me?

Struggling to grasp what we'd heard, Josh asked, "When did this happen? How could we not have known? How could you not have told us? Is this why you've been so unhappy?" The questions tumbling out of his mouth were exactly those swimming in my head.

Josh continued, "Sophie, the day you came home from camp with the bruise on your cheek. Is that the day it happened?"

My skin prickled. The air tasted thick.

Not waiting for an answer, he plowed on with his recollection of that day. "I remember asking you what caused the bruise. At first you claimed you didn't know. Then you said you played Wiffle ball and that the ball hit your face. I said a Wiffle ball couldn't make such a mark. I knew something was wrong, but you got upset and Mom made me stop asking questions. I didn't want to, but I backed off, and gave you an out. I asked if you might have been hit by the bat or by a fouled-back ball. You said it was a batted ball that was fouled back and assured me you weren't hurt."

Josh looked at Sophie, then at me, then at Dr. Shuman. He stared at the ceiling. "How could I have been so stupid? If only I had listened to my gut."

Looking up at the ceiling did not stop the flood of tears from streaming down his face.

A ball had not made the marks on Sophie's face. Neither had a bat. They were the marks left by the counselor who struck her, keeping her from screaming while he raped her.

What did it take for an eleven-year-old to keep silent? How could she have come home that afternoon upbeat, happy, full of the usual stories about camp? How could she not tell me?

Within moments Josh's sadness turned to rage. "Sophie, who was he? What's his name?"

"Dad, I don't remember."

"I want to find him and cut off his balls," Josh seethed.

In the twenty-four years I'd known Josh, he'd never used such language.

I sat numbly watching the horror unfold. How could my daughter – who had talked non-stop from the time she first had learned to speak – have kept this from me?

"Sophie, are you ready to tell them the rest of it?" Dr. Shuman coaxed.

There's more? God help me.

"I guess so," she agreed, turning to me. "Mom, remember that night I snuck out of the house? When I told you I needed to get some air? Well, that wasn't the truth."

Bracing myself, I listened as Sophie talked.

"I didn't go down to the pond. I was sneaking out to meet a man I met on the Internet. He drove me to a hotel in Delaware and we had sex." She stared at the floor, unable to look at me.

"How did you get the cut on your head?" Josh asked, again struggling to put all of the pieces together.

"When I was sliding down the sheets, I slipped and fell. I hit my head on the rocks under my window and passed out. When I woke up, I was in his car."

"Oh, Sophie," I groaned. "You could have died that night."

"Who is he, Sophie?" Josh moaned. "What kind of a creature could watch you fall and hit your head, lose consciousness, and then take you to a hotel room, worried only about shooting his rocks off?"

"Dad, you don't understand. He's a really nice guy. I love him."

The shock on Josh's face mirrored my own feelings. How could Sophie tell us this appalling story and conclude, "He's a really nice guy?"

"Sophie," Josh said, "I don't care how horny and worked up a guy is. If a woman falls, loses consciousness, and is bleeding from the head, a nice guy stops worrying about getting laid and starts focusing on getting her medical attention. The fact that he picked you up, put you in his car, and drove you to a motel to screw you is proof he's anything but a nice guy."

"Maybe he was scared and didn't know what to do. You're always so judgmental, Dad. He really is a nice guy."

"A nice guy who's scared might leave you there and anonymously call 9-1-1. He didn't worry about whether you were hurt.

His only concern was to fuck you. He's not a nice guy. He's a piece of shit."

Tears welled as Sophie began to weep silently.

Dumbstruck, Josh and I looked at Dr. Shuman.

"Sophie and I have been working on this during our sessions, and we'll continue to do so. For now, I think you'll agree Sophie telling you the truth is a huge step for her. I wanted you to be able to support her and help her as she works through this. It's going to be hard for her, but this time she's not going to live through it alone. You'll be there to help her, and so will I."

Dr. Shuman peeked at her big gold wristwatch. Our session was over.

CHAPTER 40

Surveillance

I spent a sleepless night, tossing and turning as I grappled with the horror of the day. Had the rape really happened? Sophie's proclivity to lie, and the unlikely possibility of an eleven-year-old keeping such a secret weighed in favor of this being one more of her fabrications, albeit a very elaborate and terrifying one. On the other hand, the trauma of a rape could explain many of Sophie's bizarre behaviors during the past five years. Although as a young child she had lied and been obstinate, after we moved to New Jersey when Sophie was twelve, she crossed the line from being a difficult child to being an impossible one.

Something had convinced Dr. Shuman that Sophie was telling the truth about the rape, or she never would have broken the confidentiality of the therapeutic relationship. I needed to know what that something was.

Dr. Shuman explained it was the way in which the information had unfolded that left no question in her mind. When Sophie told Dr. Shuman she'd snuck out of the house and gone to a motel with a man she'd met on the Internet, Dr. Shuman had asked whether this had been her first sexual experience. Sophie calmly said it had not and told her about the experience with the camp counselor. Hearing this, I had to concur with Dr. Shuman's conclusion.

Although Sophie refused to divulge the name of the camp counselor who had raped her, Josh phoned the camp's director and told him what we'd learned. The director could do nothing without the counselor's name, but agreed to maintain employee records indefinitely should Sophie be forthcoming with the rapist's name.

Two days after the session with Dr. Shuman and about a week after installing the surveillance software, Josh called me. He was frantic. "We hit pay dirt. You're not going to believe what I found."

"What?" I asked.

"I don't even want you to see this, it's so horrible."

"So give me the Reader's Digest version," I said.

"No, you don't get it. This is really bad," he lowered his voice to a whisper. "She's talking with a couple of perverts – and it's disgusting." The tone of his voice and seriousness of his words frightened me.

Later that evening we crept downstairs, and I read the surveillance report Josh had seen earlier.

MARCH 18, 2009 (2:49 P.M.)

GRINNER: *I miss that mouth of yours.*

SOPHIE: *I miss yours too.*

GRINNER: *On that note, I also miss the other holes you have.*

SOPHIE: *I wish I could see you.*

GRINNER: *No worries.*

SOPHIE: *When am I going to get to see you?*

GRINNER: *guh...would feel so good to slide inside you right now.*

SOPHIE: *I miss you so much.*

GRINNER: *You still need to taste my cum.*

SOPHIE: *When can I see you?*

GRINNER: *It will have to be when I have a couple days to spend with you.*

SOPHIE: *Right.*

GRINNER: *And when you can get away for a full weekend.*

SOPHIE: *Wouldn't that be great.*

GRINNER: *Without 5 a.m. drop offs and midnight pickups.*

SOPHIE: *Yea.*

GRINNER: *I would love to fuck you in your house.*

SOPHIE: *That would be breaking the rules.*

GRINNER: *Would be fun.*

SOPHIE: *Sure would.*

GRINNER: *Breaking rules always is.*

SOPHIE: *Indeed.*

I froze. What drew Sophie to someone like this? Why did she always put herself in danger? I read the words again, then again. "Josh, this is the guy she snuck out of the house with the night she tied the sheets together and shimmied out her window. It's the same guy she told us about in Dr. Shuman's office two days ago. The midnight pick-up and five o'clock drop off – it's a dead giveaway."

I read on, as the surveillance report contained a second exchange that occurred an hour after the first.

MARCH 18, 2009 (3:49 P.M.)

PHIL BEE: *get it sorted out.*

SOPHIE: *?*

PHIL BEE: *your phone.*

SOPHIE: *it was taken away.*

PHIL BEE: *I want to see you fuck yourself and I want it now. I'm so fucking horny for you right now, I could rip you apart. I want to slap your face.*

SOPHIE: *I see.*

PHIL BEE: *and hold you against the wall by your throat.*

SOPHIE: *got to go.*

Sophie was communicating with not one, but two, perverts who wanted to engage in violent sex with her. Not shocked by their fantasies, she was encouraging them. Where had she learned about such ghastly behaviors? Hadn't she listened to any of the Dangers-of-Talking-to-Strangers lectures that were first delivered while she watched *Barney* and *Sesame Street*, and continued throughout elementary, middle, and high school? How long had these conversations been going on right under Josh's and my very careful watch?

I thought about all the time Sophie spent on the computer – time she told me she was doing homework, playing games, or collecting information about colleges – and realized my hunch that Sophie was troubled had been right all along. What I hadn't understood was how sick she was. While we'd been treating ADHD, there was something more serious causing this behavior. But what was it?

Josh and I met with Dr. Shuman. We showed her the surveillance report and discussed whether to confront Sophie and make her stop the Internet chat or continue silently monitoring her. Although confronting Sophie had the potential to end her clandestine life, Dr. Shuman cautioned that, if Sophie wasn't ready to stop her risky behavior, it only would force her to modify her method of communicating with Phil Bee and Grinner from the instant messaging chat on the web – which we could keep an eye on – to something else we couldn't monitor. Believing Sophie was unlikely to stop the risky behavior, we continued secretly watching her, giving us the opportunity to intervene and protect her should they plan to meet.

This launched us into a world of lies and secrets for which I was not prepared.

Josh and I now knew Grinner was the person with whom Sophie had snuck out of the house the previous spring, but she didn't know we knew this. We made every effort to help Sophie know it was safe for her to come clean and tell us the truth. But she didn't talk to us. And she didn't talk to Dr. Shuman.

She did, however, continue talking to Grinner.

MARCH 31, 2009 (7:54 P.M.)

GRINNER: *Evening.*

SOPHIE: *Hey love.*

GRINNER: *What did I tell you about addressing me?*

SOPHIE: *Yes sir, sorry sir.*

GRINNER: *I am not your boyfriend. . . I am your master.*

SOPHIE: *Understood.*

GRINNER: *How is school going?*

SOPHIE: *Much, much better.*

GRINNER: *That's good. Keep working hard. I will be very displeased if I ever find out you are getting anything lower than a C.*

SOPHIE: *Oh, for real?*

GRINNER: *Yes. You are my pet and as such you reflect on me. Your failure looks bad on me and this I will not tolerate.*

SOPHIE: *Yes sir.*

GRINNER: *You might be in need of some discipline. Next Saturday, I suggest you find a way out of your house before 10 pm and set up a way back in around midnight. I will be passing through and will only have a couple of hours to spare. If you can't make it out, I will be passing you by.*

SOPHIE: *No can do. I'm under lock and key.*

GRINNER: *Lovely. How terribly disappointing. Why the lockdown?*

SOPHIE: *I kinda got in trouble with a boy. My parents found out I was screwing him.*

GRINNER: *I'm finding that you are far too irresponsible, which doesn't suit my purposes. Your job was to remain clean so that you had the freedom to do as I asked without anyone questioning it.*

SOPHIE: *I know, I know. I'm sorry I let you down.*

GRINNER: *Now you are under such high security that you have become almost useless to me.*

SOPHIE: *I'm sorry.*

GRINNER: *I know you are. See what you can figure out for next Saturday. I will be pleased if you can get out of the house for 2 hours during darkness.*

SOPHIE: *I will try.*

GRINNER: *I hope so. Your master really wants to slide his cock into his nice little pet.*

SOPHIE: *I promise I will do my best.*

GRINNER: *Oh, if you make it out, count on a lot of road head and a good hard fuck outdoors.*

SOPHIE: *Outdoors?*

GRINNER: *Outside.*

SOPHIE: *where?*

GRINNER: *I will find a place.*

SOPHIE: *wow, that didn't help any.*

GRINNER: *I won't have a room since I will be passing through. I'll pull the car over somewhere secluded, and fuck you on the hood or something.*

SOPHIE: *That's pretty hot. I gotta get out.*

GRINNER: *Yes so get your ass out. You won't regret it.*

SOPHIE: *I know that.*

GRINNER: *I would love to see what you've learned with your mouth. Plus being inside your pussy and ass again would be very nice.*

SOPHIE: *True.*

My mother's suicide left me with a very active imagination. This exchange gave me the creeps. The master-slave relationship, combined with his reference to her increasing irresponsibility making her useless to him, convinced me that Grinner intended to harm Sophie. She had served her master and now she needed to be destroyed.

CHAPTER 41

Julia

Okay, now what do we do?

As Josh and I wrestled with ways to protect Sophie, we sunk deeper and deeper into our parallel universe. Our conversation with Dr. Shuman had convinced us that confronting Sophie and shutting down Internet access to our home computer – the strategy parents dealing with a normal teenager would take – was not an option. Sophie was cagey and sure to resort to an alternative method of communicating with Grinner, most likely one we wouldn't be able to monitor. She would borrow a classmate's phone or connect to the Internet at one of their homes.

We wondered whether we could scare her into making better decisions. We figured that, if we could do something that would make her think about how hazardous her behavior was, she'd reverse course.

Inspired by a newspaper story in which a sixteen-year-old high school girl agreed to meet an Internet predator at a mall and later was murdered by him, I concocted a story about my colleague Jenny's daughter Julia. That night at dinner, my storytelling efforts began.

"I had a horrible day today," I started.

"Why?" asked Sophie.

"I had lunch with my friend Jenny. I hadn't seen her for months. She told me her daughter Julia, who's a year or two older than you, has gotten into some serious trouble. Jenny was very worried about her."

"Why, Mom, what did Julia do?" asked Sophie.

"Near as Jenny can tell, Julia met a man on the Internet and she's been sneaking out to meet him," I elaborated, facing my plate of spaghetti, raising only my eyes as I watched for her reaction.

"Oh, that's not so bad. Everyone does it," said Sophie.

"Really?"

"Yeah. A friend of mine's been seeing this nice guy she met on the Internet. They're talking about getting married."

"Wow, I guess things have changed since Jenny and I were young," I said.

"Mom, tell your friend Julia will be fine," Sophie said with authority. "She probably just wants to have fun."

Clearly that plan hadn't worked. A couple of days later, over dinner, I tried again.

"Dad and I have a *shiva* call to make tonight," I said.

"Why, Mom, who died?" asked Sophie.

"My friend Jenny's daughter, Julia."

"Oh my gosh, Mom, what happened?"

"The police aren't sure about all of the details, but they found her body in a hotel room near Cleveland."

"That's awful," said Sophie. "Poor Julia."

"They went through her computer. Seems Julia had been sneaking out of the house longer than Jenny realized. They think they know who the guy is, but haven't caught him yet. They know he's done it before. He meets a girl on the Internet, talks with her for months, and then gets her to meet him somewhere. He meets her several times, takes her to hotels, and eventually he starts worrying he'll get caught. That's when he kills the girl. He and Julia had been talking for at least a year, maybe longer."

Sophie listened keenly to my story, but showed no signs of distress. "Poor Julia," she said. "I've got a lot of homework to do. May I please be excused?"

Josh and I watched her walk out of the room. Had it worked? Was she connecting Julia's situation with her own? Had this convinced her to end things with Grinner? We crossed our fingers hopefully.

I was astounded at how desperate my behavior was. Each new strategy we came up with to protect Sophie had me feeling more like Alice as she tumbled down the rabbit hole. Was creating a fabricated world in order to shock Sophie back to reality crazy?

CHAPTER 42

Joker

J osh and I continued monitoring the computer. The conversations between Sophie and Grinner, grisly to begin with, escalated, and when it became clear they were making plans to meet, we contacted the police. The officer assigned to our case, Detective Walker, was a tall man with broad shoulders. He'd spent his thirty-year career working vice. He listened as Josh told him what we knew. The pain in his eyes made it clear he understood the gravity of the situation.

"We need to catch this bastard," he vowed as Josh finished talking.

"Great," Josh agreed. "What do we do now?"

"We need Sophie's help," said the detective. "Do you think she'll cooperate?"

"Not likely. She's convinced he loves her," I said.

"So how do we catch him?" Josh asked. The idea that someone could abuse his daughter made him furious. If this were the Wild West, he'd be wielding a rifle and six-shooter.

"To have any chance of arresting him and sending him to prison, we have to catch him in the act," explained Walker. "Our best chance of doing that is if we can get Sophie to cooperate and help us."

"But wouldn't that put her in jeopardy?" I asked. Having watched too many *Law and Order* shows on television, I envisioned a sting with Sophie at its center.

"I have to be honest with you," the detective said. "This is a dangerous situation. However, if we're going to stop him from hurting Sophie, this is what we need to do."

"I don't know how we could get her to cooperate," I conceded. "Unless …"

We needed Sophie to cooperate, but she wasn't likely to do so because she believed she and Grinner loved one another. We needed to deploy a strategy designed to demonstrate to Sophie the danger that Grinner posed.

"Maybe we could continue the Julia story?" I suggested to Josh.

"What do you mean?" he asked. Detective Walker listened to Josh and me bat ideas back and forth. We filled him in on our fabricated Julia story.

"That might work, but I couldn't be involved in it," the detective said. "The judge would throw me out of court."

"No, but Josh and I could tell her the story. I'll do anything to protect Sophie. I'll lie to her if I have to."

Josh and I spent the rest of the afternoon concocting our strategy. We didn't want to compromise our computer surveillance, but we needed to figure out a way to get Sophie to cooperate with the police. Continuing the Julia story would be too coincidental. We needed to fabricate a new victim and create a new story to get Sophie's attention.

Our plan set, we arranged for a friend to phone our home the next morning when we knew Sophie would be in the kitchen having breakfast with us. As I sprinkled cinnamon on the egg-soaked bread, the phone rang.

"I'll get it," Josh said.

Sophie and Aaron were setting the table.

"Yes, officer. This is Sophie Segal's father."

Sophie's ears perked up.

"Who's he talking to?" she asked.

"No clue," I shrugged, flipping the French toast.

"No, Sophie's here. She's fine, Officer," Josh responded.

"What the fuck?" asked Sophie nonchalantly reaching for the comics.

"Language, Sophie," Aaron chastised.

Josh listened intently to the phone, acting the role of a father receiving very frightening information about his daughter, as we had rehearsed. Every once in a while he interjected, "Oh, my goodness," or "Yes, I understand, Officer," or "I can't believe that." I watched Sophie watching him. We had her attention.

"Thank you for calling, Detective. I'll speak with Sophie and get back to you later today."

As soon as Josh hung up the phone, Sophie asked, "What was that all about?"

"That was Detective Walker. He told me he was investigating the death of a young girl in North Jersey. Seems she met a guy on the Internet, had been talking with him, and two nights ago she snuck out of the house to meet him at a bar. They found her body in a hotel room last night."

"That's horrible. So why was he calling you and why were you talking about me?"

"They searched her phone and computer and found she'd been talking with someone who identified himself as Grinner. They realized she and this Grinner had made a plan to meet that night. That led them to Grinner's computer account. Searching that, they found he'd been communicating with you as well as three other girls. One of those girls is missing this morning. They wanted to make sure you were safe."

Sophie paled.

"Sophie, what the hell's going on?" Josh demanded.

"I was just talking to this guy. I met him a few months ago in a chat room."

"How many times have we told you how dangerous it is to talk to strangers?" Josh sputtered. "The police want to talk to you. They're desperate to find him before anyone else turns up dead. You need to cooperate with the police."

"But he's my friend. He didn't do anything wrong," she pleaded. Even now she refused to believe Grinner could be perilous.

"Sophie. This guy killed a girl. Another girl he's been talking with is missing. You have to help the police," I said. Then, thinking about my daughter who always wanted to help the downtrodden, I tried, "Sophie, your friend needs help. He's sick. Let's help the police find him so he can get the help he needs."

"So he won't have to go to jail? Can I visit him in the hospital?"

"I'm sure we can arrange that," I said, placating her in hopes of enlisting her cooperation.

"Okay. I'll help the police."

That afternoon, Detective Walker came to our home and spoke with Sophie. After a brief introduction, Josh and I left them alone. An hour later, as the detective got ready to leave, he told us he had asked Sophie for permission to put special software on the computer allowing him to record communications with Grinner. He asked Sophie to continue talking to Grinner, not to let him know she knew about the other girls, and to let us know whenever she and Grinner communicated.

Sophie agreed to the plan.

CHAPTER **43**

Passing for Normal

Three weeks later.

A midst this total and utter chaos, we faced the Jewish holiday of Passover. In years past, I'd looked forward to celebrating the holiday with my brother Ben, sister-in-law Rebecca, and their children Sara and Allen. Could I shift from the surreal life we'd been living to the normalcy of my brother's home in Omaha?

Ben and I have always been close. As children, we squabbled as the usual sibling rivalries had us competing for our parents' attention. As adults, especially after our parents' deaths, we always knew we could count on one another. We looked forward to celebrating holidays together and enjoyed keeping our family traditions alive. We spoke often by phone, commiserating about difficult work situations, giving one another advice and encouragement, and laughing about various political gaffes.

When Sophie was diagnosed with ADHD and decisions needed to be made about medications, Ben was my first call. Although this medical problem was far afield of his expertise as a nephrologist, he read the literature, consulted with his colleagues in psychiatry, and gave me a thoughtful explanation about the medications and treatment plan that would be most effective.

Yet, despite Ben's knowledge of medicine and my close and trusting relationship with him, I hadn't told him about Sophie's more bizarre behaviors and I wouldn't tell him about her recent escapades. I'm not sure why. Maybe it was my desire to avoid facing the reality that these behaviors indicated Sophie suffered from a severe mental illness. Maybe it was to keep the sibling rivalry from our childhood at bay. Maybe it was to enable Sophie to have some semblance of a normal relationship with Ben and his family. Or maybe it was some combination of these reasons.

As we waited to retrieve our suitcases from the baggage carousel, I watched Sophie. She looked like such a normal teenager. Her petite frame had not an ounce of fat on it. She wore faded blue jeans, an olive green hoodie, and beat-up sneakers. Her long hair was pulled back from her face in a ponytail. She couldn't wait to see Sara, who is twenty months older than she, and Allen, who is fifteen months younger. From the time they were young children, Sophie had played happily with both her cousins, yet Allen's outgoing personality and playful nature made him her favorite. Relationships between Sophie and her cousins had cooled in the years after she stole Allen's cell phone and Sara's makeup, but during our last visit the rift seemed to have mended.

After we claimed our bags from the carousel, we waited for Ben to arrive. Within minutes, his red van pulled up to the curb.

"Uncle Ben!" Sophie shrieked.

Ben waved at us. He parked the van and sprang out of it.

"Dog lips!" Ben and I shouted simultaneously as we hugged and kissed. Our father had initiated this unconventional greeting years ago and it was a tradition we'd kept alive, as though by doing so, we somehow kept him with us.

As also was tradition, Sophie rolled her eyes and uttered, "I can't believe I'm related to you two nerds," and, without missing a beat, Aaron added, "Remember, Sophie, it's not so bad. We're adopted!"

Our suitcases loaded into the van, we headed for Ben's house, chatting non-stop. When we arrived, my sister-in-law Rebecca greeted us warmly as their dog Chloe barked with excitement.

Like me, Rebecca had an active professional life. A pediatric geneticist, she consulted with families whose children were at risk for various genetic conditions. As we both had a passion for cooking, when Passover came, we enjoyed whipping up traditional kugels, sweet potato casseroles, and gefilte fish. While we cooked,

Rebecca and I would talk about our work and families. However, as with Ben, I never told Rebecca about Sophie's frightening behaviors.

As Rebecca and I set to work in the kitchen, Josh and Ben conferred about the latest March Madness basketball games, and Aaron played with Chloe. When Sophie learned her cousins wouldn't be home from school for a couple of hours, she claimed she had homework to do and asked Rebecca for permission to use their computer.

I knew Sophie wouldn't be doing homework. Instead, I suspected she'd continue her chats with Grinner. But, knowing she couldn't sneak out of the house and get into trouble, I let her have her way and went about cooking and catching up with Rebecca.

After about an hour, I went to check on Sophie. As I opened the door, the screen on the computer indicated she was engaged in a game of *Sorority House*. If she had a chat window open, I didn't see it.

"I thought you were doing homework."

"All done," she answered without looking away from the screen.

"Want to help us cook?"

"No thanks, Mom. I'll hang out here until Sara and Allen come home."

I went back to the kitchen. "What time do the kids get home?" I asked Rebecca.

"You know, I'm not sure. I think they have Show Choir practice this afternoon."

How different my relationship with Sophie was from Rebecca's relationship with Sara and Allen. Because of Sophie's proclivity to get in trouble, I insisted she always tell me where she was and when she would be home. If she was even fifteen minutes late, I worried. I envied the trust Rebecca had in her children. Why can't my relationship with Sophie be like that?

I was shocked out of my jealous reverie by Chloe's bark, alerting us to Sara and Allen's arrival. Sophie embraced them happily. Aaron joined in as the four cousins grabbed handfuls of snack foods and retreated to the family room.

Rebecca and I finished setting the table. The late afternoon sun hit the crystal goblets and their glistening reflections made shadows dance on the walls. The bright yellow tulips were a sure harbinger of spring. For a fleeting moment I convinced myself that Sophie would come to her senses and have no more to do with Grinner.

"C'mon everyone. Let's get this Seder started," Ben heralded. Within minutes, the kids were jockeying for seats and we were ready to begin. Sophie squeezed between Sara and Allen and peeked anxiously at Allen's watch. What was she was up to now?

Passover celebrates freedom, as we remember and joyfully tell the story of the Exodus of the Israelites from Egypt after four hundred years of slavery. A holiday marked by order, the Passover Seder is a ritualistic prescription with fourteen well-defined steps followed by Jews all around the world for thousands of years.

The orderliness of the Passover Seder was especially comforting to me this year, as I reflected on the pandemonium that had usurped my life during the past few months. Yet, at the same time, I thought it ironic to be celebrating freedom, given the prisoner mentality I experienced hovering over Sophie in hopes of keeping her safe. Was this irony evident to Sophie? Had she ever known the joy of order? Somehow, I doubted it.

As Ben began the Seder, I was filled with memories of previous Passovers.

I was four in 1959 when my father taught me to sing *The Four Questions* in Hebrew. Traditionally chanted by the youngest child at the table, these questions ask how the Passover night differs from all other nights. We had practiced singing the questions for months until my father was sure I would deliver a stellar performance, impressing his younger brother, my Uncle Saul, as well as his wife, my Aunt Muriel, and Muriel's parents.

At four years old, I knew this night was different from all others. Not only had my mother bought me a new pink and white gingham dress with a pink bow for the occasion, but she'd also given into my pleas for ruffled ankle socks and shiny white patent leather Mary Jane shoes that went clickety-clack on the sidewalk. She'd braided my long brown hair and attached pink ribbons to the ends. And she'd ceded to my demands to polish my fingernails pink. As we drove to my uncle's house, I worried that I'd mess up and sing the questions out of order.

Arriving at my aunt and uncle's home, I made a beeline to the three silver candy dishes that graced their living room credenza. They were empty – their brilliant green, blue, and red inserts polished to perfection catching my reflection. Seeing my disappointment, my mother reminded me that we couldn't eat the delicious candies my aunt always kept in the candy dishes because it was Passover.

That night, never taking my eyes off my father's face, I belted out *The Four Questions* as the adults smiled. When I finished, there were words of praise. None, however, was more meaningful to me than those from my father.

I tried to be patient and pay attention as my father and uncle led us in the rest of the Seder, but since they read and sang mostly in Hebrew, I soon got bored, asking my mother more than once, "When do we eat?" I amused myself by watching my baby brother Ben crawl around his playpen. After a delicious dinner, complete with many of the traditional Passover foods I loved – gefilte fish, matzo ball soup, brisket, kugel, and roasted potatoes – the Seder resumed. But despite my best efforts, I fell asleep at the table, my braids falling to my lap.

Smiling to myself, I now watched as the grown-up Ben led the Seder. My thoughts drifted to the Passover in 1974 when I was twenty years old, in London participating in Michigan State's Junior Year Abroad program. It was the first and only Passover I was not with my family. Although I couldn't have known it then, that Passover was one of my mother's last. Had I known she would die so soon, would I have gone to London and missed sharing that precious holiday with her? I looked around the table. How many more Passover Seders would this group have together? Sara, the eldest of the cousins, was headed for college next year, marking the first of what would be a series of departures. Sophie would follow the next year, Allen two years later, and before long, Aaron would be on his way as well. Would they come home for the holidays? How I hoped so.

As a tear came to my eye, I realized Sophie had left the table. "Hey, Allen," I whispered, not wanting to interrupt the Seder, "Where's Sophie?" He gave me a quizzical look and shrugged his shoulders.

Thinking she may have gone to the bathroom, I waited. When she didn't reappear, I went in search of her. As I climbed the stairs, the light from the study led me to Sophie. She was staring at the computer window that I watched her minimize.

"Sophie, what are you doing up here?" I asked with annoyance.

"Talking with a friend," she answered, chewing on her finger.

"What's so important that it takes you away from the Seder?"

"It's nothing, Mom. I'm sorry," she said turning off the computer.

Returning to the table, I answered Josh's quizzical look, silently letting him know things were under control, for now.

Listening to Ben tell the Passover story, I looked over at Josh. How far he and I had come in our journey since that Passover in 1985 when I'd brought him home for the first time to meet my father, brothers, and extended family. After dating for only a month, we knew we'd marry, so my invitation to spend Passover with my family hadn't surprised him. That Passover was a stressful one for us because my Aunt Muriel was sick with cancer. Despite her illness, Muriel had prepared a delicious dinner and was keen on playing the welcoming matriarch to Josh. Although Muriel complained of achiness and nausea, she sat at the head of the dining room table orchestrating the last-minute preparations while my cousins, brothers, and I followed her orders.

My cousin Leah made the salt water, symbol of the tears and sadness of enslavement, and put it on the table. Muriel stuck her finger in the bowl and licked it. "Leah, this isn't salty enough," she complained. Seeing Brian's confusion about whether the big fork went to the right or left of the little one, Muriel corrected, "Young man, how many times have I told you the little fork goes to the left of the big one?"

"What can I do to help?" Josh asked.

"You can put the ice in the glasses and pour the water," Muriel said.

Josh did as he was asked. Within moments, Muriel scoffed, "It's clear no one ever taught you how to pour water!"

I wanted to crawl under the carpet. How would Josh respond?

"I'm sorry," Josh replied. "Please tell me what I've done wrong."

Whew!

"You fill the glass full of ice and then pour the water in, but never so much water that the ice begins to float," she explained.

I looked at her dumbfounded, shocked that she would scold someone she barely knew. How uncharacteristic of Muriel, an elementary school teacher in Detroit's inner city. This was her illness speaking. I looked at Josh, offering an apology for her words, watching as his face flushed with embarrassment.

"I'm sorry," he repeated deferentially. He understood. "I'll fix them."

My thoughts returned to the present as I reflected on our twenty-five years of marriage. How had we managed to survive the turmoil Sophie had put us through? Maybe adversity had brought us closer. Although we quarreled at times, we were rarely at odds when it came to Sophie.

After a delicious main course, we feasted on homemade raspberry cheesecake, chocolate torte, and fresh fruit served with a scrumptious crème brûlée sauce. Digesting the sugary delights, I looked around the table. Sophie was missing again. "Has anyone seen Sophie?" I asked.

"She said she had to make a phone call," Sara said.

Wondering what Sophie was up to now, I went in search of her. Like earlier that evening, I found her in front of the computer screen, which she minimized when I appeared in the doorway.

"Sophie, what are you doing?"

"Nothing."

"It's dessert time."

"I'm not hungry."

"Don't you want to spend time with your cousins?"

"Yeah, Mom. I'm coming."

If I weren't so worried about her, I'd think it comical how she'd become tethered to the computer. Like steel to a magnet, she was drawn back regardless of what the rest of the family, her beloved cousins included, were doing. And I kept rebounding after her. How I hated that I couldn't trust her and that I had to keep such close tabs on her. Watching a sixteen-year-old like I would watch a two-year-old got old quickly.

As Ben continued the Seder, I thought back to the Passover of 1996 when Sophie was four years old. She'd mastered *The Four Questions* Josh had taught her. Taking seriously his responsibility to explain the Passover story to his daughter, Josh had turned his attention to figuring out what he could do to keep Sophie engaged during the Seder.

One afternoon while I was out, Sophie asked Josh to put on one of her Shari Lewis tapes. She watched intently, giggling at Lamb Chop and Charley Horse, and Josh knew he'd solved his problem. I returned home to find Josh and his grandmother discussing ways to make the Passover story come alive with puppets.

Josh took Sophie to Jo-Ann Fabrics and they came home with bags full of colorful sheets of felt, beads, buttons, yarn, and sticks. Over the next several days, Nana and Josh made puppets, and Josh wrote a play that told the Passover story at a level Sophie would understand. Each year, as the kids got older, Josh revamped the play so that it would keep them engaged.

I smiled, thinking about how cyclical life is.

My reverie was interrupted when Allen asked, "Aunt Rachel, where's Sophie?"

CHAPTER 44

Le Klaunette

E ven though I knew Sophie was up to no good, the trip to Omaha left me feeling centered and whole again.

Pulling into our driveway, I was jarred back to my world of chaos. A playing card had been stuck in our garage door. "I'll get it," Aaron said, jumping out of the car and nabbing the card as the garage door opened.

"It's a joker," Aaron remarked. "Wonder how it got there?"

"I don't know," answered Sophie innocently.

But I had a sneaking suspicion.

That evening, Josh and I read the computer surveillance report. Sophie, knowing the police were watching her chat account, had created a new account that she was using to communicate with Grinner. She called herself "Le Klaunette," linking herself with Grinner's Joker persona.

APRIL 14, 2009 (11:59 P.M.)

GRINNER: *I might be taking a break from all this for the summer and moving to NY for a little bit. What do you have going on this Saturday? More so, Saturday after 8 pm?*

LE KLAUNETTE: *I'm being smothered.*

GRINNER: *Smothered?*

LE KLAUNETTE: *Like by my house and my parents. I'm suffocating in this hell.*

GRINNER: *So tell them you need to get out before you lose your mind. Or hell, just go for a walk or something that night and I can pick you up.*

LE KLAUNETTE: *Ha ha. That only gets me in the hospital. Yeah, last time that happened.*

GRINNER: *When is the soonest you can see me?*

LE KLAUNETTE: *Anything wrong?*

GRINNER: *No.*

LE KLAUNETTE: *I really don't know, but I want you to know that I really appreciate your missing me. It makes me smile.*

GRINNER: *Good. From now on, you aren't allowed to play with anyone else.*

LE KLAUNETTE: *Oh?*

GRINNER: *Considering it got you into this pain in the ass situation you are stuck in.*

LE KLAUNETTE: *Ha ha*

GRINNER: *Anyway, I don't want you messing around with any more boys. Understood?*

LE KLAUNETTE: *Okay, okay, I understand.*

GRINNER: *Good.*

LE KLAUNETTE: *Do you happen to have a deck of 53 cards?*

GRINNER: *Oh good, you found it.*

LE KLAUNETTE: *Actually, my Dad did. But it was found.*

GRINNER: *I figured someone would. Just frustrating to have a pet you can't see.*

LE KLAUNETTE: *And vice versa. But not so frustrated as sad.*

GRINNER: *Have you asked when you get your freedom back?*

LE KLAUNETTE: *Yeah. When I earn their trust. Great answer, huh?*

GRINNER: *Find out what it takes or how long it takes to do that.*

LE KLAUNETTE: *So there's this thing called 'second life'. You should check it out, pronto.*

GRINNER: *I don't have time for some stupid fake online world.*

LE KLAUNETTE: *Please don't get angry, but I think its really really important for you to join second life. It would mean a lot to me.*

GRINNER: *I DO NOT HAVE THE TIME FOR IT.*

LE KLAUNETTE: *You had enough patience with IMVY to meet me.*

GRINNER: *Yeah, that was when I had the time. I don't exactly lead a normal life at this point unless you didn't notice.*

LE KLAUNETTE: *And you did then? Something is wrong. What have you been doing?*

GRINNER: *Back then I hadn't started my business.*

LE KLAUNETTE: *True, true. It's not drugs, its not girls, so why do you do what you do?*

GRINNER: *Fun. For the challenge of it all. It's not about money, it's about sending a message. I do it for pure chaos and fun of it all.*

LE KLAUNETTE: *Who said that? Wasn't it from a movie?*

GRINNER: *The Joker said that in the Dark Knight.*

LE KLAUNETTE: *Figured as much.*

GRINNER: *Get this situation fixed as soon as possible. It is starting to really aggravate me.*

LE KLAUNETTE: *I understand sir. Hey, do you think you'll ever be ready for me to come out there? Forever? I mean like in a few years or something.*

GRINNER: *I don't see why not.*

LE KLAUNETTE: *Cuz if you don't want to that's okay. I mean I absolutely love the idea.*

GRINNER: *I know you do. By the time you come out, odds are I will be done with this whole thing.*

LE KLAUNETTE: *But I thought you might move on to someone else since I'm locked up.*

GRINNER: *I plan on stopping all this lovely insanity in about a year or so.*

LE KLAUNETTE: *Ha ha. And then what?*

GRINNER: *Just disappear and start over and have a somewhat normal life. Just relax and enjoy things without all the killing and violence. Well, maybe a little violence still.*

LE KLAUNETTE: *?*

GRINNER: *Violence is fun. Hard to give that up.*

LE KLAUNETTE: *You're so funny. I love you.*

GRINNER: *And I love you.*

LE KLAUNETTE: *Who you gonna fight with without getting into trouble.*

GRINNER: *Whoever has it coming. I would be really disappointed in myself if I got busted for a fight. . . considering what I have gotten away with thus far. Fix your situation. . . I want to see you as soon as possible. It has been too long since we have had some fun.*

LE KLAUNETTE: *I think at this point you should dig a hole and lie low for awhile. OK, just remember I absolutely adore you.*

GRINNER: *Yes, I know. If you want to show me get your situation fixed.*

LE KLAUNETTE: *and I'd be terribly upset if anything were to happen.*

GRINNER: *Goodnight.*

LE KLAUNETTE: *Yes sir. Sleep well.*

The playing card was the juvenile message Grinner had left as his calling card. He'd stood in my driveway and stuck the playing card in my garage door while we were gone. Chills went up my spine. How brazen he was. His control over Sophie and proclivity to violence frightened me. His plans to relocate from the Midwest to the New York area made him dangerous to Sophie and his assuming the persona of Batman's Joker character was eerie.

How much longer could we protect Sophie?

CHAPTER 45

Plans

The next day.

Although Sophie had told Detective Walker she'd assist with efforts to find Grinner, she wasn't cooperating. She figured her *Le Klaunette* persona would enable her to charm Grinner while keeping the police at bay. We knew what she was up to. The police knew what she was up to. But Sophie didn't know that we knew that she was still communicating with Grinner and trying to hide it.

Because we couldn't let Sophie know about the computer surveillance, we continued our storytelling.

At dinner one evening Josh said, "Sophie, Detective Walker needs your help finding Grinner. He's already murdered one girl. You don't want to be next. You need to do the right thing and help him."

"No," she cried. "I want to be with him. I love him."

Frustrated, I screamed, "Sophie, if that's what you want, go to him. He's a crazy person. You're putting all of us at risk."

"I love him," she wailed. "I have to be with him."

"You can't live with us and have a relationship with this pervert," insisted Josh. "We've tolerated this long enough. You're going to have to choose between him and us. What's it going to be, Sophie?"

"You don't understand. I love him. And he loves me. I can't choose."

"You're going to have to. Which is it going to be?" Josh said firmly.

"I don't know."

"Think about it and let me know."

There was quiet in our house for a few hours as a truce was drawn. Sophie finished her homework and turned on the computer. Knowing that she and Grinner would talk about what had just happened, Josh and I slipped downstairs where we watched their conversation unfold on the computer, the surveillance software revealing their every keystroke.

APRIL 15, 2009 (9:07 P.M.)

LE KLAUNETTE: *So, you know how you wanted to get away for awhile?*

GRINNER: *Yes.*

LE KLAUNETTE: *Well, we have our chance.*

GRINNER: *Oh? Oh?*

LE KLAUNETTE: *Ha Ha, yeah. Well, I'm supposedly staying at a close friend's house for a long time. A looooong time.*

GRINNER: *How long?*

LE KLAUNETTE: *Like a month, probably more. And I guess I don't really have to be there. If that's okay.*

GRINNER: *Are you saying you want to stay with me for a month?*

LE KLAUNETTE: *Yes.*

GRINNER: *When?*

LE KLAUNETTE: *ASAP*

GRINNER: *And why are you going to be at a friend's house for a month?*

LE KLAUNETTE: *My Dad is going to India for awhile for his company. They have a job for him again.*

GRINNER: *I see, and your mother?*

LE KLAUNETTE: *My mom figured that'll be hard enough, and so I'm going to Pennsylvania to a friend's house. They don't know yet though.*

GRINNER: *Don't you think your mother will tell them or at least call to confirm?*

Le Klaunette: *Maybe. I don't know, or care. We got in a big fight. I'll just tell her I went to my birth mother's or something.*

Grinner: *Odds are she will. But, just the same. I can always come grab you when I have a place set up in NY.*

Le Klaunette: *Do it. Please, I mean. When?*

Grinner: *I am going to be looking this weekend. I might even be able to line up a job doing what I did in the Air Force.*

Le Klaunette: *Well, I gotta be gone Saturday. I thought that would be convenient.*

Grinner: *Well I won't have a place that soon.*

Le Klaunette: *Damn. When can you pick me up at least?*

Grinner: *Maybe in a week or so.*

Le Klaunette: *What do I do? You said you'd be around on Saturday.*

Grinner: *I will.*

Le Klaunette: *Can you pick me up and just have me hang with you?*

Grinner: *Sure. Won't be able to get you until 8 or so.*

Le Klaunette: *Actually, can you come tonight? If possible at all.*

Grinner: *Tonight?*

Le Klaunette: *Maybe possibly yes?*

Grinner: *Not likely tonight. Let's just go with Saturday.*

Le Klaunette: *Well, I really really need you to come really, really, really soon. I'm sorry.*

Grinner: *What is going on?*

Le Klaunette: *It's urgent.*

Grinner. *I'm sorry, but I am not trusting this right now. Are you running away?*

Le Klaunette: *I can't stand my mother. I gotta get out of here.*

Grinner: *Yeah, but you bolt and they will eventually check your messenger records and find this conversation and all our old ones. And then I get totally fucked.*

Le Klaunette: *She knows I'm going somewhere.*

Grinner. *Are you telling me the truth about your Dad and your PA friends?*

Le Klaunette: *Yes.*

Grinner: *I will get you Saturday. Last until then.*

Le Klaunette: *Okay. Thank you. See you then.*

Grinner. *Very well. And this is only for a couple weeks, correct?*

Le Klaunette: *Maybe. I'm honestly not sure how long.*

Grinner: *Because I don't want to take care of you indefinitely.*

Le Klaunette: *I might not be home for awhile.*

Grinner: *I have my own plans to deal with as well.*

Le Klaunette: *I gotta get away somewhere forever. Not with you, but somewhere.*

Grinner: *Well I will take you for a bit, but I can't promise more than 2-3 weeks at a time. You might have to bounce back and forth between me and a friend or me and home.*

Le Klaunette: *That's absolutely fine.*

Grinner. *Very well.*

Le Klaunette: *Thank you for helping me out.*

Grinner: *Seriously, are you running away?*

Le Klaunette: *Not sure. Maybe yes. No. I don't know.*

Grinner: *Cause I am going to be so fucking pissed if I do this for you then find out you just bolted and then have the cops knocking on my door for kidnapping or something.*

Le Klaunette: *I feel ya.*

Grinner: *Make sure to clear out any chat logs you have on either account before you leave.*

Le Klaunette: *Will do.*

Grinner: *Are you bringing your phone with you?*

Le Klaunette: *No.*

Grinner: *You should. So they can't go through it at all.*

Le Klaunette: *I can't. They threw it out.*

Grinner: *And you are sure it is destroyed?*

LE KLAUNETTE: *Well yeah. The trash was picked up weeks ago.*

GRINNER: *Okay, good. Make sure to have a full suitcase of clothing. Will you have any funds when you leave?*

LE KLAUNETTE: *Way ahead of you.*

GRINNER: *Like, is she giving you any money for your 'trip'?*

LE KLAUNETTE: *Um, likely not. I have like $20.00*

GRINNER: *$20.00?*

LE KLAUNETTE: *Pretty much.*

GRINNER: *So I am going to have to support you then? I will have to get you food and shelter.*

LE KLAUNETTE: *I will work something out, I guess.*

GRINNER: *At times, if you are staying with me, there will be nights or even weeks where you will have to disappear.*

LE KLAUNETTE: *I'll do that if necessary.*

GRINNER: *So set up a secondary friend place so I can drop you there if need be.*

LE KLAUNETTE: *Okay.*

GRINNER: *Well, get together what funds you can and I will pick you up Saturday night. Have your secondary place set up before that. . . and have it be somewhere in New Jersey. I really don't want to drive to Pennsylvania.*

LE KLAUNETTE: *Understood.*

GRINNER: *Not going to lie. . . I have killed people and what not, but this makes me nervous. Too many variables that I don't have control over.*

LE KLAUNETTE: *Yeah. So Saturday at 8 in front of the school*

GRINNER: *Yes. I might be a little late.*

LE KLAUNETTE: *Sounds good. And thank you so much.*

GRINNER: *You're welcome. I still feel really uneasy about this all though.*

LE KLAUNETTE: *I know.*

GRINNER: *Just know. . . if this turns out to be a sting, I will kill you before I am brought down.*

LE KLAUNETTE: *I know that.*

GRINNER: *Okay. See you Saturday. Good night.*

LE KLAUNETTE: *Good night, love.*

CHAPTER **46**

Unshared Reality

R eading these words as Sophie and Grinner typed them, Josh and I watched Sophie's disturbed think-ing grow. Her story about Josh going to India and her going to stay with a friend in Pennsylvania couldn't have been farther from the truth. Josh spent most of his time working from home and Sophie had no close friend in Pennsylvania. The ren-dezvous for Saturday meant we had three days to figure out what to do.

Upstairs, Josh found Sophie sitting on the floor of the study, leaning against a bookcase and staring into space. "Dad, I've thought about it. I love you guys, but I really need to go with him."

"What? How could you possibly make that choice? You told us last week that he's violent and kills people. Is that the kind of person you want to be with?"

"No," Sophie murmured.

"Then why?"

"I don't know. I just have to be with him."

"Why?"

"Because, if I don't, he'll kill all of us."

"And that's why you're going with him? To protect us?"

"Not just that. I need to be with him."

"Sophie, do you understand he's dangerous and likely to hurt you?" Josh questioned.

"Yes."

"Do you want to die, Sophie?"

"No. Of course not."

"Good. Then why go with him?"

"I don't know. I just need to."

"So you don't want to die, but you want to go to him knowing he'll kill you. Is that right?"

"Yes, but I want to be with him," she sobbed and bolted out of the room.

Josh came out of the study, and said, "She's off her rocker, Rachel. I have no idea what to do."

Terrified, I followed Sophie as she headed for her bedroom. I gave her a minute to calm down, and then knocked on her door.

"Sophie? Are you okay?"

There was no answer. "Sophie?" I called, trying to control the shaking in my voice.

When there was still no answer, I cracked open the door. She was sitting on her bed, starring into space.

"Sophie, can I come in and talk to you?"

In an eerily calm voice, she said, "Mom, I feel like I'm going to hurt myself."

My heart pounded wildly. Although Sophie had cut herself in the past, the wounds she'd inflicted were always superficial. And while Sophie processed things differently than I did, this was the first time I realized that her ability to make a decision was severely flawed, that her emotions were abnormal, and that her fear of danger was nonexistent. Her reality was no longer mine.

I tried to calm her, with little success. I felt like I was speaking a language she didn't understand. I stopped, realizing I'd had that feeling before. Then I was sixteen years old, the same age Sophie was now. Then I listened to my mother cry as she insisted she was worthless and wanted to die.

CHAPTER 47

Losing Control

Sophie's thinking had become irrational. She was a danger to herself. As calmly as I could, I said, "Sophie, we need to take you to the hospital."

Sobbing, she said, "I have to be with him. I have to go with him on Saturday. If I don't, he'll kill you."

Josh and I looked at each other. How do we get her to agree to go to the hospital?

"What if I promise to bring you home after the doctor takes a look at you?" Josh suggested.

Sophie thought for a moment. "I'll go only if you promise I can be back to meet Grinner on Saturday. He's going to kill you and me if I'm not there. He'll think I set him up."

We agreed.

Before Josh and Sophie left, I hugged Sophie and told her I loved her. She hugged me back. As we released our holds, tears filled my eyes. Little did I know this would be the beginning of a long and difficult process of losing her.

After they left, I tended to Aaron. Having witnessed his sister's meltdown, he'd gone to his room and slammed the door. I worried about Aaron. What did he think about his sister's scary behaviors?

Josh and Sophie left home at about 9:30 that evening. They waited in the Tri-county Hospital Crisis Center intake area until noon the next day when Sophie was admitted to the Child & Adolescent Psychiatric Unit (CAPU). We later learned this long wait time was a strategy used by the emergency room personnel to calm people down. Wear them down, make sure they're exhausted, and then decide whether they need to be hospitalized. Sophie fell asleep within a half-hour of their arrival. For Josh, that night was pure torture.

With Sophie's admission to the psychiatric unit, Josh and I entered yet another foreign world. We no longer had primary responsibility for making decisions about our daughter. Josh returned from the hospital depleted. He'd been given a pass code, a phone number to the CAPU nurses' station, and a list of items we were permitted to bring to Sophie. These included reading material – but no pens or pencils – loosely fitting pants, tee-shirts, pajamas, and underwear. Anything with straps or draw stings was forbidden. Shampoo, hair conditioner, and toothpaste were acceptable, but these items had to be left at the nurses' station. Visiting hours were limited to between seven and eight o'clock each evening. Only parents were permitted to visit.

Twenty-four hours after Sophie was admitted to the hospital, Josh and I arrived for our first visit. I'd followed the instructions regarding items that were acceptable to bring and now clutched the bag filled with reading material, clothes, and toiletries. At the hospital's entrance, a security guard yawned, greeting us. We showed identification and were directed to the CAPU. "Follow this corridor until it ends. Make two rights, a left, a right, and then another left. You'll come to a locked double door. Push the call button on the box mounted on the wall. State the name of the patient you're visiting. If you're on the approved visitor list, someone will unlock the doors and escort you to the nurses' station. Be ready to show I.D. and surrender your bags for inspection." I heard his directions, but didn't process a word he said. I was humiliated, certain he must judge me to be a bad mother.

As Josh and I wound our way through the maze of beige hospital corridors, I wondered how this psychiatric hospital compared with the one my mother had been in. As a child, I'd never been allowed to visit her when she was hospitalized. I'd envisioned the hospital as grey, no black, no white, and no color. Only grey.

The door marking the CAPU had a large sign on it, "Authorized Personnel Only." I pressed the button on the keypad.

"Can I help you?" Static emanated from the box on the wall.

"We're here to visit our daughter, Sophie Segal," I said.

"Your names, please?"

"Josh and Rachel Segal," I answered.

"Just a minute."

The door opened a crack and a big woman with a pointy chin said, "Follow me."

Obediently we trailed her. The flicker of the harsh fluorescent lights made eerie shadows leap from the walls. Their buzz silenced the sounds of our footsteps. At the end of the long hallway, Sophie chatted with some of the patients. Her hair was ragged and uneven, a remnant of her recent manic episode in which the impulse to crop her hair had overpowered her promise to let only her hairdresser do so. She was dressed in the same disheveled clothes she had worn to the hospital and then slept in. When she spotted us, she smiled and ran toward us. "Mom! Dad! I'm so happy to see you." Hugging her, I gave her the bag I'd brought, but the nurse with the pointy chin intercepted it.

"Sorry. I have to check the contents of all bags." She took it behind the desk at the nurses' station.

Sophie was bewildered. Like me, she probably wondered why I couldn't give the bag to her.

The nurse rummaged through the bag. She glared at me. She waved Sophie's favorite hoodie and blanket, shaking her head. "No drawstrings. No blankets."

"I'm sorry," I apologized.

"I'm going to need to see some identification from you."

Josh and I showed the nurse our driver's licenses.

After we secured clearance, Sophie led us to the brightly lit visiting area at the end of the hall. Books and art supplies were strewn on the shelves. In one corner of the room, a middle-aged woman wearing a large cross sighed and a teen-aged girl scraped red polish from her nails.

"How are you feeling?" I asked Sophie.

"Better, but I still want to be with Grinner."

"Do you think that's in your best interest?" asked Josh.

"No, but I really love him. I need to be with him," she whined.

Sophie said she'd met her doctor earlier that morning and had participated in two group sessions. She liked the social worker, but said the nurses were mean.

I asked Sophie about the other people on the unit. She said, "I really like the people here. They're all really nice." Pointing to a glassy-eyed girl no more than eight years old who stood in the doorway, Sophie explained she was on the unit because she heard voices telling her to stab her mother with a knife. The girl picking at her nail polish had overdosed on sleeping pills because her mother wouldn't let her go out with her boyfriend. The boy hunkered in the hall had whacked his mother in a fit of anger.

I was surprised by Sophie's saying the patients were nice and enjoyable to be around, but then Sophie always liked everyone she met. Then I remembered my mother saying that the people she'd shared the psychiatric ward with – people with whom she'd played Scrabble, done art projects, and eaten meals – were nice too.

As Saturday approached, I worried how Grinner would react when Sophie failed to be at their rendezvous spot. Would he come looking for her? My imagination had him knocking at our door, a gun in hand. But we never heard from him.

Sophie had been in the hospital a couple of days when Dr. Mehta, the psychiatrist assigned to her case, called me. "I've met with Sophie several times this week," she said tersely, "I have no doubt about her diagnosis. She has bipolar disorder." Her words came at me too quickly.

Before I could respond, Dr. Mehta continued, "Several different medications are effective for treating bipolar disorder, although some people have reactions to some of them. I'm going to discontinue all the medications Sophie's been taking except Lamictal. I'm going to start Sophie on a medication called Seroquel. We've had pretty good success with it. People seem to tolerate Seroquel better than some of the other medications. She'll have to stay in the hospital for a few days while I titrate the dosage and get her stabilized."

Questions flooded me as I tried to incorporate this new information. Sophie's been seeing mental health professionals for close to five years – why didn't anyone diagnose this before? What about ADHD – does she have this as well? What side effects do the medications have? Will she ever lead a normal life? Before I uttered a single question, the doctor ended the phone call. I sat in my kitchen, my head on the table, shell-shocked.

CHAPTER **48**

The Second Diagnosis

That afternoon.

M y career as a research psychologist had me well-versed in theories about family dynamics and sophisticated analytic methodologies, but living through my mother's illness and death had kept me far from the clinical side of psychology. I struggled to remember what I'd learned about bipolar disorder in the abnormal psychology class I took as an undergraduate at Michigan State, but came up empty. A quick search of the term told me that the condition used to be called manic depression.

That was a condition all too familiar to me. It was the illness my mother had suffered from nearly forty years earlier, the illness that led to her suicide. I was terrified.

How strange that adoption, the answer to my infertility and the solution I thought would prevent my mother's genes from being passed down to my children, would yield a child with this same condition. Was this a cruel cosmic joke?

Yet Sophie's symptoms and my mother's symptoms seemed so different. My mother cried, often couldn't get out of bed, and said she wanted to die. Sophie was wound up, always seeking the next joy ride. Was there some mistake in Sophie's diagnosis? Had my mother been misdiagnosed?

I went into overdrive seeking to understand how symptoms that looked so different could result in the same diagnosis.

Josh watched in silence as book after book I'd ordered from Amazon arrived on our doorstep, each with the words "Bipolar Disorder" in the title or subtitle. I read and I read and I read. I stopped only when I thought I understood.

I learned that people with bipolar disorder experience unusually intense emotional states. An overly joyful or overexcited state is called a "manic episode," while an extremely sad or hopeless state is called a "depressive episode." Sometimes people experience both mania and depression. This is known as a "mixed state." People with bipolar disorder may be explosive and irritable. Along with mood changes, people experience extreme changes in energy, activity, sleep, and behavior often so severe they cannot function at work, school, or home.

Symptoms of mania include feeling high or overly happy and outgoing that can last anywhere from hours to weeks. During manic phases, people are extremely agitated, and report feeling jumpy or wired. Behavioral changes include talking very fast, jumping from one idea to another, having racing thoughts, being distracted, taking on a host of new projects, sleeping little, and behaving impulsively, especially with regard to pleasurable behaviors such as sex. Making matters more complex is that some people with bipolar disorder experience hypomania, which is characterized by increased energy and activity levels that are not as severe as full-fledged mania.

Symptoms of depression include feeling worried or empty, loss of interest in activities once enjoyed, and decreased libido over periods of weeks or months. Behavioral changes include feeling tired or slow, having problems concentrating, remembering, and making decisions, sleeping more than usual, and being restless or irritable.

Much of what I read was consistent with Sophie's behaviors. She had trouble concentrating in school and she frequently complained about racing thoughts. She was often giddy, blabbering non-stop. Sometimes Josh gently teased her, accusing her of talking to hear her brain rattle and her lips flap. She often stayed awake all night long. Her frenzied activities were obvious the next morning, her room looking as though a tornado had touched down. And this latest episode with Grinner had all the signs of a full-blown manic episode.

Learning there are at least four different types of bipolar disorder, I understood that the symptoms my mother had experienced and those characterizing Sophie's behavior were, in fact, related. My mother most likely suffered from Bipolar Disorder Type II, the crushing, life-interfering sadness that all but crippled her at the end of each calendar year, combined with the hypomanic state she exhibited during the summers.

Sophie's cycling was different. My guess, although none of the doctors ever said so, is that Sophie suffered from cyclothymic bipolar disorder. The behaviors caused by her hypomania, many of which we had for years attributed to ADHD, in combination with the depressive symptoms evident in her sadness and anger towards herself – evident by the cutting and self-mutilations – characterized this form of the illness. Reflecting on Sophie's behavior over the past couple of years, it seemed that she probably had shown early signs of bipolar disorder that were either missed by the mental health professionals or deemed too premature to label. Yet, in their defense, the symptoms of ADHD and those of bipolar disorder often mask one another, and accurate diagnosis of bipolar disorder is unusual before age eighteen. However, when Sophie's symptoms went untreated, they worsened until she landed up in the adolescent ward of the psychiatric hospital.

Josh joined me in the search to understand the nature of Sophie's illness. We talked about nothing else for days. We read and analyzed the information in the collection of books I'd gathered. We were hungry for answers, unwilling to rest until we figured out what this new diagnosis would mean for Sophie and how we could help her. Each morning our conversation began where it left off the previous evening.

As we learned about bipolar disorder and realized it explained many of Sophie's behaviors, relief flooded me. It is an illness. It has a treatment. She's not a bad person who hates me. I'm not a bad mother. We can fix this. Yet I knew bipolar disorder was a very serious mental illness. It had killed my mother.

To my eye, little progress had been made in understanding the science underlying bipolar disorder in the past several decades. Its diagnosis remained difficult and its treatment complex. As I grappled with understanding bipolar disorder, I wondered about the ADHD diagnosis Sophie was given five years previously. Had her condition been bipolar disorder all along? The medications she took for ADHD had beneficial effects initially, but over time, they became less effective. Was this because they masked the bipolar disorder or had they created it?

I learned that scientists agree there is no single cause of bipolar disorder. Rather, many factors likely act together to produce it. There is a genetic component, as bipolar disorder tends to run in families. Children with a parent or sibling who has bipolar disorder are four to six times more likely to develop the illness than children who do not have this family history.

Learning about the genetics of bipolar disorder, I thought about calling Jamie to ask what she could tell me about Sophie's family history, but stopped myself, recalling our conversation about ADHD years ago. Having seen how difficult it was for us to get this diagnosis even with the perseverance and financial resources Josh and I had, I knew that without them, even if a diagnosis had been made, it wasn't one in which I would have much faith.

Although there was no known cure for bipolar disorder, I learned that medications helped most people gain better control of their mood swings and symptoms. The medication the doctor in the hospital had prescribed for Sophie, Seroquel, is a second generation antipsychotic, less likely to cause the nasty side effects characteristic of first generation medications. Like most of the other antipsychotics, Seroquel relieved the severe and sudden manic episodes. Its effectiveness was generally enhanced when taken in combination with the anticonvulsant Lamictal that Sophie already had been taking. I was heartened to learn that medications could control Sophie's behavior. Yet when I learned that these same medications were used to treat schizophrenia, I panicked. Schizophrenia is a severe mental illness that interferes with logical thought and often includes hallucinations and delusions. The fact that the same medications were used to treat schizophrenia and bipolar disorder made me realize the severity of Sophie's illness. Again.

While I was heartened to learn that the medications could effectively control many of the symptoms of bipolar disorder, their side effects frightened me. Common side effects of the mood stabilizing medications were drowsiness, dizziness, headache, diarrhea, constipation, and heartburn. Common side effects of the second generation antipsychotics were drowsiness, dizziness, blurred vision, rapid heartbeat, skin rashes, and substantial weight gain. I got dizzy reading about the side effects. Would Sophie be able to pay attention in school, do her math homework, or write an English essay with all of this pandemonium going on in her head? Would the treatments be worse than the symptoms? Would she become a zombie as the medications dampened her emotions?

Grappling with how I would help Sophie cope with her newly diagnosed illness, I vacillated between optimistic determination that we would beat this mortal enemy and dread that it would demand our surrender. Knowing the illness was treatable but not curable, I hoped we could find a workable compromise.

CHAPTER **49**

Interim Events

Last week of April 2009.

W hile Sophie was in the hospital, Detective Walker identified Grinner as a twenty-five-year-old living in New York. The detective spoke with Grinner, who admitted he'd had multiple sexual encounters with Sophie, including the one when she escaped from her second story window. To questions about having sex with a minor, Grinner insisted Sophie had told him she was sixteen. He explained the violent online persona and bravado as an act he engaged in to remain true to the role he'd played in the chat room where he and Sophie had met. Laughing, he'd told the detective how Sophie loved that persona. When the detective told Grinner that Sophie was ill and had been hospitalized, Grinner expressed remorse and agreed to refrain from further contact with her.

Whether to file a complaint against Grinner was one of the few instances where Josh and I disagreed. Josh wanted him prosecuted. He wanted him on death row. I was against filing charges because I believed Sophie's illness was the root of the problem. An emotionally healthy child would not have done what Sophie did. Grinner's crime was taking advantage of Sophie. If anything, he himself needed help. I also knew filing charges against Grinner would have required Sophie to testify, making her relive the emotional turmoil, stealing even more from her than he already had.

But, the decision about whether charges would be brought against Grinner was neither Josh's nor mine. It rested with Sophie. Without her testimony, there was no case. Despite Josh's pleas, Sophie continued to maintain that Grinner was a good person, that she valued his friendship, and that he'd done nothing wrong. In the end, Sophie had her way. Although Josh filed a complaint and the police uncovered evidence supporting criminal activity, when the prosecutor spoke with Sophie, she refused to cooperate. Nothing more would be done. Despite my ardent belief that this was in Sophie's best interests, I was left with remorse. How many other young girls would suffer Grinner's abuse?

I used Sophie's stay in the hospital as an opportunity to clean and organize her bedroom. The room's disorganization was a sign of the jumble characterizing her mind, and I hoped that organizing it might aid her recovery. I entered the bedroom with trepidation. Remnants of the project she'd begun the night she was hospitalized were strewn across the floor. Beads lay scattered on the carpet. Scraps of fabric were everywhere, and a pair of open scissors, their blades catching the late afternoon sun, glistened. Straight pins and safety pins – some of them open – littered the floor. The bed was piled high with stuffed animals positioned in such a way that made me imagine she'd placed each to protect her from something frightening. Clothes rested wherever they'd fallen, discarded as she'd tried on one outfit after the next.

I moved the clutter aside and sat on her bed, breathing in the air she had breathed. What did she see in this room that I did not? How many times had she cried, "Mom, I hate my room. I hate you. I hate my life." What was it that she hated about this spacious room with its bay window, its striped purple walls, its vibrant orange comforter, its antique bedroom furnishings that had been Josh's grandmother's, its walk-in closet, and its private bathroom with chartreuse green walls painted to her specifications?

I picked up the clothes and tossed them into the hamper. I gathered the art project paraphernalia and put it away. I matched the shoes into pairs and was about to put them in the closet when something caught my eye. I stopped. There it was, one of the sketchbooks we'd given Sophie for her birthday, lying open at the bottom of the closet, staring up at me and inviting me – no, daring me – to take a closer look. And so I did. The pictures she'd drawn were artistically sophisticated. They depicted her engaged in violent sexual brawls with a man who must have been Grinner. She'd drawn herself as a harlot, complete with dark eye makeup, hair covering her left eye, dressed in Goth-style regalia. It was so realistic that it included the heavy chain link necklaces she often wore.

The sketchbook was also filled with doodles and scores of poems, some of which hinted at suicide, others of entrapment, and still others of unrequited love. On one page she'd scrawled, "I don't want to be normal." On another, she'd scribbled, "I'd rather hurt myself and bleed than feel nothing." This concrete evidence of the pain Sophie experienced flooded me with sadness. I wanted nothing but to hold her and tell her how much I loved her. I wanted to make all of her pain go away, and I ached for the days when all I needed to do was kiss a scratch on her knee to magically heal her.

Hoping to contain the pain, I gathered up the sketchbooks and hid them in the basement.

CHAPTER 50

Failure to Communicate

Last week of April 2009.

S ophie remained hospitalized for a week. The initial dose of medication made her so groggy she could barely lift her head off the table during our visits. Seeing her in this condition was almost as frightening as watching her uncontrolled mania. The nurse told me that, for the remainder of Sophie's stay in the hospital, the medication dosages would be adjusted slowly until they controlled her mania without turning her into a zombie. This, we soon realized, was a very delicate balance. Josh and I visited her every evening and were pleased to see that each day brought her more into balance. When she began asking when she could go back to school, we knew she was truly on the mend.

Other than my brief phone conversation with Dr. Mehta, there'd been no communication with the hospital staff. No attempt to explain the new diagnosis. No attempt to educate us about what it would mean for Sophie's future. No discussion of treatment. It reminded me of when my mother had been hospitalized and no one had talked to my brothers and me. I'd always assumed there had been communication with my father, but now I wondered. I didn't understand how the staff could be so lackadaisical about such a serious illness, treating it as though Sophie had a minor cold or an upset stomach.

I called the hospital and asked to speak with Dr. Mehta, but a nurse told that me the doctor didn't take calls from family members. She said I should speak with the social worker, Ms. Young. "Really?" I questioned. "My daughter's just been diagnosed with a severe mental illness, and I'm not allowed to talk with the doctor?"

"Sorry, Ma'am, I don't make the rules. I just work here," she explained apologetically. Then she suggested, "Before your daughter leaves the unit, there will be a family discharge meeting. You can ask all your questions then."

The family discharge meeting was held in Ms. Young's office, a space barely large enough to hold her small desk and three folding chairs. Ms. Young was in her late twenties. She wore pointy red high heels. This must have been her first job. On the walls of her office were pictures, most likely drawn by children on the unit – scenes of fire-spewing dragons, children wielding blood-dribbled knives, and a man stabbing a small child. Ms. Young reviewed Sophie's case, going through her checklist and canned speech. Pausing for us to answer her questions, she chewed her gum loudly. Within minutes, the lack of airflow in the room had me gasping for breath.

Josh and I acknowledged that the facts as stated in Sophie's medical record were correct.

"Where will Sophie be living when she leaves the unit?" Ms. Young asked, looking at the clock on the wall.

"With us," I answered. What other answer had she expected?

"Does Sophie have a psychiatrist she can see in the community?"

"Yes, she's been seeing Dr. Kane for years." I was sure that information was in Sophie's records. Had she or anyone else even looked at the records?

"Great, I'll send her a copy of the discharge papers. Is this her correct address?"

"Yes."

"She should be seeing a therapist or counselor as well. Do you need a referral?"

"No, she'll continue to see Dr. Shuman," Josh replied.

"Dr. Mehta started Sophie on Seroquel. Here's a prescription for a two-week supply. You'll need to make an appointment with Dr. Kane so Sophie can continue on this. Do you have any questions?"

Did I have any questions? I had a million questions, but the time for this session was limited. As was Ms. Young's expertise.

"It was my understanding that Dr. Mehta would be part of this meeting," I mustered.

"She was supposed to be, but she got busy on the ward. I can see if she has time to meet with you if you'd like."

"Yes, that would be great," I answered.

Ms. Young was gone for 15 minutes. I thought she'd forgotten about us.

"The doctor will join us as soon as she can," she said, snapping her gum and closing the door.

While we waited for Dr. Mehta, Ms. Young asked Josh and me to sign a half dozen discharge forms. They stated that we knew what medications Sophie was on, that we were aware of signs of suicidal behavior and knew how to respond to them, that we would make the requisite follow-up appointments, and that we would pay the hospital bills. She blew a pink bubble.

There was a knock on the door. Dr. Mehta had arrived.

"I'm so sorry to have missed this session. How can I help you?"

Josh and I looked at each other. Where to begin? We'd made a list of questions, yet from her body language it was clear she expected to spend no more than thirty seconds with us.

"Will she be able to function in school?" I asked, at the same time Josh asked, "What can we do to help her?"

Our distress was evident. Dr. Mehta paused. The skin under her chin wobbled as she looked from me to Josh, and back to me. "Your daughter's intelligent and charming. She's been very cooperative on the unit. I'm sure she'll do just fine." She shook our hands, wished us luck, and left the room. For an instant, the cool air from the hallway reinvigorated me. Then the door closed. We were about to leave the hospital with a very sick child and virtually no instruction about how to help her. I could barely breathe.

CHAPTER 51

Swaying Tides

Late Spring and Summer 2009.
Sophie is nearly seventeen years old.

D
espite my fears about how to help Sophie, it was good to have her home. The medications stabilized her emotions and we no longer witnessed the wild highs and lows of months ago.

Hoping to be in a stronger position to help Sophie by understanding what people with bipolar disorder experienced, I read Kay Redfield Jamison's memoir, *An Unquiet Mind.* Jamison, a professor of psychiatry, is one of the foremost authorities on bipolar disorder and coauthor of one of the standard medical texts about it. She also suffers from bipolar disorder. As Jamison pursued her very successful career in academic medicine, she experienced the exhilarating highs and catastrophic lows that afflicted many of her patients, and she poignantly described her experiences in her memoir.

The message I took from Jamison's memoir was positive: people with bipolar disorder can lead successful lives. This theme was reiterated when I attended a session about bipolar disorder at the annual meeting of the American Psychological Association. In fact, when one of the experts said, "Bipolar disorder is the new ADHD," I took solace, embracing the knowledge that, with medications and support, Sophie could look forward to a good and productive life.

With Dr. Shuman's help, Josh and I developed a contract regarding healthy behaviors for Sophie to follow. It specified our expectations and associated adherence to these healthy behaviors with rewards.

We continued to read about bipolar disorder and the medications used to treat it. We learned that second generation antipsychotics are associated with major weight gain and changes in metabolism. My concern that Sophie, like any teenage girl, would be less likely to adhere to the regimen if she knew it would make her gain weight led Josh to analyze her options. He learned that Abilify, another second generation antipsychotic, had less weight gain associated with it than Seroquel. When we discussed the possibility of switching medications with Dr. Kane, she agreed with the wisdom of doing so, wondering aloud why the hospital staff would have chosen Seroquel in the first place. Luckily, Abilify was as effective as Seroquel in controlling Sophie's symptoms.

Back at school, Sophie worked hard to catch up on work she'd missed. She completed several first-rate art projects, each of which brought notes of praise from her teacher. When the school year ended, however, it was clear Sophie needed remedial work in math. Sophie agreed to the summer online program her counselor suggested and easily earned an A.

Josh and I encouraged Sophie to get a part-time job working at a local grocery store. In addition to teaching her respect for the value of a dollar, I hoped it would provide a glimpse of what life without a college degree might be like. I pushed Sophie to befriend the middle-aged women who worked at the grocery store, knowing they would teach her volumes about why a college education is important. They did not disappoint me. One night Sophie came home surprised that her coworker had to stay at work despite feeling ill because she couldn't afford to lose a day's wages. Another of her coworkers explained to Sophie that, if she didn't work, her kids wouldn't have food to eat. Still another told Sophie she couldn't go to the doctor because she didn't have health insurance and couldn't afford to pay the doctor.

I was heartened to see that Sophie was a conscientious worker. She insisted on arriving early for her shifts and willingly completed any task asked of her. She bagged groceries, cleaned the rest rooms, straightened shelves, lugged groceries to the cars, retrieved carts from the parking lot, and helped customers find products.

Sophie continued her therapy sessions with Dr. Shuman, who made getting Sophie to confront the rape she'd experienced when she was eleven their primary goal. Dr. Shuman explained that, until Sophie confronted the rape, she wouldn't be able to move forward with her life. As part of Sophie's therapy, Dr. Shuman asked Josh and me to write letters to Sophie, telling her how much we love her, what we feared her future would be should she not confront her demons, and how much we wanted to support her efforts to lead a healthy life. Writing the letter frightened me because it forced me to confront the likelihood that Sophie might not make the same choices for her future that I would.

For a few months, things seemed to be moving in the right direction. And then, in early July, the tide turned. We were working with a videographer to produce the video for Aaron's upcoming Bar Mitzvah. Sophie was preoccupied with the computer, racing back to it constantly. She seemed happier than normal, spoke loudly and quickly, and was restless.

What alarmed me most that afternoon were the changes in Sophie's interactions with Aaron. When we adopted Aaron, Sophie had been delighted. She took her role as big sister seriously, begging to hold and feed him. Aaron, in turn, worshipped Sophie. When he was a toddler, he joyfully followed her around. On vacations to Disney World, Jamaica, and the Dominican Republic, Sophie and Aaron enjoyed the special treat of watching Cartoon Network, giggling together long after Josh and I fell asleep. Their playful banter reminded me of the relationships I had with my brothers when we were young. As Sophie approached her eleventh birthday and Aaron his seventh, Josh and I witnessed a distinct change in their relationship. It became commonplace for Sophie to wallop him, trip him, or strike out at him with little reason. She berated him with words as well as actions, taking delight in goading him in any way she could. Aaron, in turn, rushed to Josh or me with cries of "Sophie punched me" or "Sophie won't stop calling me names" or "Sophie tripped me." What once had been playfulness between siblings had been transformed into one-way unabated abuse. Josh and I tried to correct Sophie's behavior, with little success.

Unfortunately for Aaron, he was the canary in our coal mine. Sophie's poking and prodding of him that afternoon caused me to ask Josh to check the computer surveillance. In moments we learned my suspicions were justified.

Grinner and Sophie had re-established contact. Just as my hopes for Sophie's healing were taking shape, we were back to trying to protect her from herself. Not wanting Sophie to know about our computer surveillance, yet needing to make her stop communicating with Grinner, Josh and I were drawn back into our world of make-believe.

"Sophie," Josh said. "Detective Walker called. He said their records show Grinner contacted you this afternoon. We're going to file a complaint with the police tomorrow morning."

"No, Dad, you can't do that." Her eyes brimmed with tears. "I love him. You don't understand. And he loves me too. Why else would he have contacted me?"

"Sophie, you're such as asshole," Aaron scoffed. Sophie's behaviors frightened him, although mostly he hid his feelings.

The more we tried to reason with Sophie, the more combative she got.

"Sophie, how could you? All the progress you've made this summer, all the therapy sessions. What can I do to make you understand?" I screamed.

"It's not you, Mom. It's me. I have to figure this out on my own."

"Your way's likely to get you killed."

Josh clenched his jaw and ground his molars. I left the house before I exploded.

When I returned, Sophie said, "Mom, I need to go to the hospital. I think I'm going to hurt myself." As explanation, she added, "It was my fault. I contacted him. I love him. I can't let him go to jail."

Fearing Sophie had worked herself into a manic state, I called Dr. Kane. She listened to my concerns and spoke briefly with Sophie.

Then the doctor talked with me. "She sounds very disturbed," concluded Dr. Kane. "I think you need to take her to the Crisis Center."

I shook my head. Memories of the trip to the crisis center three months ago, when Josh had spent more than twenty-four hours in the emergency room, were still fresh. I didn't believe Sophie would hurt herself, but I was afraid not to take her words seriously. I tried another strategy.

"Sophie, here are your options. Stop communicating with Grinner and we won't have him arrested. Keep talking with him and he goes to jail. What's it going to be?"

"I'll stop," she pouted.

"Okay," I responded.

"Mom, I know I don't have any privileges because I lied to you, but can I watch *Family Guy* for a little while?"

"Sophie, I think that sounds like a good idea. You've made such great progress this summer. Other than today, you've been working hard. You may watch *Family Guy*. Tomorrow you start the work of earning your privileges back. I wish you'd admit what bad news Grinner is."

"When I'm eighteen, I'm going to find him," she said. She always had to have the last word. She always had to win.

"Sophie, when you and Dr. Shuman agree you're healthy and can make good decisions about whom to date, you can have a relationship with anyone you want. Now, go watch *Family Guy*. Do you want to have a sleepover with me tonight? We can kick Dad into the guest room."

"Yeah, Mom, that would be good," she sighed.

Hugging her, I said, "Sophie, it may seem like I don't understand, but believe me, I have only your best interests at heart."

"I know, Mom. I love you."

Crisis averted with no trip to the emergency room.

Aaron, having witnessed this interaction, darted upstairs and slammed the door to his room. By the time I got there, he'd calmed down and was lying on his bed.

"Mom, why does she do this stupid stuff?"

"Aaron, she's sick. Sophie has a very serious mental illness, and sometimes she does things that don't make any sense to you and me."

"Mom, I wish Sophie weren't sick. I hate it when she does this shit." He fought to keep the tears back. I remembered how I'd wished that my mother hadn't been depressed.

"So do I, Aaron. So do I. Dad does too. It might help Sophie to know how you're feeling. Would you be willing to tell her?"

"I guess," he answered.

Sophie was watching television. "Sophie, Aaron has something he wants to tell you."

"Yeah, squirt?"

"Sophie, I hate it when you act like this," Aaron mumbled.

"I'm sorry, Aaron." As Sophie tried to hug him, Aaron froze, wanting to respond but not knowing how. Tears came to my eyes.

Josh and I agreed that, for Sophie's protection, we'd get a restraining order against Grinner. Contact with Grinner had set her back and we didn't want it to happen again. Dr. Shuman agreed with our plan and suggested that we not tell Sophie.

The restraining order gave us peace of mind and a few quiet weeks. Toward the end of July, with less than two months before Aaron's Bar Mitzvah, Sophie and I started shopping for dresses. Josh and Aaron, who would easily be outfitted for the occasion in tuxedos, were our somewhat reluctant support troopers. We identified stores within a two-hour driving distance of our home and set out on our mission. Sophie found the long, fitted pink dress, complete with mermaid tail that she wanted, in the second store we visited. I was not so lucky. We visited a dozen stores and I tried on nearly fifty dresses. While I was busy looking for the perfect dress, Sophie amused herself by trying on clothes, and Aaron played his PSP or scouted out the local neighborhood in search of the next chocolate milkshake opportunity.

Finally, I found The Dress. It was black, shimmering, and elegant. Mission accomplished.

As I passed Sophie's room that evening, a pile of clothes caught my eye. Crouching to put them in her hamper, I saw the Spanx Sophie had tried on in one of the stores. Telling me they made her look hot, she'd tried to convince me to buy them for her, but I refused to pay fifty dollars for underwear. Now they were on her floor.

"Sophie," I yelled.

"Yeah, Mom?"

"What are these doing here?" I waved the Spanx, glaring at her.

"I wanted them," she said haughtily.

"You wanted them?" I shrieked. "I told you I wouldn't buy them, so you stole them? Where do you get the idea this is acceptable behavior? You need to apologize to the storeowner and pay for the Spanx."

She slammed the door of her room. How dare she shoplift! Knowing Sophie's tendency to harm herself when she was angry, I wondered what she was doing on the other side of the door. I pounded on the door, insisting she open it.

"Either leave the door open or I'll take it off the hinges," I warned.

Sophie opened the door, but sulked in her room for close to an hour. When she emerged, she was combative, insisting she'd pay for the Spanx, but not apologize.

I was at my wit's end. The lying, thievery, and combativeness in combination with her tendency to take razor blades to her skin when she was angry left me impotent, unable to parent her. I went into my bedroom, closed the door, and sobbed.

Meanwhile, Josh tried a different tactic. He sat her down and explained why stealing is wrong. She calmed down and admitted she was wrong.

Before going to sleep, Sophie said, "Mom, I'm sorry about my behavior today."

"Sophie, I hope you understand how serious this is. Not only is stealing wrong, but it could get you into big trouble."

"I know, Mom. I'm sorry I let you down. I'll pay for the Spanx and apologize to the store owner."

"Goodnight, Sophie. I love you," I said giving her a hug and kiss.

"Goodnight, Mom, I love you too."

CHAPTER 52

Finding Normal

Fall 2009 to Spring 2010. Sophie is seventeen years old.

A aron's Bar Mitzvah was one of the highlights of my life. He was well prepared, poised, and eloquent. I was so proud of him.

The best part of the weekend festivities for me was the mother-son dance. Although Aaron had scoffed at my insistence that he take ballroom dancing lessons, he proved to be a quick study. Unlike at Sophie's Bat Mitzvah, I didn't cry during the service in synagogue. Nor did I cry during Josh's heart rending toast memorializing Aaron's four grandparents, all dead before Aaron was born. However, when Aaron and I were dancing, I totally lost it. With all the stress I'd experienced with Sophie over the past several years, I reveled at the joy Aaron brought me. I also felt guilty knowing that, while my love for him was endless, my emotional resources often were so exhausted by Sophie that I had little left for him. Catapulted by the magic of our dance, I closed my eyes and wished the night would never end.

But end it did, and in the blink of an eye, we left the magical weekend of Aaron's Bar Mitzvah for the looming challenges of Sophie's senior year of high school. Sophie would be eighteen in less than a year. Then she'd have full legal responsibility for herself, including decisions about treatment for her mental illness. I was glad Sophie had a diagnosis and a treatment plan, but worried since she'd yet to learn the triggers of her mania and she still relied on me to dole out her medications each day.

Sophie worried about her senior year of high school. She knew the "good" kids would ostracize her. With close to two thousand students, the high school was much like a small town. Rumors travelled quickly and Sophie never had been good about hiding her strange behaviors from her peers. In fact, she often bragged about her escapades. While she feared being lured back by the "bad" kids, she worried even more about spending senior year without friends. I worried too, but Sophie's ability to cope won out. She renewed her relationship with Max, the boy with whom she'd gone to Sophomore Cotillion, Rick's best friend. While I contended this was another attempt to attract Rick's attention, Sophie insisted I was wrong and that she was over the boy who had impregnated her and then broken her heart.

In early February, out of the blue, Sophie announced, "Mom and Dad, I have something I need to tell you guys that you're not going to like."

This was always a bad omen.

"What's that?" Josh asked cautiously.

"I never stopped talking with Grinner," she said with a smile.

"What?" Josh screamed. We hadn't renewed the computer surveillance software subscription when more than six months had gone by without activity. During this time, Sophie saw Dr. Shuman once a week, took her medications, and, by all accounts, was making good progress. Josh and I understood that part of Sophie's healing process was enabling her to establish trust with us, so we'd loosened the reins. Now, that decision had come back to bite us.

"Sophie, how could you?" I sighed.

"Mom, I really love him."

"So all this time that we've been working to get you well, you've been sabotaging our efforts?" My voice got louder and more strident.

"He's a really nice person. I care about him."

"He's not a nice person. He enticed you to climb out your window and then, when you hit your head, he put you in his car, drove you to a hotel, and fucked your brains out," I screamed.

"That's not what a nice person does."

I stopped, thinking about how Dr. Shuman had been trying to get Sophie to stop her secret life. Was this Sophie's attempt to listen to Dr. Shuman? Rather than having a covert relationship with Grinner, she was now giving us entrée to her secret life, telling us about the harmful things she was doing, and wanting to continue them even as we watched. Before either Josh or I could say another word, Sophie added, "Yeah, and Dr. Shuman's known about this for months."

No. Could this be true?

"Sophie, I don't get it," I wailed. "Every week you go to therapy. You say you want to get well, but you continue talking with Grinner?" I stormed out of the room, frustrated at my outburst. My explosion was counter to the strategy Dr. Shuman had encouraged me to use. I was losing control. Again.

"I hate you both," Sophie screamed. "I wish you were dead!"

Of course, when I spoke with Dr. Shuman, she confirmed that, although she frequently asked Sophie whether she'd been in contact with Grinner, Sophie always denied it. Dr. Shuman reminded me that, had Sophie told her that she and Grinner were communicating, she would have been obligated to report it to us since contact with Grinner had the potential to endanger Sophie's safety.

During the conversation, Dr. Shuman mentioned her concern about Sophie's tendency to pit her against Josh and me. She reminded me how I'd called her after one of Sophie's therapy sessions, concerned to hear Sophie say, "Dr. Shuman thinks dating Max is a good idea." She'd said nothing of the sort. And now here it was again, Sophie causing a rift – what Dr. Shuman called "a split" – between us. We agreed to communicate regularly so Sophie wouldn't be able to continue this behavior.

Our quest to understand and help Sophie cope with her mental illness had Josh and me reading constantly. One afternoon, Josh picked up *The Bipolar Teen: What You Can Do to Help Your Child and Your Family*[1] by David Miklowitz and Elizabeth George. He read about the kindling theory of bipolar disorder, which states that the brain of a teenager with bipolar disorder is damaged with each manic episode. Untreated, episodes of mania will occur more and more frequently, eventually initiated by seemingly minor triggers. Treated, however, episodes of mania are less likely to occur, the loss of brain cells is minimized, and the long-term prognosis is improved. The kindling theory is controversial, but it gave Josh hope and he clung to it. He was convinced that if we could keep Sophie from experiencing the manic highs, we could keep her from worsening over time. Viewing his role as protector, Josh's battle cry was, "Do whatever it takes to keep Sophie from experiencing mania." Had he been able to wrap Sophie in a cocoon and shelter her from even the most minor of manic episodes, Josh would have done exactly that.

Like Josh, Dr. Kane wanted to minimize Sophie's manic episodes, but she reminded me it would take time to adjust the medications to the point where they would be effective in keeping her mood in check. Balancing Sophie's medications was not an easy job. Sophie complained that the medications made her feel tired and robbed her of every ounce of creativity. She no longer had the drive to draw, write poetry, or sew. Even her passion for reading Stephen King and Jean Auel novels was gone. Sophie was reluctant to report racing or impulsive thoughts, since this brought an increase in the medication dosages. In the beginning, I'd relied on behaviors I observed to help Dr. Kane manage Sophie's medications. But helping Sophie learn to recognize and report her own triggers was critical. And so I struggled, seeing the symptoms indicating Sophie was escalating out of control, yet waiting to ask Dr. Kane to increase the medications until I could convince Sophie that she needed them.

I thought about the very different reactions my mother and Sophie had to their prescribed psychotropic medications. For my mother, the medications offered relief from crippling depression, so she took them as prescribed. For Sophie, the medications robbed her of a blissful hypomanic euphoria that heightened her sexuality, energy, and creativity. Likening her to Uncle Albert who, in the *Mary Poppins* movie, floated to the ceiling when he laughed and fell to earth when he thought of something sad, I understood why Sophie would be reluctant to take these medications. They erased the color from her world. Yet, I recognized the importance of the medications; without them, she spiraled out of control and put herself in danger.

By spring, Sophie's life revolved around high school graduation activities. She continued her relationship with Max, and looked forward to going to Prom with him. One afternoon, Sophie called Josh into the study to show him a prom dress she'd found online.

"Dad, isn't this dress beautiful?"

"Yes, Sophie, it is."

"Wouldn't it look great on me?"

"I'm sure it would," he agreed, looking over her shoulder. "Sophie, did you notice the dress costs fifteen hundred dollars?"

"Yeah, but Dad, it's my Senior Prom," she whined, turning on the voice that always made him melt. "Please, Daddy? It's perfect."

"You've got to be kidding. I'm not paying fifteen hundred dollars for a prom dress."

After a few minutes of pouting, Sophie came up with a different strategy. "Dad, I'm going to talk to my fashion design teacher and see if she'll help me make the dress. I'll bet she will and it can probably be my final project for the class."

"What a great idea. I'll pay for the fabric if you'll do the work."

"Deal!" she exclaimed with delight.

Sophie printed a picture of the dress and took it to school the next day. Her teacher thought the project was perfect and agreed to supervise Sophie's efforts to make it. Sophie bought the fabric on sale for less than fifty dollars and within a few weeks transformed it into an exquisite gown. She sewed the final sequins on it the day before the dance and even made a matching vest and cummerbund for Max. When she tried the gown on and modeled it for me, she was radiant. I told her how proud I was of her for taking the initiative and using her talents in such a productive way.

The day of the Prom, I took Sophie to the beauty shop so she could have her hair and nails done. As she enjoyed her afternoon of pampering, I looked around at the dozens of mothers and daughters in the beauty shop. I thought about all the dreadful experiences Josh and I had endured with Sophie over the past few years. I wondered whether any of the other mothers watching their daughters transform into fairy princesses had any idea from looking at me what hell I'd been through. I thought not. Then I wondered which of these women, all of whom looked quite normal to me, had had their lives turned upside down and their hearts broken by the ravages of mental illness. From the statistics I knew about mental illness, that beauty shop, with about sixty people in it, should have contained three or four women whose experiences were similar to mine. But for the life of me, I had no idea who they were.

CHAPTER 53

You Can Lead a Horse to Water

Spring 2010. Sophie is seventeen and a half years old.

F rom the time Sophie started kindergarten, she knew it was my hope that she would attend college. She'd heard countless stories about my college experiences, first at Michigan State and later at Penn State, and knew how much I'd enjoyed them. I'd told her about the summer before I left for Michigan State, when my friend Pat and I planned the perfect dorm room. Pat had made curtains and matching bedspreads; I had hooked a rug. However, to our dismay, when we arrived on campus, we learned that a third, non-matching roommate had been added to our room. Sophie loved that story because she knew that her Aunt Susan was my non-matching roommate, and that Susan and I had not only ended up being inseparable during the four years of college, but also have been best friends ever since.

When Sophie was two years old, we took her for her first visit to Penn State. During that and subsequent visits to Happy Valley, we ate ice cream at Meyer's Dairy and sticky buns at the Penn State Diner. Year after year, as we strolled the campus, I reminisced about my Penn State experiences. I told the stories so often that Josh joked he was sure that he too must have been a student at Penn State. Sophie had at least a dozen Penn State shirts and other souvenirs of our visits, constant reminders of my hopes for her future.

Finding the right college for Sophie was a group project that she, Josh, and I worked on for nearly two years. By the end of her sophomore year in high school, Sophie had identified clear criteria for the colleges she would consider. Each had to offer a degree in neuroscience because, since reading *Flowers for Algernon*, she'd been fascinated by the brain. Each had to have a strong theatre program open to non-majors so she could continue to act. Each had to be within a four-hour drive from our home so she had the flexibility to visit us. And each had to be a small liberal arts college that boasted a strong faculty-to-student ratio so she'd be missed if she failed to attend a class. We had identified eight colleges meeting Sophie's criteria, visited each, and learned about the unique opportunities each provided.

For her college applications, Sophie wrote an eloquent essay describing her struggles with mental illness. She wrote of her frustration knowing she was different from other kids and not being able to concentrate in school. She explained that she wanted to study neuroscience because she wanted to learn about why her brain processed information differently than others. And, at the end of the essay, she vowed to help make the world a better place so that no child would ever have to experience what she had.

Sophie fell in love with Franklin & Marshall College. She envisioned herself working with the capuchin, rhesus, and squirrel monkeys in the primate lab. Given her poor high school grades, this option was more than a long shot, but I encouraged Sophie to apply.

As I expected, Sophie wasn't accepted at Franklin & Marshall. Reading the rejection letter, she worried that none of the other colleges would admit her either. Although I was sorry she didn't get accepted to her first-choice school, I was pleased to see her show appropriate emotions. Her disappointment and sadness were real, feelings I don't think she would have had even six months earlier.

I reminded her there were several other schools that met her criteria, each of which had the potential to be a good fit. Begrudgingly, she set off to complete the other applications. By mid-December, she had submitted all of the college applications, and I breathed a sigh of relief.

At the beginning of February, Sophie received a phone call from an admissions counselor at Dickinson College. Although we had visited the school and liked it, the morning had been chilly, our tour guide dismal, and our visit cut short because we planned to visit a second school that afternoon. The counselor's call suggested they were interested in her, so I encouraged Sophie to be thoughtful in her conversation.

After speaking with the admissions counselor for only fifteen minutes, Sophie came looking for me.

"There's no way they're going to accept me," she laughed.

"Why not?" I asked, closing the oven door.

"We had a nice talk, but when he asked me what my weaknesses are, I said academics."

"Right. You can forget about Dickinson. What were you thinking?"

She shrugged her shoulders, chuckling. "I don't know."

Not two weeks later, Sophie said, "Mom, I got an e-mail from Dickinson. I'm sure it's a rejection letter. I don't even want to open it."

"You're probably right," I agreed. "But go ahead and open it."

Within moments she screamed. "Oh, my God! I got in! Mom, I got in!"

Thinking this couldn't possibly be, I raced to the computer and read the letter. Then I read it again. I checked the name and address, making sure it really was meant for Sophie. Having recently heard about a college that had sent acceptance letters out in error, only to retract them hours later, I asked Josh to call the school to verify she had been admitted. In fact, she had.

Josh and I were astounded. This was our dream come true, the second chance we never thought Sophie would get. That Sophie had been admitted to one of the top small liberal arts colleges in the country far exceeded our most optimistic hopes.

With this victory, we encouraged Sophie to start taking greater responsibility. Within a few months, she'd be off to college. She needed to learn to take her medications at the appropriate time, and so I transitioned this responsibility to her. She needed to learn to make decisions about when to study, and so we told her we expected her to complete the last months of high school work without my policing her. Of course, we insisted she take responsibility for keeping her room clean. She was delighted by the newfound trust. She planned several social events, kept her room clean, and did her homework.

For about a week.

One afternoon, after she'd left her room a wreck before leaving for school, I gently reminded her of her responsibility to keep it clean. She promised to clean it that evening. The next day, her room was even messier. I scolded her for not taking her responsibility seriously, and grounded her for the weekend.

"But Mom," she wailed. "I was invited to Scott's party tomorrow night. I told him I'd be there. I have to go."

"You'll have to tell him you can't go."

"Can I please have another chance?" she whined.

"No, Sophie. This is about responsibility. You knew the rules. You're very good at taking the privileges, having the freedom to come and go as you please, but you've got to get the responsibility part down."

"I hate you!" she screamed, flipping over a chair and racing upstairs.

For the rest of the afternoon and evening, she scowled at me. She refused to take part in our family dinner, retiring early to her room. I hoped she was cleaning, but the next morning her room was in an even worse state. I reminded Sophie she was grounded until the room was clean. She told me she didn't care, and her abusive attitude continued.

I checked her medications. She hadn't taken them for several days. When I asked her why she hadn't taken her medications, she said, "I didn't take them because I was mad at you."

I reminded her of the importance of taking the medications as prescribed. She stomped off.

Several days later, Sophie's room was still a mess. She had a half-day of school, and called me when she got home. "I'm going to ride my bike to the nail place and get my nails done."

"Did you forget you're grounded until your room is clean?"

"You never told me that."

"I did. Remember last week when I told you that you couldn't go to the party – and you flipped the chair over?"

"What does 'cleaning my room' mean?"

"You know what it means. All the clothes picked up from the floor. All the surface areas cleaned off. And I'm going to check, so make sure you don't just pick everything up from the floor and stuff it into the drawers."

"Do I have to fold my clothes?"

"No. But you can't just move the papers and things from the dresser and desk into the drawers."

"I'll have plenty of time to clean after I get my nails done."

"Wrong order. Why are you fighting this? Cleaning your room is your responsibility. Once it's clean, there's plenty of time to get your nails done."

"Fuck you! I hate you!" She slammed the phone down.

This pattern was typical. Sophie enjoyed the freedom to make decisions and spend time with her peers, but wanted no part of the responsibility for keeping her room clean and doing her homework. Her response to the consequences we gave her when she failed to live up to her responsibilities was to fire back with rage and abuse.

By early April, Sophie was expressing concern about not having the study skills and discipline needed to succeed at Dickinson. She said she wanted to go to the community college for a year, develop the skills she lacked, and go to Dickinson the following year.

I bristled at the idea. I was ready to launch her and put the nightmare of the past several years behind me. I wanted Aaron to have a few years with Sophie out of the house so he could live a more normal life. And I believed Sophie had the intelligence to be a high achiever if only she'd find the discipline to do so. I encouraged her to work hard during her last two months of high school, and did everything I could to get her pumped about college. I spoke joyfully about her future roommate and the classes she might take. I even bought the matching comforter, towels, and pillows Dickinson sold, hoping it would motivate her.

But it was not to be. The more I tried to kick Sophie out of the nest, the more she refused to try to fly. Rather than embracing the responsibility to complete homework on her own, Sophie stopped doing her homework. She used the poor grades that followed as evidence that she wasn't ready to go to Dickinson.

Though I pressed my case that she'd do fine if only she would try, it finally became clear to me that Sophie wasn't ready for college when she failed the math and science placement tests Dickinson required of incoming freshmen. It wasn't merely that she failed the tests, but that she didn't even try. Although two hours were allocated for the tests, she spent no more than fifteen minutes on them.

We scheduled a family session with Dr. Shuman to discuss our options. When Josh suggested Sophie's idea to spend a year at the community college was reasonable, Sophie breathed a deep sigh of relief, and said, "Finally, you heard me. What took you retards so long?"

Sophie requested, and was granted, a one-year deferral from Dickinson. I accepted the new plan and championed Sophie's insight and wisdom. But, would she really implement it?

Chapter 54

Splitting

Summer 2010. Sophie is eighteen years old.

From the time Sophie was old enough to know what adoption meant, she knew that Josh and I had adopted her and that Jamie was her birth mother. The warm relationship Josh and I had established with Jamie and her grandparents before Sophie was born had been challenged over the years, but Jamie's importance in our lives never wavered.

As I'd expected, Sophie's curiosity about her roots grew as she entered her teenage years and, as I'd hoped, Jamie was more than willing to answer her questions. I encouraged Sophie to talk with Jamie, respecting and valuing the biological bond that linked them.

Now I worried. Sophie said Jamie was encouraging her to get a fake driver's license so she could go to bars. She also said Jamie had said going to college was a waste of time. Of course I didn't believe Jamie had said these things. Jamie wanted the best for Sophie. Even in the first conversation Jamie had with Josh, before Sophie was born, Jamie had made it clear that she hoped Sophie would go to college. What was Sophie up to now?

I suspected Sophie's comments were a ploy to split Jamie and me, just as she'd pitted Dr. Shuman against Josh and me. When I refused to engage in these conversations, Sophie raised the bar by telling me about Jamie's invitation for her to visit Texas and her intention to go. I told Sophie that a visit with Jamie was fine and asked her how she intended to pay for it. I also reminded Sophie that she needed to find a job and start putting aside spending money for college.

Was Sophie's newfound focus on Jamie a genuine expression of her need to explore her biological roots or some mean-spirited delight she derived from sparking turmoil? Her ability to maintain a frosty calm while pushing Josh's and my buttons provided weighty evidence that it was the latter.

The calmness of a Sunday morning disintegrated when Sophie came downstairs with fire in her eyes. "Mom, would you disown me if I pierced my lip?" Here was yet another of her questions meant to rile. Her fascination with piercings had been the subject of countless conversations over the past several years. She knew where Josh and I stood on this, as we'd told her time and time again that, as long as she depended on us for financial support, piercings and tattoos were out of the question. I reminded her of how we'd removed her from camp the summer she'd pierced her nose. Yet, here she was, pushing my buttons. Again.

"Sophie, I'm not going to have that conversation with you again. You know my answer."

"But Aunt Jamie has piercings. She thinks they're great."

"That's her choice, and when you're ready to be financially independent and take full responsibility for yourself, you can make decisions about whether or not to have them."

Hours later, frustrated that her initial attempt failed to spark my fury, Sophie launched the second missile. "Mom, I'm not asking. I'm telling you that I'm going to dye the top of my hair bright yellow and leave the rest brown."

"I don't think so."

"But you said I could do anything I wanted with my hair," she whined.

"Right, but now you're working with two-year-olds at the synagogue's day care. Do you think screaming yellow hair is appropriate?"

"The kids wouldn't care."

"Right, but their mothers might. Besides, you need to find a part-time job so you can pay for that car you want. In this lousy economy, you have to do everything you can to make yourself appealing to a potential employer. Do you think looking like a freak when you go on a job interview is a good idea?"

"You never let me do anything fun," she howled. "I hate you!" She stomped upstairs.

Hours later, Sophie was still bellyaching. "But Mom," she pleaded, "you said I could do anything I wanted with my hair. Why do you always change your mind? It's not fair."

She'd worn me down. "Sophie," I screamed. "This has to stop. I'm sick and tired of your nonsense. If you can't follow our rules, why don't you go live with Jamie?"

Hoping to give me an opportunity to calm down, Josh suggested we take the dogs out for a walk. When we returned, Sophie was getting off the phone. I'd dealt with the piercing and hair dyeing announcements too effectively. Sophie upped the stakes.

"I'm leaving. Aunt Jamie said she'd pay for the plane ticket. I'm moving to Texas. I'm not going to college."

"Yeah, right," I said.

To my complete and utter surprise, Sophie persisted with her plan. She spent hours on the phone with Jamie, and that evening she told me they'd decided on a travel date.

Josh came unglued. Shaking his head, he sighed. "How could she make such a terrible decision?"

I left Sophie alone for most of the night. Before she went to bed, Sophie came looking for me, gave me a hug, and told me she loved me. I seized the opportunity to encourage her to think about the practicalities of moving to Texas and what her life might be like if she didn't go to college.

"Sophie, you know how important your medications are. How will you afford them in Texas?"

She looked at me blankly. "I don't know, Mom."

"You'll need to find a psychiatrist. He'll probably charge you between five and seven hundred dollars for the initial visit. Then you'll need monthly med checks, and of course you'll need to pay the co-pays on your medicines. Even though you're covered on our insurance until you're twenty-six, you're still looking at significant costs each month. How will you pay for them?"

"Maybe Aunt Jamie could pay for them."

"Maybe, but remember Jamie has two little kids to worry about."

She paused, saying nothing.

"What about school?"

"I could go to the community college in Texas."

"How would you pay for it?"

"Maybe Aunt Jamie would pay for it," she answered. The attitude of entitlement was amazing. She always assumed someone else would pay her way. Did I create that?

"You should probably talk with her about that. And don't forget, you'll have other expenses – transportation, food, and clothing. How are you going to pay for those? How will you afford your cell phone?"

"I'll get a job," she answered with confidence.

"What about your friends?" I asked, hoping to shake her back to reality.

"I'll make new ones." She was not to be dissuaded.

For the next three days, Sophie and Jamie planned the trip. They were constantly on the phone. Sophie made plans to ship boxes of her possessions to Texas. She said goodbye to Dr. Shuman and left notes on Facebook telling her friends of her plans.

I panicked. Maybe, just maybe, this trip might happen. Amidst my panic, an all-encompassing sadness descended. The thought of Sophie turning down a chance to go to a great college and leaving our family devastated me.

That evening, my sister-in-law Denise sent me a chatty e-mail. She told me about Brian and their kids and asked how we were doing. I wrote back telling her about Sophie's plan to move to Texas. I wanted to tell her more, but I couldn't. Denise was the perfect mother, the mother I wanted to be. She'd not been employed since her first child was born and she'd created her life around her three children. Maybe if I hadn't spent so much time pursuing my career, things would have been better for Sophie.

Within the hour, Brian called. "Rachel, what the hell's going on? Denise tells me Sophie's moving to Texas. Let me talk to her."

Brian has a heart of gold, but his understanding of Sophie's mental illness was limited. Over the years, I'd told him even less about Sophie's behaviors than I'd told Ben. Five years younger than me, Brian had been only seven when our mother got sick and sixteen when she died. As difficult as things had been for me, for Brian they'd been far worse.

Thinking like the rational engineer that he is, Brian was hell-bent on assessing the problem and fixing it.

"Be my guest," I warned, "but it won't do any good."

Brian spent the next hour lecturing Sophie. I don't think that Brian and Sophie had ever had such an extended conversation. When they had finished, Brian called me.

"Wow, Rach, she's tough. I let her have it with both guns. I painted a picture for her of what life in Texas would be like, without you and Josh and her friends. She doesn't believe me."

"Join the club. She doesn't believe me either."

"Why don't you send her out here? Denise and I'll set her straight."

I sighed. How could I begin to explain what Josh and I had lived through with Sophie? How could I make Brian understand his offer wasn't a good idea?

Wanting to see how Sophie was faring, I knocked on her door. "What?" she growled. "Uncle Brian's an asshole."

"He was only trying to help you, Sophie. Like Dad and me, Uncle Brian loves you and wants the best for you."

She stared into space and asked, "Mom, can I go visit Aunt Jamie for six months? I want to do some self-exploring."

Happy to see a glint of reality to her thinking, I said, "You need to be in college. That's a great place for self-exploring."

"How about if I go to Texas for two months?"

"Classes start in four weeks. How about if you go for a few weeks, but come home before school starts?"

"Deal."

"No tattoos or piercings," I reminded her.

"Okay," she repeated, her eyes closing as though a great burden had been removed from her shoulders. "Mom, I love you."

"Sophie, I love you too. Good night."

After that evening, Sophie made no further mention of going to Texas. The phone calls with Jamie dwindled. Sophie started working at a new grocery store, and said she looked forward to starting college.

Had I been to *The Twilight Zone* and back? Was this a manic episode? Was it a test of the extent to which Josh's and my love for her is unconditional?

CHAPTER 55

"I'm 18 and I Can Do Anything I Want"

Fall 2010. Sophie is eighteen years old.

For many, 1972 was a dark year. Arab gunmen murdered eleven Israeli athletes at the Munich Olympics. Five White House operatives were arrested for burglarizing the offices of the Democratic National Committee, launching the Watergate scandal. The last American ground troops were withdrawn from Vietnam, ending a sad and bloody chapter of the first war in United States history without widespread public support.

But for me, 1972 was a year of exhilaration. I was eighteen and I could do anything I wanted.

I was bound for Michigan State, a school I chose because it was two hours from home. In addition to worrying about whether I'd get homesick, be able to do my own laundry, and make friends, I agonized about my mother's health. Her manic and depressive cycles were directly tied to the seasons. Autumns brought her crashing down as depression left her unable to get out of bed. In recent years, she'd attempted suicide several times and made many trips to the psychiatric hospital. How would she survive this year? Would my leaving push her over the edge?

Sophie's giggle jolted me back to reality.

It was 2010 and we were celebrating Sophie's eighteenth birthday. I was hopeful she'd embrace her growing independence, yet frightened since she'd shown little evidence she had the where-withal to do so. I'd not only come to terms with her decision to defer her admission to Dickinson, but believed her plan to spend the year at the community college was mature and thoughtful. We agreed I wouldn't hover as I had when she was in high school and she'd take full responsibility for her schoolwork. I hoped she'd achieve her goals of developing good study skills and learning the math that frustrated her in high school.

In an effort to respect Sophie's growing independence, Josh and I established only the most nominal rules for her. We expected her to go to school, work a part-time job, keep her room clean, and treat us with respect.

As though a switch had been thrown, Sophie's determina-tion to take responsibility for her life reversed itself weeks after she turned eighteen. Like a train gathering momentum, her initial rum-blings about not studying intensified. The textbooks she insisted I buy on the first day of class remained in their bags, unopened. She used the laptop computer we had given her as a birthday present only to watch *Sponge Bob* and *Adult Swim* cartoons. Sophie's new-found independence had her taking glee in igniting Josh's and my ire in any way she could. She left food-encrusted plates and silver-ware from midnight snacks strewn around her bedroom. She made plans to attend a rock concert on Yom Kippur, the holiest day on the Jewish calendar. Several nights a week, she came home with glassy stoner eyes. There was no evidence she was studying.

By the beginning of October, in hopes of lighting a fire under her, Josh reminded Sophie that, if she didn't earn at least B's in her classes, we wouldn't pay for the spring semester. Because Sophie was notorious for her "but you never told me" whine, we put our agreement in writing. She confessed she hadn't been doing her homework and had failed more than one math test, but promised to change her ways.

Again – as always – she did not.

At the end of October, when Sophie had failed so many tests that it was clear she couldn't possibly meet the goals to which she'd agreed, we took our family conversation to Dr. Shuman's office. Resolved to hold Sophie responsible for her actions and force her to face the consequences of them, Josh and I encouraged her to think about taking time off from school and getting a full-time job. She cried, she yelled, and then she threw her hoodie over her head. "One more chance, please give me one more chance. I promise. I'll do my homework. I want to go to college."

Despite her pleas, we told Sophie we wouldn't pay for the spring semester. We explained, however, that if college was important to her, she could get a job, pay for spring semester, take her work seriously, and then we'd pay for Dickinson the following year. My fantasy of her going to college refused to bend to reality.

She continued to whine and wail.

Josh cajoled her, "I'll go one better. If you take a full load of four courses this spring and earn a B or better in all four, Mom and I'll reimburse you for the semester's costs." More than she deserves. Josh never could stand to see Sophie cry, but at least he had the sense to refuse to give in without making her deliver first.

"Deal," she agreed bounding across the room to hug him.

Friday evening, Sophie told me she had a date Saturday afternoon and was scheduled to work at the grocery store that evening. She planned to get up early to complete her math homework before leaving the house.

Saturday morning, I met Sophie in the back hallway as I returned from an early morning Pilates class. She was getting ready to leave the house. "Mom, I did as much of the math homework as I could, but I couldn't do some of it because the teacher was behind in the lesson."

"Oh," I said skeptically, still calmed by the Zen of exercise. "Can you show me what you did?"

Sophie turned on the computer, went to the website where homework was to be uploaded, and screamed, "Oh no, it's not there. I must have not saved it right."

Of course, more likely the truth was that she hadn't done the work. This was one of her theatrical performances designed for my benefit.

"You'd better call your friend and let him know you won't be able to go until your homework is done." My endorphin high was beginning to dissipate.

"No way," she insisted. "I'm going. I can't let my friend down. He's almost here."

"Work before play," I reminded her. "You agreed to take responsibility for your school work. Sometimes you have to make tough decisions."

"I'm going, and there's nothing you can do about it," she screamed.

"Go and you're done with community college. If you leave the house without completing your work like you promised in Dr. Shuman's office the other day, you can forget about the rest of the semester and a future with college. You can get a job and pay rent."

"You'd never do that," she fired. "You believe college is too important. You'd never take that away from me."

Sophie clutched her purse and work clothes, and slammed the front door behind her.

"Watch me," I screamed.

But she was already gone.

I didn't hear from Sophie until ten thirty when she called, asking for a ride home from work.

Getting into the car, she said with a snooty tone, "Do you think we can be civil to each another?"

I didn't answer her, so she continued talking. "I watched the final episode of *Lost* this afternoon. It wasn't very good."

"Sophie, it's late and I don't want to have this conversation now. We can talk in the morning."

A half hour after we got home, Sophie knocked on my bedroom door. "Mom, I cut my wrist. I feel like I want to hurt myself. I need to go to the hospital."

She had what looked like a paper cut on her left wrist. I gave her a tissue and told her to apply pressure to it.

"How long have you been feeling like you wanted to hurt yourself?"

"I don't know. For a while, I guess."

"Did you feel like you wanted to hurt yourself while you were hanging out with your friend this afternoon?"

"No."

"What about when you were at work? Did you feel bad then?"

"No. I had a good day at work."

"So, when did you start thinking about wanting to hurt yourself?"

"I guess when I was in the shower. If I can't go to college, I don't have any reason to live."

It took every part of my being not to scream back at her. Are you kidding? How manipulative can you be? You don't want to take responsibility for your life, and then when you're called on it, you pretend to be suicidal? Get a life! I wanted tell her what real suicidal behavior looked like. I wanted to tell her how much my mother had suffered.

But I did not. I had no desire to put ideas in her head.

"If you want me to drive you to the emergency room, Sophie, I will. But I won't sit there with you all night like Dad did last time. I'll take you, check you in, give them my insurance card, and then I'll leave. Is that what you want?"

"Yes," she nodded.

On the way to the hospital Sophie said, "Mom, I'm sorry I let you down."

"Sophie, I don't care whether or not you go to college, but flitting from one party to the next is not acceptable. You're eighteen and you need to take responsibility for yourself."

When we reached the hospital, I asked her again whether she wanted to admit herself. I reminded her how the last time she was admitted to a psychiatric hospital she'd spent more than eighteen hours in the emergency room first. She assured me this was what she had to do.

It took everything I had to check Sophie into the emergency room, give the admissions clerk my insurance card, hug Sophie, and say goodbye without crumpling. I got into my car and started the ignition. Can I leave her here? Would a good mother leave her sick child alone? But I had to do it. Although I'd done everything I could to help Sophie deal with her mental illness – had held her hand at every nasty turn – in the end, I couldn't fix her problems any more than I could fix my mother's problems years ago. Then I was a child with no tools. But now, even with my advanced degree in psychology and my years of maturity, I was still powerless.

I turned the radio on and crept out of the parking space as B101's disk jockey introduced the next song, Leeann Womack's *I Hope You Dance*. Of all the songs he could play, why this one? It was the song Josh and I picked for the end of the video we made commemorating Sophie's Bat Mitzvah five years ago. It was the song that conveyed all the hopes and dreams we had for the daughter we loved more than life itself. Its melodic message to be humble, to take nothing for granted, to not settle, and to embrace life's challenges with gusto had accompanied photos showing Sophie's maturation from a baby to a young child to the beautiful, talented thirteen-year-old she had become. The hope then in her eyes, the optimism in ours, was gone now. Mental illness had defeated me once again. I was crying so hard that I couldn't see. Sophie was disappearing from my life and there wasn't a damn thing I could do about it.

CHAPTER 56

Love on the Psych Ward

Fall 2010. Sophie is eighteen years old.

T he jangle of the phone startled me. I looked at the clock. It was 3:18 A.M.

"Hello," Josh answered. He handed me the phone. "It's the hospital. They want to talk to you."

The caller identified herself as a crisis worker. She explained that she hadn't wanted to call "too late or too early."

Great, so she calls in the middle of the night. How sane is that?

She asked why Sophie had come to the emergency room. I told her about the day. When she asked whether I thought Sophie was suicidal, I said I did not. Unlike my mother, Sophie never really had done anything to hurt herself. Even when Sophie had cut herself, she never did more than break the skin. However, I told her that Sophie was troubled and that I didn't want to be responsible for any harm that might befall her. I agreed that Sophie's request to be admitted as an inpatient made sense.

Several hours later, after Sophie was transported by ambulance to Weston Behavioral Health Center, a psychiatric inpatient hospital, she called and told me she was on the Adult Dual Diagnosis Unit. She gave me a password enabling me to speak with her health-care providers, new protocol for us now that she was of legal age.

I called the unit and spoke with a nurse named Shirley. Her voice was chilly. She confirmed Sophie had been admitted hours ago, had met her roommate, and was settling in.

"I want to make sure the staff knows Sophie has parents who love and care about her," I said, remembering the girl I'd watched pick through the trash in San Francisco years ago. "Has she told you why she's there?"

"Sophie told me she tried to hurt herself because you said she couldn't go to college. She said you made her go to the community college instead of Dickinson."

"Oh my," I gasped. During the next twenty minutes, I explained how Sophie had begged to go to the community college, claiming she wasn't ready to go to Dickinson. I told Shirley that Sophie had been partying rather than studying for the past few months and how it had all come to a head the previous day when Sophie decided to play rather than do her work.

"You know, I figured there was more to the story than what Sophie told me," Shirley said, warming to me. "I have four kids of my own, and I knew that child wasn't telling the truth." Shirley oriented me to the rules of the ward and invited me to call her anytime. Hanging up the phone, I shook my head in dismay.

I spoke with Sophie a few hours later. She was tired and asked me to bring some of her clothes to the hospital. Entering her bedroom to gather them, I found clothes, papers, jewelry, and pieces of art projects scattered on the floor, on her desk, on her bed, and on her nightstand. Dirty clothes and clean clothes were strewn about and hanging halfway out of her dresser drawers. Opening a drawer in search of underwear, I found an unopened pregnancy test, her toothbrush, a plate with cake crumbs, and a fork. Opening another drawer in search of pajamas, I found a notebook, some underwear, one of Josh's hammers, several razor blades, and one of Aaron's Gameboy games.

I finally found a couple of pairs of pants, a few tee-shirts, and two sweatshirts to take to Sophie. Failing to find clean pajamas, underwear, and socks in her room, I went to Target, purchased these items, and delivered everything to the hospital.

That evening Sophie called.

"Hi Mom. How are you and Dad and Aaron?"

"We're fine," I said. "How are you?"

"Not so good. They messed up my medications and they've been giving me only 200 rather than 300 mg of Lamictal each day. I'm having crazy, wild mood swings."

Figuring Sophie had reported her medication doses incorrectly, I suggested she clarify the doses to the nurses.

"It's boring here," she complained. "Will you promise to call me every day while I'm here?"

"Of course I'll call you, Sophie. I love you and want you to get well." Her request for daily contact surprised me; before the hospitalization she had little but disdain for me. "What did you do today?"

"We had a bunch of therapy groups and I did a couple of art projects. I just got back from a smoking break."

"Smoking break?"

"Yeah, if we go to group therapy sessions, we get to smoke cigarettes as a reward."

"Have you taken up cigarette smoking?"

"Would you rather see me smoke cigarettes or cut myself?" she offered.

Not wanting the conversation to escalate, I changed the topic. "So, tell me about the other people there."

"They're nice. I like my roommate a lot. She's a heroin addict. She's nice, but she's troubled. I don't think she wants to get well. She keeps sneaking drugs when the nurses aren't looking."

Sounds like a wonderful person.

"Mom, can I ask you a question?"

"Sure."

"Are you serious about withdrawing me from classes? I really want to stay in school."

I was flabbergasted. How could she say this when time and time again her behavior indicated otherwise? Were my values so firmly ingrained in her that she couldn't shake them loose? Or does she want to stay in school so she can continue the party life?

"Sophie, the main thing now is to figure out what's troubling you. We can worry about school later. But right now, it's not where you need to be."

Over the next two days, I spoke with Sophie frequently. Her anxiety decreased and she attended both group and individual therapy sessions.

On the fourth day Sophie was in the hospital, there was an unexpected thrill in her voice when she called. "Mom," she whispered. "There's the cutest boy here. I really like him."

"Sophie, you've got to be kidding." I didn't want to incite her, but wondered why she saw the psychiatric hospital as a pickup bar. "Sophie, you're in a psychiatric hospital. People there have very serious problems. Probably not the right place to find a boyfriend."

"But Mom, you don't understand. He's so cute. His name's Rick. I like him a lot. He understands me, and I understand him." Here we go again. Sophie was so quick to attach to people she barely knew.

Trying to take the high road, I asked why he was in the hospital. She told me he was a recovering heroin addict who'd gone back to the drug, overdosed, died, and been resuscitated. This can't be for real. It's got to be a bad dream. Pinch me. My explanation about recidivism rates among heroin users fell on deaf ears.

"He'll never do it again. He nearly died. He told me he'll never use heroin again. I believe him. He's a great person and he's my friend. He's helping me, and I'm helping him."

Hoping to change the conversation, I asked, "How are the therapy sessions going?"

"Good. I decided I want to quit school and work full-time."

"Sounds like a good idea."

"Mom, I've got to go. We're going outside for a cigarette break."

How was it that both Sophie's roommate and her new heartthrob were heroin addicts? A call to Geoff, the hospital's Director of Social Work, revealed that patients on the Dual Diagnosis Unit had a diagnosed mental illness as well as a drug problem. Geoff said Sophie's bipolar diagnosis and her positive test for cannabis upon admission qualified her for the unit. To my queries about the wisdom of putting an eighteen-year-old college kid who smoked weed on a ward with heroin addicts, he said, "That's the rule here. She was eligible for the unit and that's where we had a bed."

That evening as we did the dishes, I told Josh about my conversation with Sophie.

"A heroin user? Is there no end to the bad decisions she'll make?"

He paced as I loaded dishes into the dishwasher.

"Wait a minute," he said. "Did you say this guy's name is Rick?"

"Yeah."

"Rachel, did you ever realize that every one of Sophie's boyfriends has been named Rick? There was that neighborhood kid I caught groping her on the way to school shortly after we moved to New Jersey. Then there was the kid who got her pregnant. Although the police never did tell me Grinner's last name, his first name was Rick. And now there's this guy. That can't be a coincidence."

A shiver ran down my back. "Do you suppose the guy who raped her was named Rick too?"

"I'll bet it was," Josh concurred, his eyes blazing.

The next day I checked in with Nurse Shirley. Before I even asked about Sophie, she laughed and said, "Oh yeah, we have our own little budding romance here. Sophie's been telling us she's met the man of her dreams and she's madly in love."

How could they let this happen?

Later that afternoon, Sophie called and said she was scheduled for discharge the following morning. She added that Rick was also scheduled for discharge and said they'd made a date for the weekend.

Incensed, I called Geoff. Hearing of their plans and my intent to hold him and the hospital responsible for any harm that befell Sophie, he agreed that discharging Sophie was not in her best interest and extended her stay.

When Josh and I visited her the following day, Sophie was furious. "How dare you try and keep me from Rick. I really love him and he loves me. You know, no matter what you do, I'll figure out a way to see him."

"Sophie," Josh said calmly, "we love you more than you'll ever know and we'll do anything we can to help you get healthy. I wish you'd work with Dr. Shuman to rescue the little girl we love so much and haven't seen in years. But, if you insist on smoking pot and dating a heroin addict, you cannot live in our home. I won't let you destroy Mom, Aaron, and me."

Those were the most difficult words I'd ever heard Josh say and I don't think I'd ever loved him more than I did at that moment. How hard it must have been for him to give Sophie an ultimatum.

Sophie, however, seemed not to hear a word he said. She continued to be adamant about her intention to date Rick, yet unable to think through the consequences of no longer living with us. As always, she refused to take responsibility for her behavior.

"Where do you think you'd live if you left home?" I asked.

"With my classmate, Kay."

"Have you discussed this with Kay?"

"No."

"You understand that if you leave home you'd be responsible for all your living expenses?"

"Can I keep my phone?"

"No," I replied.

"What about my computer?"

"No."

"But Mom, that's not fair," she protested, tears streaming down her face.

"Sophie, it's all about choices and responsibilities," Josh explained.

Unhappy with our resoluteness, Sophie tried to strike a bargain. "I'm willing to give up my relationships with the community college kids, but I'm not giving up Rick. He's too important. I need him. I wish you'd meet him and see what a great kid he is."

We told Sophie she needed to get healthy before she would be ready for any romantic relationship and suggested she and Rick put their relationship on hold until then. We tried to make her see how dangerous it would be for her to have a relationship with a heroin user. We pointed out that, when her community college friends smoked weed, she smoked weed, and when her hospital friends smoked cigarettes, she did too. But, like my mother in the conversations I had with her years ago, Sophie seemed incapable of understanding the language Josh and I spoke.

As visiting time drew to a close, we urged Sophie to reconsider her decision to leave home. She slouched in her chair and stared at the clock on the wall, waiting for visiting hours to end.

This visit reinforced the severity of Sophie's problems and convinced me that we needed to be clear about our expectations for her behavior if she wanted to come home. To that end, Josh updated the contract detailing her responsibilities that we'd developed when Sophie returned home from the CAPU. She was to work at her part-time job, keep her room clean, and attend the outpatient therapy sessions recommended by the Weston staff. As before, the contract made it clear Sophie would need to earn privileges, and it spelled out exactly what that meant.

I wanted to present the contract to Sophie in a neutral environment and make sure she understood what we expected from her, so I requested that Josh, Sophie, and I meet with Geoff prior to her discharge.

Armed with our contract, Josh and I arrived at the hospital. As we entered the unit, the smell of stale cigarette fumes filled my nostrils. To my right, a door opened to an outdoor courtyard. Half a dozen patients dressed in mismatched clothing were gathered. Each held a lit cigarette. A cloud of smoke wafted above them.

"I thought this was a healthcare facility," I whispered to Josh.

"Did you see Sophie out there?" he asked.

I had not, but when I looked closer, I spotted her. She wore tattered pink slippers, torn jeans, and a paint-splattered shirt. She was smoking a cigarette.

Geoff came out of his office and welcomed us. I couldn't resist asking him why patients were smoking on hospital property. "It's the only way we can get them to go to therapy sessions," he sighed, stroking his salt and pepper beard. "For each hour of therapy they attend, they get a fifteen-minute cigarette break."

Geoff read our contract and confided, "I wish the parents of all my clients were as thoughtful and caring as you are. This is clear and appropriate, exactly what she needs."

After a few minutes, Sophie joined us. As she entered the room, I stood up and went to hug her. She barely embraced me. Her hair was disheveled and her eyes were empty. I handed the contract to her and Josh said, "Sophie, I want you to know how much we love you and how glad we are you're ready to come home. This secret life you've been leading has got to stop. This contract is much like the one we used when you came home from the CAPU a couple of years ago. Dr. Shuman thinks it's in your best interests, and so does Geoff."

As Josh spoke and Sophie read the contract, I watched her body language. Her eyes filled with tears, her face reddened, and she slumped down in her chair, her shoulders sagging.

"You can't take away my texting. I have to be able to talk with my friends."

"You'll earn back the texting privilege when you demonstrate you can follow the rules," Josh assured her.

"No way! I need to text. My friends are all I have. I have to be able to talk to them," Sophie glowered.

Silence.

"Sophie, your parents are being very reasonable," Geoff said. "I wish all the people on your unit had parents who care as much as yours do."

"Bullshit," sputtered Sophie. "No way. I need to be able to text my friends." She pounded herself against the back support of her chair for emphasis and crossed her arms. Her piercing eyes stared ahead, fuming.

"Sophie, if you don't think you can follow your parents' rules, I'll have to discharge you to a half-way house," Geoff explained. "And frankly, I don't think a cute little eighteen-year-old from the suburbs is going to do very well in that kind of place."

Sophie was sobbing. She stood up, ripped the contract, and screamed, "Fuck you all!" as she dashed from the room.

Could Sophie continue living in our home? The anger she displayed terrified me. Had we been home, she'd have ranted and raved and then barricaded herself in her room. Most likely she'd have threatened to hurt herself.

CHAPTER **57**

The Final Piece of the Puzzle

Fall 2010. Sophie is eighteen years old.

"Have any of Sophie's doctors ever suggested she may have borderline personality disorder?" Geoff asked, thumbing through the pages of her medical record.

"I don't think so," I said. How many more psychiatric labels could they slap on this poor kid? How could it be that the doctors came up with so many different diagnoses? Was it that psychiatry didn't have enough science behind it to understand which neural circuit in Sophie's brain was malfunctioning?

"She may be young yet to have this diagnosis, but I would almost bet my life on it," Geoff said thoughtfully.

"Dr. Shuman mentioned Sophie might be borderline shortly after she found out about the rape," said Josh. "She suggested many of the behaviors Sophie was exhibiting could be connected to PTSD or might be indicative of borderline personality disorder. Of course, she also thought these behaviors might be due to bipolar disorder and that it was premature to make the diagnosis."

"Once Sophie calms down and figures out how to get out of here, I think she'd benefit from a program at Horizon House," Geoff said. "The program is for women who've been raped. It's based on a therapeutic protocol called DBT – Dialectical Behavioral Therapy. It was developed years ago for patients with borderline personality disorder and they've had a lot of success with it. I'm going to recommend it for Sophie. I think it could help her."

At home I searched for information about borderline personality disorder. The National Institute of Mental Health website[1] explained that borderline personality disorder, abbreviated BPD, is "a serious mental illness characterized by pervasive instability in moods, interpersonal relationships, self-image, and behavior." This instability, it went on to say, "disrupts family and work life, long-term planning, and the individual's sense of self-identity." People with BPD suffer from the inability to regulate their emotions. While less well studied than schizophrenia or bipolar disorder, BPD is more common, affecting two percent of adults, most of whom are young women.

I continued reading.

"While a person with depression or bipolar disorder typically endures the same mood for weeks, a person with BPD may experience intense bouts of anger, depression, and anxiety that may last only hours."

Sophie's moods could turn on a dime. One minute she was happy and giggly, the next she could turn mean and abusive.

"These episodes may be associated with periods of impulsive aggression, self-injury, and drug or alcohol abuse."

The aggression she displayed toward Josh, Aaron, and me. The razor blades she cut herself with, despite my attempts to remove them from her room. The unexplained burn mark on her arm. Her frequent use of marijuana. Suddenly everything fell into place.

"Distortions in cognition and sense of self that are characteristic of BPD can lead to frequent changes in long-term goals, career plans, jobs, friendships, gender identity, and values."

I thought about how Sophie could never stick to a plan she made, how she eagerly had started ballet classes, ice skating lessons, piano lessons, and voice lessons, and how just as quickly she'd lost interest in each. She didn't have a single long-lasting friendship, and the plans she made for her future vacillated wildly, from being a neuropsychologist to being a seamstress to working in a grocery store to being a medical technician – sometimes within the course of a twenty-four hour period.

"People with BPD tend to view themselves as bad or unworthy; they feel unfairly misunderstood or mistreated, bored, empty, and have little idea who they are."

How often had Sophie said things like, "I'd rather feel pain than nothing at all," as she tried to explain why she cut herself and played with razor blades?

"Symptoms tend to be most acute when people with BPD feel isolated and alone and can result in frantic efforts to avoid being alone."

Sophie often ranted about not having friends, blaming Josh and me for her inability to connect with her peers. She tried to make the "bad" kids in high school like her by having wanton, promiscuous sex. Even at eleven she was afraid to be alone and so we had gotten Dunkin to keep her company. How accurately the description of BPD characterized Sophie.

"People with BPD often have highly unstable patterns of social relationships. While they can develop intense but stormy attachments to people, their attitudes towards family, friends, and loved ones can suddenly shift from idealization, love, and admiration to intense anger and dislike."

Sophie's pattern of falling madly in love with one boy after the next, with only days between the end of one tumultuous relationship and the start of the next, certainly fit. She always drove wedges between the adults in her life – she split allegiances between Dr. Shuman and me and between Jamie and Josh.

"People with BPD tend to form immediate attachments with others whom they idolize, but when a slight separation or conflict occurs, they switch unexpectedly and accuse the person of not caring for them and even hating them."

Whenever Sophie connected with someone at school, the relationship was brief and intense. Sophie would quickly and easily tell anyone the most intimate details of her life, unable to distinguish an acquaintance from a good friend. Yet, none of these relationships lasted more than a few weeks. When I'd ask Sophie about her latest friend, she invariably would say, "She's an asshole" or "She's become a real snob" or "She sings/hums/talks all the time and gets on my nerves."

"Even with family members, people with BPD are highly sensitive to rejection, reacting with anger and distress to even a hint of emotional distance on the part of the other person."

When either Josh or I were angry with Sophie, she always knew it, but rather than try to repair the damage she'd caused to the relationship, she'd dig her heels in and refuse to admit she'd caused the rift.

"These fears of abandonment seem to be related to difficulties feeling emotionally connected to important persons when they are physically absent, leaving the individual with BPD feeling lost and perhaps worthless."

Josh and I were amazed how whenever Sophie was away from us for weeks at a time – when she went to camp or to Wellspring – she totally cut us out of her life. There were no letters or phone calls. Similarly, while fellow campers were the center of her life when she was at camp, the minute she came home, it was as though they ceased to exist.

"People with BPD often exhibit impulsive behaviors that include risky sex and stealing."

Sophie's interactions with Grinner, her reckless sexual escapades with the boys from high school, and the many times she'd stolen – all of it began to fall into place. How odd that the longest relationship she'd had was with Grinner.

Geoff had nailed the diagnosis. Understanding this diagnosis gave me the same immediate peace of mind I'd had when Sophie was diagnosed with ADHD and with bipolar disorder. It is an illness. She is not a bad child; I am not a bad mother. Yet how difficult it was to get a diagnosis and how tenuous each felt. My quest for certainty was desperate.

If indeed Sophie suffered from BPD, what had caused it? I continued searching the National Institute of Mental Health's website.

"Although the cause of BPD is unknown, both environmental and genetic factors are thought to play a role in predisposing patients to BPD symptoms. Studies show that many, but not all, individuals with BPD report a history of abuse, neglect, or separation as young children. Researchers believe that BPD results from a combination of individual vulnerability to environmental stress, neglect or abuse as young children, and a series of events that trigger the onset of the disorder as young adults."

Sophie hadn't been abused or neglected by Josh and me. If anything, we were guilty of being over-involved, doting parents. Did the separation explanation refer to the adoption – from being separated from her birth mother?

"40 to 71% of BPD patients report having been sexually abused."

Bingo! The rape.

Like pieces in the jigsaw puzzles Josh and I loved to do, Sophie's behaviors started fitting together and I understood the progression of her mental illness. Her constant singing and talking, characteristics associated with the hyperactivity aspect of ADHD, banished her from her peers as these behaviors annoyed the other kids. As her peers shied away from her, choosing to play with children more like themselves, Sophie was left to her own devices. She was lonely, her self-worth reduced to ashes. By the time Sophie was eleven years old, she was not only vulnerable to the flirtations and exploitation of the camp counselor, she probably sought them out. An older boy paid attention to her and made her feel important. She was ripe for his perverted attention. Her pent-up rage, a vestige of the hidden rape, had blossomed into borderline personality disorder.

Her bipolar disorder probably evolved from a different set of circumstances. Although scientists agree there is no single cause for bipolar disorder, the tendency for it to run in families and the clear structural and functional patterns identified by brain-imaging studies suggest it has a strong genetic link that may or may not be influenced by the environment. Thus, my guess is that the bipolar disorder is an unfortunate, but separate condition. While it may have been exacerbated by her experiences, it's also likely that, had they not occurred, she still would have had the unfortunate luck to develop bipolar disorder.

Given how many of Sophie's behaviors could be explained by borderline personality disorder, I turned my attention to understanding its treatment. The DBT Geoff suggested was lauded as highly effective. However, unlike the pills Sophie could easily swallow each morning to combat the attention deficits characterizing her ADHD and the mood swings of her bipolar disorder, the success of this treatment required insight, determination, and volumes of hard work. Inasmuch as Sophie had never shown a willingness to work hard at anything, I feared this disorder would be the most seriously debilitating of all.

CHAPTER 58

Outpatient Care

Within twenty-four hours, Sophie called saying she wanted to come home. She agreed to abide by the contract, asking only that she be allowed to talk with Rick by phone. While Josh and I were opposed to this, we agreed that she could talk with him, but only if one of us were within earshot.

I picked her up from the hospital on a chilly, raw afternoon. As we carted the trash bags the hospital staff had helped her fill with her belongings to the car, I told her I loved her and was glad she was coming home. She seemed happy, too.

I reminded Sophie that her first priority was to clean her room. Until that was done, she had no privileges. Although she didn't like it, she agreed to comply. As I was scheduled to leave town for a weeklong conference in New Orleans the next day, I encouraged her to cooperate with Josh while I was gone.

I wasn't out of the house for six hours when Sophie laid down the first gauntlet.

"Dad, I'm going outside for a smoke."

"It's fine if you want to go outside, but you may not smoke a cigarette."

"Bullshit. I can do whatever I want. I'm eighteen."

"Sophie, remember, you agreed to follow the house rules. Smoking is against the rules."

"You can't stop me from smoking."

"You're right, Sophie. I can't stop you from smoking or from other destructive behaviors, but you'd better be prepared for the consequences of making bad decisions."

"What are you going to do if I smoke? I have a right to know."

"Sophie, life doesn't always warn you of the consequences of bad decisions, but the consequences do occur. That's how things are going to work from now on."

"But Dad, what will you do to me if I smoke a cigarette?"

"Sophie, do you understand smoking cigarettes is unhealthy?"

"Yeah."

"So why would you want to smoke if you want to get well?"

"Smoking isn't a problem. Everyone does it."

"Your mother and I don't smoke, so clearly not everyone does it."

"Everyone at the hospital smoked."

"Right, Sophie. And people in the hospital aren't healthy people. So, do you want to be a healthy person or not?"

"You're crazy. I'm going outside to smoke."

"Sophie, if you want to live here you need to respect the house rules."

"I don't respect your fucking rules."

"Okay Sophie. You don't have to respect the rules, but as long as you live here you have to follow them. You can think they're stupid or dumb, but you have to follow them."

At the height of the argument, Aaron blurted, "Hey Dad, can we cut up that coconut we bought this afternoon?" Distracted from the smoking conversation, Sophie abandoned her interest in smoking and eagerly dived into the coconut. She didn't raise the smoking issue again.

The next day, Josh took Sophie to the intake session at Horizon House. He stepped out of the office to phone me while Sophie spoke with the intake worker.

"I have to tell you what's going on here. It's surreal," Josh began. "I wish you were here. We've been sitting in the waiting room for close to an hour. It's a room full of crazy people who are trying to act normal. The staff is going about their business and, one by one, calling the patients in and admitting them. Sophie got all excited when this one guy came in. Turns out he was at Weston with her – on the same unit. It was like an old-time reunion. They hugged each other, he bought her a soda from the vending machine, and they've been talking non-stop."

"Wow," I commiserated. "Sorry I'm missing it."

"The most amazing part is I found myself looking around at the people here and I realized that Sophie's one of them. The other parents sitting in the waiting room looking at Sophie probably think she's a crazy person."

Later that evening, Josh told me about the intake process. He and Sophie had met with Dr. Zahavi, an older Israeli psychiatrist. To Dr. Zahavi's question about what brought her to Horizon House, Sophie provided only limited information about her recent stay in the hospital and almost no details about her past. She withheld information about Grinner, said nothing about the rape, and barely mentioned the strife surrounding her community college experiences.

Did Sophie lack the insight to report correctly or was she trying to put on a good face?

Josh filled in the missing pieces for the doctor. Thinking about the many patients he'd seen that afternoon in the waiting room who didn't have family members, Josh asked, "How can doctors develop a treatment plan and help people without accurate information?"

Alone in my hotel room, I tormented myself. Was I to blame for Sophie's problems? Was I too lenient? Was I too harsh? Did I expect too much from her? Did I expect too little? Did we spoil her? Did my experience with my mother make me overly protective? Should we have moved to New Jersey when we did? Of course, I had no answers. I never did.

The treatment plan called for Sophie to participate in a combination of group and individual therapy sessions at Horizon House on a full-time basis for several weeks. Eventually, they would step her down into a part-time program and then she'd resume her therapy sessions with Dr. Shuman. The professionals involved in Sophie's care stressed the importance of her having clearly structured days. To that end, she participated in the outpatient program from nine o'clock in the morning until three o'clock in the afternoon and she worked at the grocery store in the evenings. Her demeanor improved. However, she made no move to clean her room. In fact, she rejected every attempt I made to help her get started.

Instead, Sophie spent hours on the phone with Rick. She laughed and sang to him, told me what a wonderful person he was, and asked me to reconsider letting her spend time with him. I encouraged her to work on getting well instead of talking to Rick so much.

We'd settled into the schedule when, one evening, without warning, Sophie announced she was being moved to the part-time program beginning the next day. This meant she'd be involved in therapy sessions three days a week from nine o'clock in the morning until noon, creating too many unstructured hours alone.

When Josh expressed concern about the change, Dr. Zahavi apologized. He acknowledged that Sophie was deeply troubled and needed a lengthy course of behavioral therapy. However, he explained that the move to part-time therapy was dictated by insurance regulations. Staff reports indicating Sophie wasn't an imminent threat to herself or others made her ineligible for the full-time program.

Although Sophie was virtually mute about her treatment sessions, on one of her more talkative days she said, "My group therapy leader Celia thinks I'm not over the rape, but that's such bullshit. I'm over it. I've moved on. It doesn't affect me."

Over the next several days, Sophie's comments gave us glimpses of how she was using the therapy sessions.

"Mom, Celia thinks Rick is really, really good for me. She doesn't understand why you won't let me see him."

"Sophie," I reminded, "heroin is a very serious problem. People who use it have a very high recidivism rate."

"But Mom, Rick's not like that," she lamented. "He hasn't used drugs in twenty-four days. Celia thinks I should be allowed to see my friends whenever I want to and that the house rules contract is ridiculous."

Fully aware by now of Sophie's tendency to split the adults in her world in order to achieve her objectives, I suggested, "Maybe you, Dad, and I should meet with Celia. Does that sound like a good idea?"

"Yes," she smiled. "That would be great."

When Josh and I arrived for the meeting, we were ushered into Celia's office. There we found Sophie sobbing and blowing her nose as she talked with Celia, a heavy-hipped woman who couldn't have been older than twenty-five.

"Thank you for joining us, Mr. and Mrs. Segal," Celia greeted. "Sophie's been doing very well in therapy sessions and she's ready to take on more responsibility. She wants to start making choices about what she'll do and whom she'll spend time with. She's been talking a lot about her friend Rick and she's frustrated that you don't want her to date him." The middle button on her blouse looked like it might fly off and hit me in the eye.

"Celia," I interrupted, "Did Sophie tell you that Rick was at Weston because he overdosed on heroin?"

"Mom, you're such an asshole," Sophie hissed.

"Yes, she did. But Sophie's eighteen and she has a right to decide whom to date."

I cannot believe what I'm hearing.

"Of course she does. However, she doesn't have the right to bring a heroin user into our home. I won't allow Sophie to put our lives in danger so she can date a heroin user." I wasn't going to let this woman make me yell.

"I hate you. You're such a bitch," cried Sophie. "You never let me do anything."

"Sophie, stop it right now. You may not talk to your mother like that," Josh said, gritting his teeth.

"Let's all take a deep breath," Celia suggested. "Mr. and Mrs. Segal, I understand your concerns, but Sophie needs to start taking responsibility for decisions about her life. What would it take for you to agree to let Sophie date Rick and decide for herself whether this relationship is a good one?"

Is this woman for real? I want to have her diploma revoked. Here was yet another time when I kicked myself for not using my credentials and being Dr. Pruchno.

"Honestly, Celia, if Sophie wants to have a relationship with Rick, she's going to have to find someplace to live other than our home. I want to be clear that, under no circumstances, may Sophie date a heroin addict while she's living in our home."

That ended our meeting. Why was this so difficult for Celia to understand? Josh and I were so outraged by Celia's attempt to enable Sophie to have a relationship with a heroin user that we scheduled a meeting with her supervisor, the Director of Social Work.

The director's brow furrowed as she listened. She acknowledged that, while Celia was an enthusiastic advocate for her patients, Celia lacked experience and understanding about family perspectives. "Are there strategies you've used that have helped Sophie make good decisions on her own?" she asked.

Wow! She's stumped and asking us what to do with Sophie.

Dr. Zahavi met with Josh afterwards. The doctor had taken a liking to Josh, perceived how distraught he was, and tried to assuage his pain.

"I'm sorry," the doctor began. "I wish there were something more I could do to help Sophie. She is very, very ill, but under our healthcare system, because she's eighteen, Sophie has to be treated as an adult. She has the right to make decisions about her health care that include whether or not to get counseling, and whether or not to take the prescribed medications."

"But, Dr. Zahavi, you told me Sophie lacks the capacity to make these decisions," Josh reiterated. "How can someone like Sophie possibly take responsibility for her own health care when you and all the other doctors say she's not able to do so?"

"You could try to have her declared incompetent and ask that you and your wife be made her guardians, but that would be a long and costly process, and at best would last for just a few months. Afterwards you'd be thousands of dollars poorer and right back where you are now."

"What about institutionalizing her? Is that a possibility?" Josh asked.

"Unfortunately, no. The few institutions that exist are for people with severe schizophrenia who are an imminent danger to themselves or to other people. To be institutionalized, a person has to be wielding a knife or a gun or have already hurt someone. Sophie's not sick enough to be institutionalized. Besides, she wouldn't get the care she needs in an institution."

"So what do we do?" Josh asked.

"The best thing you can do is try and convince Sophie to cooperate with you and work hard to get well. She has to want to get well and she has to cooperate in her treatment. If she doesn't, she will never get well."

Dejected, Josh and I left. We were in a never-ending loop: the doctors can't help Sophie until she decides she wants to get well. Her illness prevents her from understanding how ill she is and from cooperating with her care. She cannot be committed, either to our care or to an institution, because she's reached the age of maturity. So she gets to make decisions about her mental health care that she lacks the capacity to make. And if she doesn't agree to seek help, the doctors can't help her until she's ready to work hard at getting well. But her illness prevents her from knowing she's ill and being motivated to get well and cooperate in her care …

How much did Sophie understand about her illness? Did she realize how terrified I was about her future?

As we struggled to help Sophie, her hostility toward Aaron, Josh, and me increased daily. She was happy to go to her therapy meetings and happy at work. When she came home, however, she morphed into a mean, angry person.

One evening, as Josh drove Sophie home from work, he asked about her morning therapy session.

"It was fine, Dad," came the cold response, followed by silence.

"I'm glad. The Horizon House program is a great one. I wish you could be there longer than the week or so you have left. I hope they're helping you explore the effects of the rape."

"Everyone keeps talking about the rape. I'm so over it. It's a non-issue."

"I don't think so, Sophie. Dr. Shuman doesn't think so. And Dr. Zahavi doesn't think so either. You need to stop thinking you know better than all the doctors," advised Josh.

"Why do you always pick on me?"

"I'm not picking on you. I'm trying to help you."

"No, you're not. You always bust on me. It's why I hate you guys. Do you want to know what I told my therapy group today?"

"Sure. What did you tell them?"

"I said if I had a gun, I'd kill my parents."

"Why would you say such a thing, Sophie? Is that how you feel about Mom and me?"

Sophie thought for a moment. "I don't know." More silence. "I guess you don't have to worry about it being just another week at Horizon House. What I said about killing you should buy me at least another two or three weeks."

CHAPTER 59

Think Horses, Not Zebras

Winter 2010. Sophie is 18 years old.

William of Ockham, a fourteenth century English logician and Franciscan friar, is credited with developing Occam's Razor. This principle of parsimony holds that, when multiple explanations are possible, the simplest version is best. Occam's Razor has been translated to many shorthand adages, including the popular KISS principle – "Keep It Simple, Stupid" – and the axiom taught to medical students, "When you hear hoof beats, think horses, not zebras."

Ever since we learned about the rape, Josh and I wondered how it could have occurred under our watch without our having even the slightest inkling of it. We were very involved parents. We talked with Sophie and Aaron constantly. We had dinner as a family every night. We took family vacations. How could we have not known about such a horrid experience?

In hindsight, Occam's Razor had led us astray. We saw the warning signs that had been there all along. Yet each sign had a different, much simpler explanation to which we, sometimes guided by Sophie's lies, attributed cause.

When Sophie came home from camp with a bruise on her face, she said she'd gotten hurt playing Wiffle ball. I believed her. Kids sometimes get hurt at camp. Josh saw the bruise and asked about it. When Sophie told him the story about the Wiffle ball hitting her, Josh didn't believe it. He asked her dozens of questions.

However, Sophie's detailed fictional account, her lack of concern about it, and my insistence he not upset her forced Josh to drop his questioning. In reality, Sophie's rapist had made the bruise. This certainly was not the most likely explanation. We were thinking horses when we should have been thinking zebras.

Sophie's behavior toward Aaron changed dramatically after the rape. She went from being a bossy big sister who lovingly bantered with her little brother to a mean, aggressive child who found delight in tormenting him. Josh and I were aware of this change and struggled to make Sophie understand that her behavior was unacceptable. We doled out time-outs, redirections, and positive as well as negative consequences immediately, consistently, and fairly. While we didn't condone her behavior, we attributed it to the turbulence of adolescence. Once again, we were thinking horses when we should have been thinking zebras.

One afternoon, as Josh and I were driving to the grocery store, we started one of our many How-Could-We-Not-Have-Known conversations. Shaking his head sadly, he said, "I suspected her Wiffle ball explanation was a sham, but I didn't pursue it. If only I'd questioned her more."

"Don't beat yourself up over that again," I pleaded, seeing the hurt in his eyes. "You did what any father would have done, and more. You saw a bruise. You asked about it. She gave you an explanation. You questioned it. I begged you to drop it. There was nothing more you could have done. If one of us should feel guilty about not pursuing things that day, it's me. You kept insisting something was wrong. As usual, I wanted to put it behind us and not make a big deal about it. I can't tell you how sorry I am that I made you stop."

"I wish I could turn the clock back to that summer. I would have been much more persistent."

"She never would have told you, no matter what you'd have said or done. Remember, that camp counselor was an older boy who was paying attention to her. He made her feel special. There was nothing you could have done to make her talk."

There was silence in the car. "Josh, let's think about that summer again. Summer of 2003. Sophie went to camp. She got raped and came home telling us she was hit by a Wiffle ball. Her behavior toward Aaron changed. What else was going on then?"

"I was doing consulting work. You were at Boston College. Not much else. It was the summer before we moved to New Jersey."

"Wait, wasn't that the summer we adopted Dunkin? Sophie loved that silly mutt. Remember how she was having trouble sleeping and was afraid to be alone?"

"Yes, you're right," Josh said thoughtfully.

"Dr. Gilloway started Sophie on Strattera and it seemed like a wonder drug. She had such a great beginning to the sixth grade school year. Remember? Some of the girls in her class even went out of their way to tell Sophie what a great person she was and how much calmer she was than in previous years."

"Right," Josh remembered. "But you're forgetting that the calm didn't last very long. Her year started out great, but then there was that big fight with Kate over Christmas break."

Silence.

"Oh my gosh," I exclaimed. "Kate. Sophie must have told Kate her secret. Kate knew and when she and Sophie had a fight over the break, Kate told all the other girls in the play."

"How do you know?"

"Because one and one is two. Kate was Sophie's best friend. Sophie always has been quick to tell even the most casual acquaintances too much. She had to have told Kate."

"Why would she tell anyone she'd been raped?" Josh asked, with annoyance.

"She didn't. Think like an eleven-year-old girl. Sophie told Kate that she'd had sex, not that she'd been raped. Kate got her period first. Sophie was envious. So, to compete, Sophie told Kate she was the first of them to have sex. It was a notch on her belt. She was bragging. When Kate turned on her, she told the other girls Sophie's secret. Sophie was devastated as one by one the girls ostracized her. They knew what she had done was not normal. Remember how she didn't want to go back to school after the break? How she cried bitterly? How she hid in the bathroom stall at school, not wanting the girls to see her cry? She even wanted to drop out of the play."

"You know," Josh said thoughtfully, "I don't think Sophie ever referred to the camp incident or the encounter with Grinner as a rape. Does she even understand the difference between sex and rape?"

"You're right. And it certainly explains why she's not taking her therapy sessions seriously. She thinks she's different than those other women. She's not thinking rape. She's thinking sex. So why does she have so much rage?"

"Maybe deep down she knows it was rape," Josh sighed.

Finally it looked like we'd put it all together. But now, the million-dollar question: was there anything we could do to help Sophie?

CHAPTER 60

Last Straw

January 2011. Sophie is eighteen years old.

I awoke to a dark room in a cold sweat. I'd been running. This time it was from East Lansing to Southfield – not that I ever could – knowing my mother would kill herself, hoping I could stop her. But I could not. Not this time. Not in any of the countless dreams I'd had in the past thirty-five years.

Classic rock radiated from Sophie's room, so I went to check on her. She was fast asleep. I turned off her radio and kissed her cheek.

How these two tortured me – one from the grave, the other from down the hall. Both of whom I loved desperately, neither of whom I could reach.

Sophie's emotions had stabilized and her behavior improved. She went to her outpatient program, apprenticed at a local tailor shop, worked at the grocery store, and finally cleaned her room. Yet her insistence on talking with Rick several times a day continued. Monitoring their calls annoyed me. She insisted he was a wonderful person and kept trying to get me to agree to meet him and "give him a chance." I told her she needed to work hard to get healthy and only then would she be ready for a romantic relationship. As always, my words fell on deaf ears.

Sophie knew her privileges would be minimal until she terminated the relationship with Rick, so she staged a breakup. One afternoon, I came home and found her weeping.

"What's wrong?" I asked.

"I broke up with Rick," she sobbed. "I told him I couldn't talk to him anymore."

"That sounds like a healthy thing for you to have done. Give yourself a chance to heal. Give him a chance to heal."

Continuing the charade, the next day, her Facebook status changed from "in a relationship" to "single," and her postings mourned the end of their relationship.

Over the next several days, Sophie told me she and Talia, a girl she'd met at the college, were making plans to go to the mall, have lunch, and see a movie that Saturday. The day before the outing, Sophie went to her morning therapy group and came home in a good mood. She said she decided to enroll in and pay for two classes at the community college. When she asked me to help her register for the classes, I agreed, sending her to the school's website to find the course numbers. Because she needed to get ready for work, I told her I'd help her sign up for classes the next morning.

That evening, after Josh and I had gone to bed, Aaron sent Josh a text message. It read, "Sophie went downstairs. You might want to check on her." Annoyed, Josh put on his bathrobe and headed to the basement.

He found the door to his office closed and heard Sophie's voice. "Who are you talking to?" Josh asked, opening the door.

Sophie jumped. "Talia."

"Please get off the phone. Your phone conversations are limited to those either mom or I can monitor. You're grounded."

Speaking into the phone's receiver, Sophie sighed, "Talia, I'm sorry. I can't see you tomorrow."

She ran to her room and slammed the door.

About fifteen minutes later, Sophie knocked on my bedroom door.

"Come in," I called.

"Mom," she sobbed, "I'm feeling suicidal."

"What?"

"I hate my life. I need to go to the hospital." As evidence of her fragile state of mind, Sophie showed me a tiny puncture wound on her left thumb.

I sprang out of bed. More than anything I wanted to shake her and scream. Every time Sophie got caught doing something she wasn't supposed to do, she'd feign suicide and run for the security of the psychiatric hospital rather than accept my consequences. Can you say manipulation?

But I didn't shake her and I didn't scream at her.

"How long have you been feeling this way?"

"A few days."

"Did you talk about it with your group this morning?"

"No."

"Why not? Isn't that the point of the group?"

"Well," she hedged. "Not really for days. I guess I've been feeling this way for the past half hour or so."

"What were you doing in the basement?"

"Talking to Talia."

"Did she say something that upset you?"

"No," she sobbed.

"So what got you so upset?"

"Mom, it's deeper than that. I really need to go to the hospital."

"Sophie, I don't understand. You seemed so happy this afternoon. You were talking about going back to school and getting together with Talia. What happened?"

"Mom, I need to go to the hospital. Please, will you take me?"

"Sophie, it's nearly midnight. Are you sure you don't want to sleep on this and see how things look in the morning? You know they'll keep you in the emergency room all night long."

"No," she sobbed. "I need to go to the hospital now. Please take me."

Josh and I looked at each other. "I guess we need to take her to the hospital," I sighed. "Your turn. I went last time."

Josh drove Sophie to Tri-county Hospital's Crisis Center, gave the intake worker our insurance information, and left her there. When he returned, we realized Sophie's plan to get together with Talia had most likely been a ruse, and more likely than not, she and Rick were going to rendezvous. Our suspicions were confirmed the next morning when I asked Aaron to check the phone number that had been dialed from our phone around midnight. Not only did I recognize the number, but I also called it, and spoke briefly with a woman who identified herself as Rick's mother.

As before, Sophie was admitted to Weston Behavioral Health Hospital, but this time she was put on the adult psychiatric unit. When she called and asked for some clothes, I got them together and Josh delivered them. After her first full day in the hospital, Sophie called and told me that Rick had come to visit her. Appalled, I called Geoff and asked why a known heroin user was able to visit her. He agreed this was an error and banned Rick from further visits.

That afternoon Sophie called in a rage. "Why did you tell them Rick shouldn't be allowed to visit me?"

"Because, Sophie, Rick is a heroin addict. Besides, I thought you said that you and Rick broke up."

"I hate you," she screamed.

"Sophie, are you ready to tell me what happened last night?"

"No."

"Who were you talking with last night?"

"Talia."

"Really?"

"Yes."

"Sophie, you're busted. I know you called Rick."

"I want to move out of the house. I hate you."

"Fine," I said as calmly as possible. "You cannot live here and continue to lie to us. We've given you every opportunity to work on getting well, but you don't seem to want to do that." Even as I said these words, I wondered how much of Sophie's behavior was under her control and how much was a function of her illness. But at this point it didn't matter. I couldn't let her jeopardize the rest of us with her poor decisions.

"I hate you," she insisted. "I'm leaving."

Why did Sophie always make bad decisions? Had a classmate sought her advice about the wisdom of jumping out of a window to meet a pervert or dating a heroin addict, Sophie would have counseled against these choices. Yet when it came to making decisions for herself, she invariably chose the wrong one. Did she want harm to befall her? Was she on a mission of self-destruction?

Two days later, Geoff invited Josh and me to attend a hospital discharge meeting. When we arrived, Sophie was talking with a young man wearing a white lab coat. Her face was pale and swollen, her hair disheveled, and her eyes glassy. The ripped over-sized sweat pants and paint-splattered sweatshirt she wore dwarfed her. I went to give her a hug, but she turned her back on me.

Geoff introduced us to Dr. Agassi and then said, "Sophie, I understand from talking with you and your parents that you won't be going back home. Where do you think you'll live?"

"I'm going to live with Talia."

This surprised me. Sophie had told me that Talia lived with her mother, several miles from our home. I asked, "Have you discussed this plan with Talia and her mother?"

"No," she scowled.

"How will you get to your job?" I wanted Sophie to think through the practicalities of her new living situation.

"Rick will drive me. We're going to get an apartment together."

"How are you planning on paying the rent? Between the two of you, there's one part-time job and no money."

"Rick's parents are going to help us. They really like me."

Having spoken with Rick's mother earlier that day, I knew that wasn't going to happen.

Geoff tried to get us back on track. "Maybe it would be productive if we spend some time talking about what your options are, Sophie. There's a residential program in New Hampshire where you could take classes, work, and participate in therapeutic sessions."

"No," she interrupted. "I'm not going to New Hampshire."

"What about Dickinson?" asked Dr. Agassi. "Do you think you're ready to go to college?"

Sophie rolled her eyes. "No way."

"Aunt Jamie invited you to go to Texas and live with her for a while. Would you like to do that?" I asked.

"Who's Aunt Jamie?" asked Geoff.

"Sophie's birth mother," I explained. "We've had an ongoing relationship with her since before Sophie was born. Jamie's as worried about Sophie as we are. When I spoke with her last night, she offered to have Sophie spend some time there. Maybe going to Texas would be a good idea. What do you think, Sophie?"

There was silence. Sophie slumped further down in her chair.

"I hate you. You suffocate me. You treat me like I'm five years old," she huffed.

"Sophie, we love you, but you're very troubled and it's not in your best interest or ours for you to live with us. We're trying to help you figure out where you can live – some place where you can be safe, happy, and have a chance to get on with your life," I explained.

Silence.

"Sophie, do you feel like you've hit rock bottom?" asked Dr. Agassi.

"No," she answered.

"Do you know what rock bottom is?" Geoff queried.

"No."

"Rock bottom is the lowest point a person can reach," Geoff explained. "It's the point at which a person says, 'Hey, something's wrong in my life and I need to do something about it.' What's interesting about rock bottom is that it's a different place for every person and, most importantly, you get to decide what it is. I'll give you an example. For some people, getting a diagnosis of diabetes is enough for them to change their lifestyle, give up eating sugary foods, and start exercising. For other people with diabetes, rock bottom doesn't come until one of their legs has to be amputated. For still others, it happens after their second leg is amputated. So Sophie, the cool thing is you get to decide where your rock bottom is."

Sophie stared at the floor.

I thought about all the times I was sure Sophie had hit rock bottom. When she stole from her cousins. When she got pregnant. When she was expelled from school for fighting with a girl. Each time I thought it couldn't get worse, it did.

Turning to me, Dr. Agassi said, "Until she hits rock bottom, there's very little any of us can do for Sophie. Even Sophie won't be able to help herself until that happens."

There was an uncomfortable pause. Nobody was happy.

"Why don't I work with Sophie to develop a plan and we'll get back to you?" Geoff suggested. And then the meeting ended.

A couple of days later, Geoff called me with news that Sophie was going to live with kids from the community college, the same kids with whom she had cavorted and smoked marijuana prior to her previous hospitalization. When I asked who would pay for this, there was silence. Clearly, important details of the plan had not been developed.

Incensed, I spoke first with Geoff, then with Dr. Agassi, and then with the hospital administrator. How could they, in good conscience, discharge Sophie to such an environment?

Dr. Agassi called me late one afternoon. "It's very clear to me that it's not in Sophie's best interests or the rest of your family's for Sophie to live with you."

"But how can we let her go when she's so sick? Can't she be committed somewhere where she would get the help she needs?" I asked.

"You're right about how sick she is," he confirmed. "But I can't commit her involuntarily to treatment."

This was the second time we'd heard this frustrating news.

"Until Sophie's ready to embrace treatment on her own, there's little I or anyone else can do for her. Involuntary commitments to places like a state psychiatric hospital involve a long process in which psychiatrists and lawyers wrangle with one another. Even if I could get her committed, which I can't, a state psychiatric hospital wouldn't be the place where she would get the help she needs."

Nothing he told me was new. The system was broken.

"What about one of those wilderness programs?" I asked desperately. Josh and I had explored that option when she was younger, but on the advice of her therapists, we had not pursued it.

"You could try that, but Sophie would have to agree to go. Given her state of mind, I doubt she'd consider it."

"Aren't there any residential placements where she could get the therapy she needs? Geoff mentioned someplace in New Hampshire." I was grasping for answers. "Those places are expensive, but we could use the money we saved for her college education to pay for it."

"There are a number of those facilities all over the country," he explained. "The problem is they're very expensive and because they're voluntary, patients can walk in the front door and out the back door whenever they want. I don't recommend you go that route."

He heard my desperation. "I'm sorry there's nothing I can do to help Sophie. It's clear to me how much you love her and how much you've done for her over the years. Unfortunately, the system in our country for treating people with severe mental illnesses isn't a good one. Requiring a person with a mental illness to have the insight needed to ask for help when, in fact, lack of such insight is an inherent symptom of the illness, is a problem I run into several times a day. I wish there were something I could do, but there really isn't. You have no idea how sorry I am."

I believed what Dr. Agassi told me, yet I kept thinking there must be something more I could do to help Sophie. My conversation with the hospital administrator only confirmed that, as Sophie is eighteen years old, she could do anything she wants.

Unwilling to accept this, Josh found an attorney specializing in guardianship law. The lawyer explained that the process of declaring a person incompetent was very expensive. Hearing the details about Sophie, the attorney agreed to take on the case, but conceded it could take three to six months to get it before a judge. During that time, Sophie would be free to make decisions on her own. And, he warned, even if Sophie were declared incompetent, the decision would be valid for a couple of years – and more likely, for only six months – at best. Then we would be right back where we started.

Finally, hoping for a miracle, I called my cousin George, a seasoned attorney who specializes in healthcare law, whose opinion I valued. After I told him all that had happened during the past several months, George said, "I wish I could tell you something different, but I can't. This crazy system can't help people like Sophie. We have to hope she'll wake up one day and figure out that she wants to get well. Only then can you help her."

Heeding the advice of the doctors and lawyers, Josh and I did not attempt to have Sophie declared incompetent. We had hit a wall, and we had lost her.

CHAPTER 61

Rock Bottom

Winter 2010. Sophie is eighteen years old.

My conversations with Dr. Agassi and my cousin George led me to conclude that the mental health system itself is psychotic. Requiring a person who is not competent to make treatment decisions on her own to make such decisions is not only irresponsible, it is immoral. Yet, these seemed to be the operating rules. My eighteen-year-old daughter, who is dependent on antipsychotic medications to stabilize her and therapeutic sessions to enable her to function safely in society, had the right to refuse any and all treatments. I had absolutely no say in the matter.

As awful as our situation was, many families have suffered fates far worse as they sought to protect a loved one with severe mental illness. Most frightening are the scores of cases documented by Fuller Torrey, a psychiatrist and leading schizophrenia researcher, in which persons with untreated severe mental illness murdered family members or strangers. [1]

If it is true that a society is judged by the manner in which it treats its most vulnerable members, ours has failed miserably.

As I thought about this, and my experiences with Sophie, I had an eerie déjà vu experience I didn't understand for months.

One afternoon, I had lunch with a psychiatrist friend from the university. Although Sophie's doctors and the lawyers we'd consulted had told me that there was nothing we could do, I wasn't ready to accept that. My friend listened sympathetically as I told him about Sophie. Then he explained that, "unless a person is a danger to herself, to others, or to property, she cannot be treated involuntarily." He added, "And *danger* means she's wielding a knife or gun, not that she's making bad decisions that are likely to lead to future suffering or death."

His words didn't give me new information, yet they explained what had caused my déjà vu feeling. The last time I'd studied mental health laws was in 1990. At that time, I was developing a research project about mothers of adult children with chronic disabilities. The study contrasted the experiences of two groups of women, one having an adult child with a developmental disability and the other having an adult child with schizophrenia. Attempting to understand the experiences of these women and develop hypotheses to guide my research, I'd sought out women in these situations who would be willing to educate me.

My colleague and friend Amy had reminded me of a tragedy that occurred in 1985. On the day before Halloween, twenty-five-year-old Sylvia Seegrist, dressed in olive green military fatigues, a knit cap, and shiny black boots, and armed with a semi-automatic rifle, fired twenty rounds of ammunition inside a crowded suburban Philadelphia shopping mall. Within four minutes, two people were dead and eight were seriously wounded. A few months later, one of the wounded victims died. Having gotten married only four days before the tragedy, I'd paid little attention to the media coverage. Amy, however, recalled that Sylvia's mother had been interviewed by reporters and later testified at her daughter's trial. She encouraged me to call Ruth Seegrist.

Ruth invited me to her home where she talked, and I listened, for hours. Not only had she been involved in her daughter's trial, but also in the years after, she'd actively worked to change legislation regarding persons with mental illness.

Now, more than twenty years later, I tried to recall our conversation, frustrated that I was able to retrieve only bits and pieces of what Ruth had said. Remembering I'd included a summary of our conversation in a grant application, I ransacked the files in my office. There I found not only the summary I had written, but also a full transcription of our conversation.

Ruth told me Sylvia had been diagnosed with paranoid schizophrenia when she was fifteen. As a sophomore in high school, Sylvia was very bright, but her performance in school had deteriorated as her illness escalated out of control. Sylvia's bizarre behaviors included cutting off all her hair, spray-painting herself, and writing hostile expressions on the walls of her bedroom. Expelled from school, she was admitted to a mental hospital where she stabbed a counselor in the back with a paring knife. Over the next ten years, as her illness spiraled out of control, Sylvia was committed to psychiatric hospitals more than a dozen times.

Ruth knew that her daughter was dangerous; years before the shooting, Sylvia had tried to choke Ruth to death. Fortunately, the police intervened. Sylvia was committed to a psychiatric hospital for three weeks, but couldn't be held longer despite the poor prognosis noted in her psychiatric report. There was one violent episode after another, yet psychiatrists could keep her hospitalized for only brief periods. This was the law. Sylvia hated the side effects of the medications needed to control her behavior – weight gain, loss of muscle control, dry mouth, and vision problems – so she often refused to take them. Sylvia's escalating illness left her hostile and aggressive, alienating her family and friends. She was often disoriented, couldn't hold a job, and was unable to support herself. Neighbors complained that she raked leaves in the middle of the night, played loud music, and shouted threats. She dressed in army fatigues and berets, and she preached angry political propaganda on street corners.

Ruth had said that, on the morning of the tragedy, Sylvia was obsessed with "negative energy." Her thinking had been disorganized for days. These were signs to Ruth that Sylvia had stopped taking her medications, but even more distressing to Ruth was that she also knew Sylvia had bought a gun. Seeing the distress her daughter was experiencing, Ruth pleaded with Sylvia to admit herself to the hospital. But Sylvia resisted, claiming she'd rather go to prison than back to the hospital.

Sylvia was about to make the front page of national newspapers. Her mother knew it. The doctors knew it. The police knew it. But no one could do anything about it – until three innocent people died.

I remembered forcing back tears, feeling the impotence Ruth must have experienced. How could such destruction be allowed to happen while an immobilized audience of concerned professionals and loved ones stood by? Now, thinking about Sophie, I shuddered. Clearly, in three decades, we hadn't made much progress in helping people with mental illness.

Sylvia was found guilty, but mentally ill, and condemned to three consecutive life sentences. Ruth's story became even more poignant when she told me about how well Sylvia was functioning in prison. "She's so stabilized now. The protective environment gives her the structure she needs. Her delusions are controlled by her medications. She works in the laundry four hours a day and she usually jogs in the morning. She takes college courses. That keeps her day very structured." Ruth concluded, "The sad thing is, she could have been stabilized in the community if only the laws and services had been different. Because of her illness, she couldn't make a rational decision about whether or not to take medication, whether or not to take part in a hospitalization program, and so forth. But no one could force it on her. Left to fend for herself, things fell apart quickly."

And so, here I was now, twenty-five years later, faced with a mental health system that hadn't changed in any substantive way. Days before Sophie left home, Jared Loughner, a twenty-two-year-old man with schizophrenia and a history of drug possession coupled with violent and disruptive behavior, gunned down eighteen people, including Congresswoman Gabrielle Giffords, in a Safeway parking lot outside Tucson, Arizona. My fear about what might happen to Sophie, and what she might do to others, paralyzed me. Although Sophie had said more than once that she'd kill me if she could, I doubt she'll kill anyone. Unlike people with schizophrenia, people with bipolar disorder and borderline personality disorder are not likely to unleash violence upon others. What's more likely to happen is that Sophie will be unable to support herself, become homeless, take up with the wrong people, and get herself killed.

The doctors encouraged us to hope Sophie would hit her rock bottom, sympathetically informing us that neither they, nor we, nor Sophie could do anything to help Sophie until she did. Yet hoping for a child to hit rock bottom is antithetical to being a good parent. We're programmed to support children, nurture them, help them soar, and – at all costs – protect them. I wanted someone to explain to me how I was supposed to sit back and wish that my daughter, whom I loved more than life itself, would sink to the unimaginable depths and horrors of rock bottom.

CHAPTER 62

Martin Luther King Day

January 2011. Sophie is eighteen years old.

D espite my fervent attempts to dissuade the administrators and doctors from releasing Sophie, she was discharged from Weston Behavioral Health on Martin Luther King Day.

She called and asked whether she could stop by to pick up some of her clothes. I told her she could. Rick picked her up from the hospital and brought her to the house. She knew better than to invite him inside.

Sophie rang the doorbell. I answered. Her pasty-skinned face smiled back at me. Her hair was disheveled and pulled back in a ponytail. The sweat pants and tee-shirt she wore hung on her slender frame. She wore flip-flops, despite the chilly January evening.

"Hi, Mom."

"Hi, Sophie."

"Can you get me a couple of trash bags?"

I grabbed three white trash bags and followed her as she sprinted up the stairs. At the top of the landing, I handed the bags to her.

I stood outside the door of her room, not trusting her to have free reign in the house, fearing she'd pocket something that didn't belong to her while hating myself for thinking this. I blinked and saw her rosy cherubic face and the dazzling smile that had made me melt when she was two as I read *The Rainbow Fish* or

Goodnight Moon to her. I blinked again and saw the grey, troubled young woman whom society and I had failed miserably.

I watched as she opened one dresser drawer after the next, gathering tee-shirts, hoodies, pants, makeup, underwear, and her toothbrush. Each item was thrown willy-nilly into one of the bags. As she packed, our eighteen-year relationship was dissolving before my eyes. It broke my heart. Where would she go? How would she survive? What kind of horrible situations would find her? Would I ever see her again? Tears welled in my eyes. There was nothing I could do to stop her. She was eighteen and, although there was no doubt she was seriously ill, the mental health system couldn't confine her any more than I could. She had the right to make decisions about where she would live, with whom she would consort, and whether she would take her medications.

After fifteen minutes, Sophie said, "That's all I need for now. When I figure out where I'm going to live, I'll come back and get more of my things, if that's okay with you."

"Yes," I answered, "that's fine." Although I hoped she would come to her senses and want to return home after a few days, I knew it wasn't likely. Sophie never had been able to admit to making a bad decision. She was digging the biggest hole she had ever dug for herself, and I feared it would be a hole from which she never would emerge.

"Can I have my phone?"

"No," I said. Although giving her the phone would enable me to stay in touch with her, it wasn't in her best interest. She wouldn't hit rock bottom if she continued to rely on me for support. "If you want to see what life's like on your own, it means getting your own phone and paying the bill."

"What about my laptop?"

"No."

"What about my Bat Mitzvah money? It's mine and I want it." She had almost ten thousand dollars in a savings account earmarked for the down payment on her first house. If she had access to that money, it would be squandered within weeks.

"No."

She lugged the bags downstairs and set them in front of the door. Storming past Josh and Aaron, she grabbed her coat from the back closet.

Before Sophie arrived, I'd gathered her medications and listed the phone numbers of people she could always call should she need help. I hoped that maybe, if she didn't want to call Josh or me, she might call one of her uncles, Jamie, or one of our friends. I handed her a bag containing her medications and the phone numbers.

As we approached the front door, all I wanted to do was put my arms around her and tell her how much I loved her, beg her to stay, and reassure her that we could figure this out together. But that was not in her best interests. And it probably wasn't true. She needed to hit rock bottom, run into the fire, get burned, and see how ugly life could be. How many times had she said, "I can't learn things if I don't experience them myself"? Maybe she was right. Maybe another ability that her mental illness robbed her of is the ability to learn vicariously.

As she opened the front door, we were hit by a blast of frigid air. Sophie picked up her three plastic garbage bags. And then she walked out of my life.

CHAPTER 63

Roller Coasters

Days after Sophie left home, the phone rang.

"Hi, Mom," she said haltingly. I hoped she was calling to tell me she wanted to come home.

"Hi, Sophie. How are you?"

"I'm okay. I wanted to tell you I took my meds today. I also wanted to tell you I wasn't able to go to the outpatient program because I couldn't get a ride."

"I'm sorry to hear that." I wanted to keep her on the phone forever. "I love you, Sophie."

"I love you too, Mom."

I hung up the phone and sobbed.

These have been among the longest two weeks of my life as I wait, hoping Sophie will realize the importance of adhering to the treatment plan that I know she must follow. But I'm sure she will not.

Instead, the roller coaster ride that Sophie and my mother have taken me on for most of my life continues. I detest roller coasters, yet the highs and lows of my mother's and Sophie's illnesses have taken me on one wild ride after another. I've been whipsawed back and forth as the slumps of their depressions and the frenzies of their manias tossed me about, propelling me from one crisis to the next. I've seen my mother and Sophie drop into bottomless black pits and then emerge, turned upside down. I've cringed as they descended to their lows and winced as they soared to their highs. I like neither the highs nor the lows of the roller coaster and I've never enjoyed scary thrill rides; the gentle carousel is more to my liking.

And now Sophie's gone. I linger by her bedroom door. My stomach plummets. My heart pounds. I can't breathe. Nothing has changed in her room since the last time I walked by. I stand in the doorway gazing at her clothes, her bed, and the stuffed animals she left behind. I cannot bear to enter the room. I expect to see her, but I don't. I start to tell her something, and then I stop myself. My baby doesn't live here anymore. My sadness isn't balanced by knowing she's left the nest to pursue her dreams and live a promising life, as it should be.

I look up at the framed, poster-sized picture of Audrey Hepburn that Sophie created from scraps of newspaper. It's but one of many high school art projects now gracing our home. Her artistic talents awed me from the time she was five, especially in light of my own inability to draw even stick figures. When she'd brought this project home and told me how impressed her teacher had been, I'd envisioned a future for her in the world of fine art. How sad to realize that this bright, talented young woman would be lost to the terrors of mental illness. Just like my mother.

My sole connection with Sophie is Facebook. It's a tenuous link at best, because I only lurk. Several times a day. I'm terrified. Her mania is out of control. She's pierced her nose and sports a ring that looks like it belongs on a bull. It's a statement, literally as obvious as the nose on her face, that she's left and wants nothing more to do with us. For years, Sophie heard our clear and consistent messages that piercings were unacceptable, to be considered only when she no longer wanted our support. If there were any doubt to the meaning of her nose ring, the caption under the picture that reads, "A new face for a new life," makes her intent clear. This nose piercing is her emancipation proclamation. She's free of my conventional life.

Because she now depends on her peers for computer access, it's not uncommon for her to go days without posting a new entry. I fill in the spaces between entries with my imagination. She's hurt.

She's dead. When a new post finally appears, I breathe a sigh of relief. She's unharmed. She's alive.

A week after Sophie left home, Rick ended their relationship. Within days, her Facebook page revealed she had begun a torrid new relationship with another boy from the psychiatric hospital. New Psycho Boy, now the love of her life, had been hospitalized when, in a manic state, he tried to kill himself. The kids make rude comments to her. They call her "bitch" and "slut." Someone asks her if she's a hobo. She's exploring her sexuality and claims to have made out with a girl with "big titties." She takes the last name of her birth father and she moves farther away from me. When she changes her Facebook name to Anne Obahdy, her friends mock her. Is she sliding into the rock bottom the doctors said she had to hit? Although I understand what the doctors have said, I worry that Sophie will die before she hits rock bottom.

I agonize about my daughter. Is she scrounging for food? Is there a blanket warming her at night? Does she miss the life she left behind? Part of me hopes she does, for maybe that will help her reach her rock bottom sooner rather than later.

I worry about Aaron and what he must think of Sophie, of Josh, and of me. Like most teenage boys, he's not a big talker. I try to give him opportunities to talk about how he's feeling, but his responses are only grunts. The best he can muster is, "No, I don't miss that psycho bitch." I can't say I blame him. Sophie was mean to him.

I fear the sad look will never leave Josh's face and hope our marriage survives this horrible crisis.

I watch Sophie spin out of control on her latest roller coaster ride. Could I have done anything to stop her?

I don't know how I'll make it to tomorrow.

CHAPTER **64**

Goodbyes

Two months later.

S ophie lived in the apartment with the kids from the
community college for close to seven weeks. During
that time, she called me twice. Sophie spoke more frequently with Jamie, and Jamie, in turn, called me often.

The more Jamie talked with Sophie, the more worried she
became. Jamie learned that, in addition to the two boys living in the
apartment, there was a girl living there who hated Sophie. The kids
were rude to Sophie, often asking her when she planned on leaving
and why she was such a slut. She slept on the floor of one of the
bedrooms closets, engaged in sex with multiple people, and was
stoned most of the time. One day Jamie told me that Sophie had
called, sobbing. She'd been smoking dope with a boy she barely
knew, fell asleep, and when she awoke her clothes had been ripped
from her body and damp semen marked the bed.

With every new episode, Jamie and I worried more and
more. At the beginning of March, Jamie said, "Richard and I are
having a party to celebrate our fifth anniversary. What would you
think about my sending Sophie an airline ticket so she can come to
the party?"

"I think that would be a great idea," I said, hoping that if
Sophie spent time with Jamie, maybe she'd gain a fresh perspective
on life.

Sophie was delighted to be invited to the party and accepted Jamie's invitation to spend a week in Texas.

Sophie called me about a week before her trip and asked when she could stop by for her passport. I told her she could come anytime, but asked that she call ahead to make sure I was home.

I didn't hear from Sophie until seven o'clock the evening before the trip. Irked with her for waiting until the last minute and assuming that I would be at her beck and call, I didn't answer my phone. After a few minutes, Josh's cell phone rang. "Don't answer it," I hissed. He heeded my request. The house phone rang. When we didn't answer it, the answering machine picked up.

"Hi, Mom. Hi, Dad. It's me, Sophie. I'm two minutes away from the house and I'd like to get my passport. I'll be there soon."

Mental illness creeps into families and poisons even the sanest of people. I didn't want to enable Sophie. I resented her waiting until the last minute to get her passport, and I was infuriated by her assumption that I would always be available whenever it suited her. But mostly, I knew this wouldn't be a one-week trip. Sophie wasn't coming back anytime soon. This might be the last time I ever saw her. I didn't want to say goodbye. Goodbyes are too final. I was no more ready for Sophie to leave my life than I was for my mother to leave. I didn't say goodbye to her either.

"She's on her way," I yelled to Josh and Aaron. "Don't answer the door."

I turned off all the lights in the house and locked the dogs in the laundry room as we do when we leave the house. Then I hid in a corner of the laundry room where she wouldn't see me from the window.

Travis and Dunkin barked as the car came up the driveway. My heart pounded. Sophie laughed as she and the driver approached the house. When we didn't answer the doorbell, Sophie tried to open the garage door, but we had changed the access code. She talked to the dogs, trying to calm them, letting them know it was she and not an intruder.

What had I become? Just weeks ago I'd begun my term as Editor-in-Chief of one of the premier gerontology journals, charged with making decisions that would guide the field as well as make or break careers. And now, here I was, cowering in my laundry room.

After what seemed like an eternity, she said, "I guess they're not here. Let's go." The hum of their voices faded as they walked away from the house. The car doors slammed and the engine ignited.

"Is lockdown over?" Aaron asked, as I emerged from the laundry room with the dogs.

"Yes," I muttered.

"Good," he said. "I'm going back downstairs."

"Okay," I managed to say.

Josh was furious.

"Do you realize that in your unwillingness to be available out of some silly pride, she won? Look what you did and look what you made Aaron and me do. Rather than simply happening to be home, you hid in your own house and insisted we hide too. This is the last time I'll be a party to this kind of charade."

I was stunned – both at my behavior and at the accuracy of Josh's analysis. Tearfully, I apologized. "I can't believe I did that. I'm so sorry. I panicked when I heard her voice on the answering machine."

Josh shook his head, put his arms around me, and held me.

I relaxed, safe in his embrace. How had our marriage withstood the strains of the past several years? Josh and I balanced one another perfectly. When I was out of control, he was strong; when he melted, I stayed tough. My nature was to persevere, to develop one concrete course of action after the next, determined to be a good mother, no matter what. Josh was more even-keeled, easygoing, willing to roll with the punches. Yet when Sophie pushed his buttons, as she invariably did, Josh would explode and yell, calming down only after I'd insisted Sophie stop. Josh always had been better than I at knowing what he could control and accepting what he could not. When things were out of control, as they had been for me this evening, I panicked, and it was up to Josh to pick up the pieces.

CHAPTER 65

Jamie's Turn

Spring 2011. Sophie is eighteen and a half years old.

For weeks, I tried to prepare Jamie for the Sophie she was about to welcome. I told her about Sophie's laziness and her unwillingness to do anything other than sleep, party, and watch television. I don't think she believed me.

Sophie arrived in Texas with the clothes on her back, two tee-shirts, one pair of shorts, one extra pair of underwear, and some makeup. Surprised by Sophie's lack of luggage, Jamie happily took her shopping for new clothes. Hoping to make Sophie feel welcome, they went out for dinners, stayed up late at night, and smoked cigarettes together.

Shortly after Sophie had arrived in Texas, her Facebook picture revealed a prominent butterfly tattoo on her chest. I cringed. Had she given this decision much thought? Did the physical pain she must have experienced getting the tattoo dull her emotional pain? Was the tattoo an even more deafening statement than the nose piercing, declaring that Sophie's new self was independent from Josh and me? Or was it more akin to the cutting she'd done as an adolescent – further evidence of her belief that feeling pain was preferable to not feeling?

Cast in my new role as Jamie's advisor, I suggested she'd be most likely to get Sophie to confide in her if she acted more like a big sister or favorite aunt, rather than like a mother.

Sophie had been in Texas for about a week when Jamie called, saying, "I'm worried about Sophie. She's been telling me about that apartment and the boy she's been dating. I don't think that's a good place for her."

"I agree with you."

"What would you think if I kept her down here for a while?"

I'd thought about that for days. With Sophie in Texas, I was much less worried about her than when she lived with the community college kids. Jamie loved Sophie and wanted the best for her. I no longer felt compelled to stalk her Facebook page and I was able to sleep at night. On the other hand, Sophie wouldn't hit rock bottom living with Jamie and so she would have little chance of recovery.

"I think that's a great idea," I said. The words tumbled out of my mouth before I could stop them. Knowing that Sophie was always stoned, sleeping on the floor of a closet, and having sex with one boy after the next frightened me. I couldn't stand by and watch her hit rock bottom. "But, how do you see that happening?"

"I got her a one-way ticket to come down here. Money's tight. I could tell her I don't have the money to send her back right now."

"Sounds like a good plan to me."

Mardi Gras was celebrated a couple of weeks later. Heeding my advice to treat Sophie as a friend, Jamie took her to a gay bar. Although Jamie knew the bar would be wild, she figured Sophie would be unlikely to get in trouble in a gay bar. Amidst the tumult of a drag show, Sophie told Jamie she was going out to smoke a cigarette. When Sophie didn't come back after a half hour, Jamie went in search of her. But Jamie couldn't find Sophie. Hours later when she returned, Sophie claimed she'd gone for a walk and had gotten lost.

A couple of weeks later, Sophie complained of feeling bloated. Her stomach was distended, so Jamie took her to a doctor. As Sophie filled out the paper work, Jamie looked over her shoulder. To the question "Are you pregnant?" Sophie wrote, "Maybe."

"What? How could that be?" Jamie asked. Weeks earlier, when she suspected that Sophie might be pregnant, Jamie had insisted Sophie take a home pregnancy test. The test was negative.

Since then, Jamie thought Sophie hadn't been out of her sight long enough to get into trouble. Jamie was stunned that, once again, there was the possibility that Sophie was pregnant.

"Remember when we went to that gay bar during Mardi Gras and I went out for a cigarette?" Sophie asked.

"Yes," said Jamie.

"I met this really nice guy who bought me a drink and told me I was hot. He said he was a lawyer, that I could trust him, and that he didn't have any diseases. He even gave me his card."

"And?"

"And I had sex with him in the bathroom."

Jamie screamed at Sophie, told her that not only could she get pregnant, but also that the likelihood of contracting AIDS from someone in a gay bar was great. Sophie said she didn't care.

As Jamie told me the story, I tried to calm her down, explaining that Sophie's bad judgment and impulsive behavior were the result of her being off the medications she so badly needed. Jamie listened to what I told her, but remained shocked at the terrible decisions Sophie made. Like me, Jamie had hoped that once Sophie felt safe with her and could trust her, she'd stop making bad decisions. Yet another bullet was dodged when subsequent tests showed that Sophie was not pregnant.

As Sophie's impulsive behavior and bad judgment followed her to Texas, so too did her laziness. One afternoon, Jamie called and greeted me with, "I'm fixing to kill her."

"What did she do now?"

"You know I babysit for my neighbor's kids sometimes. The kids are two, three, and four years old. I had a bunch of errands to do, so I asked Sophie if she would babysit them for me. She told me she would. I left the house at about nine o'clock this morning and, when I got home at about three o'clock, I found Sophie fast asleep on the sofa. One of the kids had hand lotion in her eyes and was crying. The other two were breaking eggs in the bathtub."

While Sophie's behavior didn't surprise me, I was amazed that Jamie would leave Sophie in charge of young children. Jamie still didn't understand how sick Sophie was.

"I'm so mad I can't see straight. She's going to have child protective custody knocking on my door, and those guys are mean here in Texas. When I called her on it and told her she was going to get me in trouble, she smiled and told me I was getting worked up over nothing. She claimed she was tired. I swear – I'm ready to kill her. She's the laziest thing I've ever seen. She quit the job I got her at the restaurant, and she won't go to school."

"Let me guess," I ventured. "She's up all night, watching television and playing on Facebook, right?"

"Yep."

"Jamie, this behavior is consistent with Sophie not being on her medications. If you can get her to listen to you, make her take them."

"That's it. I'm calling the drug store right now and getting that prescription renewed. She's going to take those dang things if I have to sit on her and shove 'em down her throat."

"Good luck with that. This is one of the battles we've had with her for years."

Sophie took her medications for about a month. She settled down and accepted her role as babysitter while Jamie waitressed. Then, when Sophie moved with Jamie and her family to East Texas, she said her medications had disappeared.

CHAPTER 66

Getting the Story Straight

Summer 2011. Sophie is almost nineteen years old.

S ophie had been in Texas for about three months. With the medications out of her system, she again spiraled out of control. Sophie called only when she had a sore throat or an upset stomach and wanted access to our health insurance. Jamie called often, each conversation beginning with "You're never going to believe this."

I was never going to believe it? I'd lived with Sophie for years.

During the July Fourth weekend, Josh, Aaron, and I travelled to the west coast for the wedding of a friend's daughter. On the evening we arrived, we found ourselves nestled in the restaurant of a lodge in Olympic National Forest. Although it was summertime, a toasty fire crackled, its embers warming us. I lingered over a glass of Dungeness Red, a silky pinot noir from the Olympic Cellars winery. We took turns marveling at the rippling lake and the beauty of the Pacific Northwest.

The ringing of Josh's cell phone startled me. He answered it. Aaron and I continued talking. With one ear, I listened to Josh. "Yes? Oh, hello, Richard."

Richard was Jamie's husband. We'd never met him, but knew he'd been supportive of Jamie's inviting Sophie to live with them. How had he coped with the very needy interloper he'd welcomed?

"I'm so sorry to hear that," Josh said.

Puzzled, Aaron and I looked at each other. "Wonder what she did now," Aaron said.

I often worried about Aaron and how living with Sophie had affected him. For years, he'd suffered her verbal abuse. Her taunts were always exacting, cutting him at the vulnerable points that she as his sister knew so intimately. Sophie couldn't walk by Aaron and not wave her fingers in his face, slap his arm, or trip him. While our household revolved around Sophie, Aaron receded to the sideline. The more Sophie escalated out of control and Josh and I struggled to rein her in, the more distant Aaron had become. Since she'd left, however, a new, more self-assured Aaron had emerged. He initiated conversations at the dinner table, asked for privileges he hadn't asked for before, and invited friends to our home. He worked hard at school and his grades improved. Yet, he didn't want to talk about Sophie. I often tried to engage Aaron, explaining it was Sophie's illness that made her do the things she did. I encouraged him to talk about his feelings. But, as is typical of most teen-aged boys, he wanted no part of these conversations. I was sad that Aaron hadn't had the opportunity to have a normal sibling relationship, especially given the close relationships I've had with my brothers. To whom would Aaron turn when Josh and I were no longer here?

"Richard, I understand. You need to do what's best for your family," said Josh.

"Sounds like something awful," I offered.

"I wish I could be more helpful, but she doesn't get it. She refuses to take responsibility for her behavior. Don't let her hurt you or your family," Josh advised.

Their conversation went on for close to ten minutes. When it ended, Josh put his phone back in his pocket, shaking his head.

"So, what did she do now?" I asked, wanting and not wanting to know.

Josh hesitated. He glanced at Aaron as if to suggest this could wait. I blinked and nodded silently, communicating that Aaron was old enough to hear. Although we'd shielded Aaron from as much of Sophie's abnormal behavior as we could when he was younger, we recently had brought him into our inner circle. I wanted him to understand Sophie's mental illness as much as possible.

"She had oral sex with her new boyfriend Steven in a moving car."

"You've got to be kidding," I said. "How did Jamie find out about it?"

"I don't know."

"Why did Richard think we needed to know about this?" I asked.

"I don't know."

Typical man-to-man conversation. What startled me was that this news didn't faze me. Was it the calming effects of the wine and crackling fire, or was I becoming numb to Sophie's bizarre behaviors?

When we returned from our trip, I called Jamie.

"So, I heard what she did, but I got the man version," I teased. "What happened?"

Jamie laughed. "Sophie and I were sitting on the couch. I was eating a bowl of pasta that I really shouldn't have been eating but, whatever, I was hungry. Out of the blue, Sophie says, 'I'm madly in love with Steven.' Steven is a friend of the boy Sophie was madly in love with last week. That kid was a racist who hated Jews. He was a KKK member."

"Great. She's still making good choices and picking winners."

"I'm so mad at her I could spit. So then Sophie tells me she was riding in a car with Steven. Another kid was driving, and there were a couple of other people in the car. And Sophie says, 'I sucked his dick off.' I swear, Rachel, I hurled that bowl of pasta at the wall. I called her a slut and asked her why she keeps making these stupid decisions. Sophie insisted she loves Steven and he loves her. I told her Steven didn't love her, that no guy worth having would let his girlfriend have oral sex with him in a car with other people watching. Sophie said they weren't really watching."

I listened as Jamie continued.

"She got mad at me and kept talking back, telling me that I didn't know what I was talking about. I finally had it. I kicked her ass out of the house. When she came back three hours later, she was even more abusive. She hauled off and punched me when I said she was acting like a slut. Then she dropped the bombshell."

"What was that?"

"She told me one of the kids in the car was fourteen. That's when I lost it. That's a felony in Texas. I told her she could go to jail for three years. Here in Texas, there's no leniency for that kind of stuff. Do you know what she had the nerve to say to me?"

"No, what?"

"She told me to go ahead and call the cops. She didn't care. She added that the kid was really mature and acted more like a twenty-five-year-old than a fourteen-year-old."

"Oh, Jamie, I'm so sorry."

"There's more. Turns out Steven just broke up with his girl-friend, who's a couple of months pregnant. His mother Amber and I are friends. Amber told me last week she walked in on Sophie, buck-naked, riding Steven like a bronco on her living room sofa. It was the ending to their second date."

This sounded more and more like the X-rated plot line of an episode of *Hillbilly Peyton Place*.

"I don't know how much more of this I can take," Jamie said. "I don't think Sophie has a rock bottom."

"She may not. Sometimes I don't know her at all. I don't believe I raised her."

"Rachel, you and Josh didn't do anything wrong. You were great parents. You gave her every opportunity, and she just walked away. I can't believe she's my flesh and blood. I'm so sorry. I know she looks like me, but I keep thinking she was switched at birth. I want my real baby back."

"So do I," I said sadly. "So do I."

Nature or nurture – what explains Sophie's behavior? While in my heart of hearts I knew that Sophie would act no dif-ferently in Texas than she had in New Jersey, I'd hoped I would be wrong. I'd hoped she would reconnect with her birth mother and by some miracle be made whole. But it was not to be.

CHAPTER 67

Gooky

Summer 2011. Sophie is almost 19 years old.

G ooky was Sophie's oldest possession. Given to Sophie as a baby present, Gooky was the blanket that lived first in her crib and later on her bed. He – Sophie always referred to Gooky as a he – comforted Sophie when she was frightened, dried her tears when she was sad, and warmed her when she was cold. When she was a baby and I would check on her each night before going sleep, I'd smile at her tiny fingers interlaced in the blanket's yarn as though she'd been stroking Gooky before a gentle slumber overtook her. Listening to the rhythm of her soft breathing, I would kiss her cheek and close the door.

Unlike the security objects that some kids carry from room to room inside and even drag outside, Gooky didn't leave Sophie's bed except when we traveled overnight. On these occasions, Sophie would either put Gooky in the suitcase or carry him to the car. It always worried me when Gooky left Sophie's bed for I knew that, if we should happen to leave him in a hotel room, we'd be on the next plane back to claim him. Luckily, that never happened.

When Sophie first left home, I couldn't bear to enter her room. A combination of sadness and anger would overtake me as I stood in the doorway gazing at her clothes, her bed, and the stuffed animals she'd left behind. Although I was astounded that she had left her beloved Gooky, I took solace in his presence. I fancied that leaving Gooky was a sign Sophie had left for me, a sign that she would be back. Had she purposefully left Gooky to comfort me?

Gooky, a fusion of pink, yellow, blue, and green acrylic yarn, measured approximately two feet by four feet when my friend Miriam gave it to Sophie. Now, more than eighteen years of love later, having been pulled and wrapped around her on countless occasions, Gooky stretched to at least three feet by six feet. Had I stretched myself as much as I could for Sophie? Did Sophie know how hard I had tried to shield, comfort, and protect her? Gooky's colors had faded and he had more than a few holes. How sad he looked lying on her bed. Although Sophie had battered me for years, like Gooky, I waited patiently for her return.

One rainy Saturday afternoon, I was caught in a wave of despair. I was beginning to forget the sound of Sophie's voice, the way she laughed, the silly way she rubbed her nose. Aaron and Josh were out doing errands, leaving me home alone with Dunkin and Travis. Glumly, I walked upstairs, the dogs playfully following. Dunkin seized one of his tennis balls; Travis picked up a chew toy. What did they think about Sophie's absence? Did they wonder where she was? Did they miss her? Dunkin had been Sophie's "baby." She would often encourage him to pounce on her bed and snuggle with her. More than once since she'd left, I'd watched Dunkin slink into her room and sniff around as though he were looking for her. Sometimes he'd jump up on her bed and wait. When she didn't appear, he would emerge from the room, his big brown eyes drooping.

I sat on her bed and picked up Gooky. He was limp and soft. Dunkin put the ball he'd been playing with near my foot, his invitation for me to play fetch with him. Was he trying to distract me from my pain or just being a dog? I picked up the ball and gently tossed it, watching him retrieve it, chew it for a few seconds, and then bring it back to me, fully slobbered. Travis gazed out the window, watching a bird fluttering in a nearby tree, his tail wagging wildly.

Should I have known all along that Sophie was mentally ill? Was her lack of fear of strangers as an infant the first sign? Was her insistence at age two that the flu shot wouldn't hurt something to be concerned about? Should I have worried about her extraordinary ability to understand Josh's early science lessons? Were the intricate stories she created about her fabled baby sister and the Tooth Fairy indications that her view of reality was distorted? Did her resistance to being punished by her Pre-K principal foretell her defiance as a teenager? Had I missed what now looked like big flashing warning signals? I still do not know.

I put Gooky to my face and inhaled deeply. Lost childhoods run in my family. My mother lost her childhood at age three when her mother died. Sophie lost her childhood just before she turned eleven when a camp counselor raped her. I lost my childhood at age twelve when my mother became ill.

Sophie's scent on the blanket soothed me and I was flooded with memories. How ridiculous it seemed now for me to have ever questioned whether I could love an adopted child as much as a biological child. Sophie didn't grow in my uterus; she grew in my heart and in Josh's. She grew and she challenged and she fought and she left. She suffered from severe mental illness. A blood tie wouldn't have changed any of that. There were many times I didn't like her. Many of her behaviors frustrated and angered me, while others made me cringe in embarrassment. But never once did I stop loving her.

I smiled as my scientific mind fancied the experiment that would allow me to objectively test whether I could love an adopted child as much as a biological child. But then I stopped myself. It wasn't possible to love anyone more than I loved Sophie and Aaron.

But what would Sophie say about the role adoption played in her mental illness? If only Gooky could talk – what secret worries had Sophie shared with him? Did she feel abandoned by her birth family? Did Sophie think her adoption was connected to her mental illness?

I think not. Sophie knew how much Josh and I loved her, and even in her most delusional state, she had to have understood all we'd done as we prepared her to succeed in the world. She also knew how much Jamie loved her and why Jamie had made the difficult decision to allow Sophie to be adopted. From the beginning, even before Sophie could talk, we normalized adoption. We read books about adoption to her. Her first friends were the kids in our adoption playgroup. Josh's best friend and his wife had two adopted children, and Josh's cousin and his wife had an adopted daughter. In Sophie's childhood world, adoption was common-place, not the exception.

I'd embraced an open adoption because I believed it would be in Sophie's best interests. Jamie loved Sophie, and we made sure Sophie understood that love. Jamie played a critical role in Sophie's life that I could never play. She was the bridge to Sophie's genetic makeup. It was Jamie, not me, who could tell Sophie why her breasts were small and her feet were big.

Once it became clear how bright Sophie was and what a vivid imagination she had, I was even more fervent in my insis-tence that she have an ongoing relationship with Jamie. This was a child who, absent a real and honest relationship with Jamie, would have fantasized about being lost by a fairy princess in a forest. She would have convinced herself that Jamie and the handsome prince who was her father were riding around on a white horse searching for her. Our open adoption enabled Sophie to know Jamie and to see what Jamie's life was like.

I also had the benefit of watching Aaron grow and prosper in our home. Unlike Sophie, Aaron is well-grounded, self-assured, and responsible. He may not like studying for midterm exams, but he does it. He has lied to me, but his lies aren't habitual and they aren't pathological. He's never stolen anything, and he's never jumped out his second story window in the middle of the night. He's rolled his eyes and scowled at me, but he's never hit me.

And so this conflict between nature and nurture continues and important questions remain unanswered. With all that has happened, would I have adopted Sophie had I known then what I know now? Would I have felt differently had I gotten pregnant and my biological daughter inherited my mother's mental illness? These are critical questions and ones for which I don't have ready answers.

Looking down at Gooky, tears ran down my face.

CHAPTER 68

Replaced

Summer 2011. Sophie is almost nineteen years old.

Shortly after Sophie arrived in Texas, she called as I was cooking dinner. She complained of a painful sore throat and wanted information about our health insurance so she could see a doctor. Although Josh and I had agreed to keep her on our plan, we didn't give Sophie the account number, knowing it provided a reason, albeit a tenuous one, for her to contact us.

"Sophie," I explained for the third time, "All you have to do is have the doctor's office call me. If they accept our insurance, I'll give them the number and you'll have to pay the co-pay. If they don't, you'll have to pay out of pocket, send me the receipts, and I'll submit them to the insurance company for reimbursement."

"What?" she said, the frustration mounting in her voice.

"Call the doctor's office and ask them if they take our insurance," I said patiently.

"Can you just call them?" she pleaded.

"No. If you're old enough to be on your own, you're old enough to make a simple phone call." The loud voices in the background must have distracted Sophie.

"Mom?" Sophie yelled, "Can you please turn the radio down? I can't hear her."

The room tilted sideways as I realized "Mom" was Jamie and I was "her." Anguish stabbed me.

Over the next several months, in a multitude of ways, it became clear that both Josh and I had been replaced. Sophie's birth father Gary had been absent from her life for eighteen years. There'd been no contact with him. No cards exchanged on birthdays, no phone calls, and no visits. Sophie had found Gary on Facebook during her senior year of high school. She'd looked forward to meeting Gary, but he insisted on having a paternity test first. As soon as the results confirmed that Gary was Sophie's birth father, he enjoyed a meteoric rise in stature from sperm donor to "Father of the Year." It was Gary whom Sophie feted that Father's Day and Gary who would take her to dinner on her nineteenth birthday.

From Sophie's words and actions, it seemed she no longer considered Josh and me her parents. Jamie had become Mom; Gary was now Dad. There was no room for us. What did Sophie think when she remembered the past eighteen years? Did she remember I taught her to ride a bike? Did she remember how Josh sang to her every night before bed, and how he put her in the car and drove her around the neighborhood when she couldn't fall asleep? Did she remember that I had bandaged her scraped knees and kissed her boo-boos? Did she know Josh had saved her from running into a fire as a toddler or care that he had taken her to the foot surgeon and held her hand last year when the doctor removed the needle she'd stepped on?

Sophie's distorted reality wreaked havoc with me, but Josh suffered even more. I was used to sharing the mother role and, in one way or another, had done so with Jamie for eighteen years. Josh never had any competition. Until now. And it was killing him.

CHAPTER 69

Beginning to Heal

Summer 2011. Sophie is almost nineteen years old.

F amilies and households develop unique rhythms. So routine are the little idiosyncrasies of a home – the whir of the coffee grinder and smell of fresh coffee signaling the start of the day, the morning trip outside to retrieve the newspaper, the leisurely talk and shuffle of plates indicating that dinner is over – that those living there may not even be conscious of them. The rhythms that provide the backdrop for our lives are often so subtle that they become evident to people only when they are disrupted.

Although Sophie was only one of the four people living in our home, for at least ten years, her needs reigned supreme. Our household was in a state of high alert because of her erratic behavior. Yet it was only after she left that I realized how she had dominated the rhythms of our household, often to the detriment of the rest of us.

Our home is now calm, something I value. Dinner times are filled with interesting conversations as Josh, Aaron, and I catch up with one another. Voices rarely are raised, other than in goodnatured laughter. When tasks need to be done, it is with a spirit of cooperation and goodwill. My makeup, Josh's tools, and Aaron's games are where we leave them. I no longer fumble at the grocery store cash register, cursing Sophie for pilfering my cash yet again. I no longer experience the incessant worry I once had that Sophie was playing with razor blades behind the closed door of her bedroom.

By the time Sophie was out of the house for four months, I knew she'd never again live with us. Doing so wouldn't be good for her, and it would have destroyed the rest of us. After a brief honeymoon period, things would have gone right back to where they had left off. We would be faced with the never-ending fights and the pervasive daily tumult. We would worry that, when the door to her bedroom was closed, she was doing something destructive. We would fear that her inability to distinguish good people from bad people would put us all in danger. Even under the best of circumstances – if Sophie entered an intense therapeutic program and developed the skills to live independently – returning to our home wouldn't be good for her.

The pain Josh and I suffered around this issue was immense. While most kids leave home at age eighteen as Sophie had done, her departure was a very different experience. She wasn't off to college, with plans to return over school vacations. She was gone, off her medications, and spiraling out of control. It would be years at best before we would see her again.

Our grief, and the different ways that Josh and I experienced that grief, finally propelled us to seek help from a therapist. Josh always had to get to the bottom of things – just like when Sophie told her Wiffle ball story. He was intent on removing all doubt from his mind that we'd done everything we could have for Sophie. Memories of Sophie flooded him. He wanted to remember and talk about each. I had haunting memories of Sophie, too. For months, I couldn't walk into the grocery store where she'd worked because the disappointment of not seeing her overwhelmed me. I couldn't bear to make Passover dinner, knowing she wouldn't be with us. But I didn't want to talk about all the hurt. I wanted to put it in a box and bury it.

For years, while we'd shuttled Sophie from one therapist to another and worried about her mental health, Josh and I had muddled by on our own. How odd it now seems that seeing a therapist never occurred to us; even more surprising, it never was suggested by any of Sophie's therapists. Agreeing about the importance of rebuilding our lives without Sophie, Josh and I began seeing Dr. Shuman. Not surprisingly, we were unable to convince Aaron to join us. Looking back, however, seeing a therapist was one of the smartest moves Josh and I could have made and one that I wish we'd made years earlier.

Our first concrete challenge was Sophie's bedroom. It remained as she had left it, a shrine to our smashed hopes. A grey pallor of dust pervaded the room, which compounded the sadness I experienced whenever I ventured in there. Josh and I talked about what to do with Sophie's room, but we could never finish these conversations, as one or both of us ended up in tears.

In our sessions with Dr. Shuman, I acknowledged that, although being able to go into Sophie's room had comforted me initially, the room had become an eyesore that now brought more sadness than relief. "You need to get the toxins out of your house," Dr. Shuman suggested. Even as I was taken aback by the callousness of her statement, I nodded in agreement.

Josh has always been a pack rat, albeit a loveable one. There was no way the room would get cleaned if he were involved. Every stuffed animal, every piece of clothing, every memento would be mourned, the subject of endless debate – do we keep it or toss it? Bemoaning this to my friend Susan in a phone call on a late spring afternoon, she threw me a lifeline: "I'll come and help you. No problem." I accepted her offer and we chose a weekend two months from then for her visit.

As our clean-up weekend approached, my anxiety increased. I called Sophie and told her about the plan to clean her room. I asked her several times to send me a list of anything she wanted, telling her I'd gladly pack it up and send it to her. Although she acknowledged she was thinking about what she wanted, she never asked for anything. This made the clean-up task even more difficult. The last time Sophie's room had been cleaned, a couple of months before she left, we had done it together. We'd stuffed and thrown out dozens of garbage bags, so the worst of the task already was done. Yet I kept coming back to the question of whether I could get rid of all of Sophie's possessions.

The week before Susan arrived, I sat on Sophie's bed, estimating the magnitude of the task ahead of us. Sophie hadn't worn the clothes she'd left behind for more than eight months. Jamie told me Sophie had gained about fifty pounds since she'd arrived in Texas, so the clothes would no longer fit. It wouldn't be hard to pack them up and give them to the Salvation Army. I comforted myself knowing that Sophie's desire to help people less fortunate than she would make her happy to give away clothes that others could wear. The makeup she left in her bathroom was old and caked, and many of the hair ties were stretched out or broken. All of that could be disposed of easily. Remnants of art projects Sophie started and abandoned wouldn't be difficult to discard.

I closed my eyes, recalling the morning six months after my mother died when my father had said, "Rachel, we have to clean out Mom's closet. I can't keep looking at her things every day."

I had frozen. I couldn't tell him there had been times when I was alone in the house that I sat in her closet, her clothes surrounding me, inhaling her scent as I had imaginary conversations with her.

"Okay," I'd said reluctantly. "I'll help you."

That afternoon, trash bags in hand, I'd opened the door to the walk-in closet that held my parents' clothes. I'd gazed at the sparkly blue-grey gown my mother had worn at a cousin's Bar Mitzvah. How beautiful she had looked that night, floating across the dance floor in my father's arms. Gently I'd taken the dress off its hanger, folded it, and put it in the garbage bag. One by one, my father and I took her clothes off the hangers and slid them into the bags. The scraped-up Hush Puppies she'd worn every day, her summery white sandals, and her fancy black patent leather shoes were relegated to the Salvation Army bag, soon to be invaded by the feet of strangers. More than once I'd feigned having to make a phone call so I could leave the closet to cry.

We were nearly done cleaning when I saw it – the pastel silk shirtwaist dress, a duplicate of the one she'd made for me when I was seven, the dress she'd worn when we'd played a duet at our piano recital. I'd long ago outgrown and discarded my dress, but she had kept hers. Had she loved it as much as I'd loved mine? Were her memories of sitting so close and being so in tune with me that night as important to her as they'd been to me? I thought about keeping my mother's dress, but didn't. Although difficult, cleaning out her closet had brought me a sense of peace. Keeping the dress would only have caused me pain later.

Getting rid of Sophie's things wasn't going to be as onerous as I'd feared. It would be cathartic, a chance to do something constructive in a situation where I had little control. I was ready to clean out the room; Josh would come around as well. Most importantly, I thought about Aaron: cleaning up and redecorating Sophie's room would be concrete evidence that his world had become more orderly, that Josh and I were finally starting to take positive steps toward making our lives less about Sophie.

Then my eyes turned to Pink Bear, the four-foot stuffed animal that had lived on Sophie's bed for years. My Uncle Saul had given Pink Bear to Sophie when she was born. How could I get rid of Pink Bear? Josh would never agree to that.

Hoping to come up with a solution, I broached the topic during our therapy session. Josh's immediate response was predictable. "Pink Bear? You can't get rid of Pink Bear!"

"What do you want to do with Pink Bear?" I challenged, hoping the practicalities involved in saving Pink Bear might make Josh think more seriously.

"I don't know. But how can we get rid of Pink Bear? I mean, it's Pink Bear."

"Pink Bear is worn out, dirty, and full of holes."

"We could sew her back together and take her to the dry cleaners."

"Right," I scowled.

"We could put her in the basement."

"Why? So we can dig her out years from now, have all our Pink Bear memories come back, and then throw her out?" This is why I hadn't kept my mother's dress years ago when my father and I had cleaned out her closet.

"Maybe you should set Pink Bear aside and keep her for a while," Dr. Shuman counseled. "Or maybe you need to have a ceremonial goodbye for Pink Bear."

This wasn't the help I wanted. Glaring, I suggested with a laugh, "Maybe Pink Bear should spend her retirement years as a therapeutic bear in your office?" Josh would hear none of it. When he saw Pink Bear, he thought of the cherubic little girl in pigtails who worshipped her Daddy.

Clean-up weekend arrived and I headed off to pick Susan up at the airport. As we caught up over lunch, I confessed my apprehensions about Pink Bear. Susan said, "Don't worry, kiddo, we'll get through this."

We entered the bedroom, determined to complete our task in a thoughtful, efficient manner. Using a divide and conquer approach, Susan started at one end, I at the other. Clothes, shoes, and purses that were in good shape were set aside for the Salvation Army. Sophie's yearbook, Gooky, and photographs, cards, and mementos that might be meaningful to her one day, we put in a storage box. We saved books likely to be of interest to Aaron, and put the others in the Salvation Army pile. Almost everything else was relegated to the trash.

As we worked, Susan said, "Not nearly as bad as I thought it was going to be. It's just lots of crazy teenage clothes and some goofy souvenirs."

"Remember, this is what was left after the major cleaning Sophie and I did back in December," I said. "That's when I found the dark poetry and razor blades. Last week when I was in here, I found an empty bottle of Champagne under her sink."

From her spot on the bed, Pink Bear watched us, perhaps wondering what her fate would be. When we were almost done cleaning, I picked up a stuffed dog resting on Pink Bear. There was a gaping hole in Pink Bear's stomach. Black stuffing tumbled onto the bed.

"Looks like a little mousy may have gotten into Pink Bear," Susan said.

The image of a rodent munching on Pink Bear was more than I could take. Within minutes, Pink Bear had her head in one garbage bag and her feet in another and was on her way to her final resting place. I would find a way to break this news to Josh.

Now, at last, the room was empty. Our healing could begin.

CHAPTER **70**

Losing Part of Me

Summer 2011. Sophie is almost nineteen years old.

H ealing does not have an on-off switch. Rather, it is
a process that I expect will last for years.

One Saturday morning, sweat dripping from my face as I left
my Pilates class, a woman greeted me. I recognized her, but couldn't
place her.

"You look familiar. How do I know you?" she asked. Standing there, it came to her. "You're Sophie's mom, right?"

Then I recognized her. She was Lydia's mother. Sophie and
Lydia had been friendly in middle school, but had drifted apart
during high school. I hadn't seen Lydia's mother for years. "How
are you?" I asked.

"How's Sophie doing?" She had a concerned look on her
face.

"Not well," I choked, tears welling in my eyes. "She's suffering from some very severe mental illnesses."

"I'm so sorry. She was always such a sweet girl. I knew she
had some issues in high school, but I'd heard she'd gotten her act
together."

Her expression of sympathy felt like a dental drill hitting a
raw nerve. Despite my attempts to muffle the torrent of tears, I was
powerless. I started blubbering.

"I understand. Lydia's had her own issues." She hugged me.

As the room emptied and the other women returned their weights to the racks, they turned from the spectacle Lydia's mother and I created. I continued weeping.

"I haven't done that for a long time," I apologized, drying my eyes.

"It's okay," she comforted. "Do you want to talk?"

"Yes," I answered. "But first, remind me of your name."

"Valerie," she answered. "Yours?"

"Rachel."

My emotional outburst surprised me, especially as it came just days after a chance meeting in the grocery store with Ellen, a faculty member from the university whom I hadn't seen for months. Telling Ellen about Sophie hadn't been difficult. I'd given her much of the same information I'd shared with Valerie, but without any of the tearful drama.

I think the difference in these experiences was a function of how I defined myself in relationship to these two women. Ellen and I had talked about our children, but they were not the basis of our relationship. We'd also talked about university politics and grant-writing strategies. But to Valerie, I was "Sophie's mom" and to me she was "Lydia's mom." We had talked about nothing else but our daughters. I don't think I even knew her name when the girls were middle school friends.

Part of the person I'd been for so long – Sophie's mom – no longer existed. The hurt of having this part of my identity ripped from me was tremendous.

CHAPTER **71**

An Earthquake, a Hurricane, and a Birthday

August 28, 2011. Sophie is nineteen years old.

As I wrote, I wondered how I would know when my memoir should end. Mother Nature came to my rescue.

On the afternoon of August 23, 2011, a 5.8-magnitude earthquake struck Virginia. Its impact jarred the Northeast Corridor of the United States, sending shock waves through our world. Here in South Jersey, chandeliers swung, floors in high-rise buildings wobbled, and walls vibrated for close to twenty seconds. Days later, Hurricane Irene lumbered across the Atlantic Ocean and officials issued mandatory evacuation orders for people living on Cape May. The Atlantic City casinos suspended gaming operations, the Phillies rescheduled their weekend baseball games, and all public transportation systems stopped service. Josh, Aaron, and I cleaned the gutters, moved the furniture from the sun porch inside, secured the grill with rope and bungee cords, and moved the outdoor potted plants inside. We bought batteries and candles and filled the bathtub with water. At five-thirty-five A.M. on August 28, Irene became the first hurricane to make landfall in New Jersey since 1903.

By eight o'clock the rain had diminished to a sprinkle and a slight breeze blew the leaves. The hum of the air conditioner assured me we hadn't lost power. Although many leaves and a few branches were strewn about the yard and our pool's water was murky, there was no evidence of flooding. The basement was dry. We had survived both the earthquake and the hurricane without a problem.

Breathing a sigh of relief, I looked ahead with trepidation to the day ahead of me. Unlike the unanticipated earthquake, I knew for months this day was coming. Unlike the predicted hurricane, I had neither a survival plan nor a first aid kit for this day. It was Sophie's nineteenth birthday, the very first of her birthdays I would not spend with her. This wasn't like a child going off to college and being away for her birthday. No, this was Sophie's first birthday since she'd walked out of my life nearly eight months ago.

I rode each wave of sadness as I remembered the birthdays I'd celebrated with Sophie. I thought about Sophie's first birthday, how Josh and I had woken her with a serenade of *Happy Birthday*. We'd watched with joy at Sophie's amusement, opening the dozens of presents she received from family and friends and plunging her fingers into the chocolate icing on her birthday cake. I remembered when Sophie turned six and we took her and a dozen of her friends to the Peoria Zoo, where they watched and listened with fascination as the zookeeper talked about snakes and tortoises. I remembered when Sophie turned eight. She'd insisted on having her birthday party at the gymnasium where she'd learned how to do cartwheels, walk the balance beam, and swing on the parallel bars. I remembered her Bat Mitzvah – how poised she was during the ceremony and how pleased she was that her friends and family were gathered to celebrate her entrance to Jewish adulthood. Much like the rains of the previous day, the ebbs and flows of my emotions varied in their intensities.

Toward the end of the afternoon, the phone rang. It was Jamie.

"I think this has been the worst day of my life," she sobbed.

"Why? What happened?"

"I'm about fixin' to kill Sophie. You're probably the only person who understands what I've been going through. I'd been looking forward to spending this day with her – for the first time in nineteen years, I was going to get to spend her birthday with her. Richard and I took her out last night for a birthday dinner. We bought her a little tiara, some sunglasses, new shoes, and a couple of other little things. We had a really nice time. She and I were going to get manicures and pedicures this morning, have cake with Richard and the boys, and then she was going to spend the afternoon with Gary."

Did Jamie have a clue about the hurt I was experiencing that afternoon? Did she know I held Sophie's hand when she took her first step? Did she know it was me who comforted Sophie when she broke her arm? Did she realize how much I struggled to help Sophie do well in school? Did she not understand that it took all I had to answer the phone and hear her voice, knowing it was she and not I who Sophie now called "Mom"?

"She refused to get out of bed until after eleven o'clock. At that point, there wasn't time to have our girl time before Gary picked her up. I'm so angry and hurt. I've spent the afternoon crying. I don't know what to do."

"Oh, Jamie, I'm so sorry," I sighed, putting my grief on hold to console her.

"She knew I was upset and all she could say to me was, 'I wish you'd stop crying and carrying on. You're stressing me out and ruining my birthday.' And you know the worst of it? On her way out, she grabbed the birthday cake and the candles I bought for our celebration with her."

Nothing Jamie had told me thus far surprised me. This was typical Sophie. Then she said, "I swear, dealing with Sophie is just like dealing with my mother."

My stomach lurched.

When Josh and I had first met Jamie, she told us of her mother's lifelong addictions to alcohol and drugs, as well as her proclivity to violence. We'd wondered whether this was a red flag. But my sister-in-law Rebecca, a pediatric geneticist, had told us that the violent behaviors and drug and alcohol abuse could easily be explained by environmental factors. She probably said that genetics may have played a part, but I'm sure I wouldn't have heard those words. I was too desperate to become a mother. Since then, Jamie and I hadn't spoken about her mother, and I'd given little thought to Sophie's connection with her maternal grandmother.

"Do you know if your mother was ever diagnosed with a mental illness?" I asked cautiously.

"I saw her medical records years ago. She had bipolar disorder, multiple personality disorder, maybe schizophrenia, and borderline personality."

So there it was. Not only had Sophie inherited her maternal grandmother's wiry build and small breasts, she'd also inherited her mental illnesses.

Had Jamie seen her mother's medical records before Sophie was born? I didn't ask. It didn't matter now.

Hanging up the phone, I thought about the horrendous twist of fate I'd just discovered. What was the likelihood that both Sophie's biological grandmother and my mother would suffer from severe mental illness? I'd accepted my infertility and adopted Sophie, happy that my mother's mental illness genes wouldn't be passed down to my children. Yet, my daughter had inherited those genes anyway.

This realization, coming on the heels of the two natural disasters, made me understand that there are things in life that I can control and things that I cannot. I could no more control Sophie's mental illness than I could my mother's. And I could no more control their mental illnesses than I could the earthquake or the hurricane. I could try to minimize potential hurricane damage by making sure we had candles, water, food, and batteries. But I couldn't have stopped a tree from falling on our house. For years I'd done all I could for Sophie – taken her to the best doctors, made sure she took her medications and went to her therapy sessions, and encouraged her to do well in school. But I couldn't keep mental illness from destroying her.

In the wake of natural disasters, people rebuild their destroyed homes. Now, with Sophie gone, my challenge was to protect what was left – my marriage, my relationship with Aaron, and myself. This was the day to let go, the day to hope Sophie finds her way in the world and that, perhaps someday, she might remember and value the love I always will have for her.

CHAPTER **72**

The Box

I n about half of all cases, signs that a person suffers from severe mental illness emerge in childhood and become clear by early adulthood. These signs include responding to situations with unusual fear, defying rules and acting destructively, disorganized thinking, and persistent sadness, anger, or rapidly changing moods. Family members, teachers, and even peers often know something is different about these people. This certainly was true in Sophie's case.

Yet I did not know about my mother's mental illness until she was forty-two years old and I was twelve. How could this have been? Were there earlier signs that I'd missed? Or was she part of the fifty percent of people with manic depression who are not diagnosed until mid-life or later? If so, what made her become unhinged?

I began searching for answers to my mother's story after I had experienced Sophie's mental illness. By this time, however, I was approaching age sixty. My father, my mother's sister, and many of the other people who at one time may have been able to help me understand her illness were dead. Her hospital and psychiatric records had been destroyed long ago.

A forty-year reunion with my childhood friends from Detroit led me to search for the pictures I'd taken with the Kodak Instamatic 100 camera my parents had given me for my ninth birthday. That day and in subsequent weeks, I'd taken candid photos, capturing the childhood grins of my friends Thea, Joanne, and Julie. Now, I was sure the pictures would make us laugh, and knew they'd be great fodder for reminiscing at our reunion.

Within minutes, I found the box in which I'd put the pictures. It had remained undisturbed in the basement of each of the five houses in which Josh and I had lived, touched only by the moving men who carted it from one location to the next. I dipped my hands into the box, caressing one photo after another, smiling as I looked at the faces of my childhood friends, the decades melting away.

It didn't take me long to find some of the other treasures I'd put in that box nearly forty years ago, and little by little, they offered clues to my mother's story.

Her autograph book, signed by friends, teachers, and family members as she graduated from eighth grade in 1937 revealed that, at age thirteen, Mom was smart, driven, well-liked and respected by her peers. She was President of her class, listed her college-to-attend goal as "Harvard," and indicated her motto was "Always keep your chin up."

On the front page of her autograph book, her teen-aged handwriting showed that her favorite song was *Never in a Million Years*. Not being familiar with the song, I searched for its lyrics. I was mystified to find there were two songs, both popular in 1937, with that name. One came from the film *Wake Up and Live*. It was a love song. Ozzie Nelson wrote the words to the other song. It told a much darker story – of sadness, of isolation, of waking up screaming in the middle of the night, of thinking about suicide, and of hoping that each new day will bring love and a sunny new beginning. There were no other clues in the autograph book to help me figure out whether my mother's reference was to the love song or to Ozzie Nelson's song.

Four years later, in 1941, when she graduated from James Madison High School, just over her school picture in the yearbook my mother had written, "Don't stop till you reach the top." She took great pride in being President of Arista, an honor society that awarded her five gold scholarship pins. After graduating from high school, she became a stellar college student and earned her bachelor's degree in 1946 from the City College School of Business and

Civic Administration. There, she was President of Hillel and the Economics Club. In 1947, she completed a master's degree in economics at the University of Wisconsin. Although her major professor encouraged Mom to continue her education and earn her Ph.D., she decided she was ready to join the labor force.

I see no evidence of mental illness here.

From August 1947 until March 1950, Mom worked as research assistant at the National Bureau of Economic Research, a private, nonprofit research organization in New York dedicated to promoting a greater understanding of how the economy works. After that, Mom worked for the U.S. Department of Labor, Bureau of Labor Statistics, where she was part of a team lauded for producing critical wage surveys. Glowing letters of recommendation, yellowed slightly by time, reveal that she was a highly efficient employee who discharged her duties with great skill, responsibility, and intelligence.

These documents offer no hint of the mental illness that ravaged her years later.

The termination of her position at the Department of Labor at the end of August 1952, due to a funding cut, in combination with a long-term promise to visit a beloved aunt brought my mother to Detroit. There, the quick work of her aunt and a matchmaker introduced my mother and father to each other. Mom thought one date would get the aunt and her matchmaking friend off her back, but the date was the beginning of a romance that would usher in the next phase of her life. Mom and the handsome engineer, who had arrived in Detroit from Europe in November 1951, fell in love almost immediately. She moved to Detroit and they were married on August 30, 1953, her twenty-ninth birthday.

As a child, I'd spent many snowy afternoons looking at their wedding pictures. The smile on Mom's face that day gives no hint of the pain she later experienced.

Just thirteen months after my parents married, I entered the world, weighing in at six pounds, fifteen ounces and measuring twenty and a half inches. My mother approached her new role with fear, but with all of the zeal and sense of purpose she previously had devoted to her career.

The operating manual for her new baby was the original 1945 version of Dr. Spock's *Common Sense Book of Baby and Child*

Care, which rested on her nightstand for years. Small page creases and pencil notations annotating her self-taught introduction to motherhood marked its well-worn pages. How ironic it must have been for this woman, whose mother had died when she was three years old, to read Spock's advice to "trust yourself." When she had doubts about feeding schedules, bathing, unexplained crying, or toilet training, and when she wanted to understand how I should be behaving, she consulted her baby bible. At four years old, when I threw myself on the floor of the Sunday school room, kicking and screaming for fear she would leave me, she followed Spock's suggestion and patiently sat in the corner of the classroom reading a book.

Three years after my birth, my brother Ben was born; Brian followed two years later. For the next seven years, my brothers and I enjoyed halcyon childhoods. Mom was always there to dry a tear, settle a fight, or wipe a nose. She held my hand as I nervously started kindergarten, lovingly reprimanded Ben when he and his best friend Ricky followed the birds after school, got lost, and were escorted home by a police officer, and patiently followed through with the therapeutic foot exercises recommended by Brian's podiatrist to straighten his pigeon-toes. She read and corrected every paper we wrote for school and checked our homework nightly. She cultivated a love of music in us and began teaching each of us to play the piano on our fifth birthdays. Summers meant carefree time spent in the neighborhood building forts, playing baseball, and spending a quarter at the Good Humor ice cream truck.

There was no hint of mental illness.

And then everything changed. On August 2, 1966, we moved from our family friendly neighborhood in Detroit to Southfield's suburban sprawl. That fall, my father, Ben, Brian, and I witnessed Mom change from what she called the good Dr. Jekyll to the evil Mr. Hyde. She was overwhelmed by a sadness we never had seen.

What happened?

Initially, I thought Mom had hidden her illness, first by immersing herself in school and career, and later by embracing the role of ideal mother. That didn't square, however, with what I knew about severe mental illness: it overwhelms and suffocates its victims. It doesn't allow them the luxury of masking their pain with mundane activities.

Had I missed signs of Mom's mental illness that were there all along? Probably not. Like me, my father and Ben first knew something was wrong with Mom shortly after we moved. Even Brian, who was only seven years old, knew. No, if Mom's symptoms had existed before the move, surely I would have known.

CHAPTER 73

Coming Out

Summer 2012. I am fifty-eight years old.

For almost forty years, my relationship with mental illness was shrouded in secrets. Before I went to college, I helped keep my mother's illness a secret. After I left for college, I became one of the outsiders, privy to little of what my father and brothers witnessed. Although my mother wrote weekly letters to me when I was in college, they included no hint of her annual cycling. Even the letters she wrote to me in the weeks preceding her death were upbeat, newsy, and thoughtful. Was this her attempt to shield me, to allow me to focus on my studies, and to provide me some sense of normalcy? Or were secrets kept because I had become one of the people who didn't need to know?

Over the years, I've had conversations with my brothers about my mother's illness and her death. I learned about some of the secrets kept from me. Only recently did Ben tell me about coming home from school in November 1974 to find her passed out after a suicide attempt. She'd overdosed on aspirin. In early spring of 1975, Ben came home and again found Mom collapsed after overdosing on her depression medications. That time she'd written a three-page note, a note Ben read and then gave to my father. In the note, Mom inventoried her inadequacies and apologized for not being a good enough wife and mother. Ben had watched as Dad folded the note and put it in his jacket pocket before following the ambulance to the hospital. When Dad returned from the hospital and Ben asked about the note, Dad denied its existence. Similarly, Brian told me recently that, in the fall of 1975 shortly before Mom's death, Dad woke him early and asked him to stay home from school to watch Mom because earlier that morning she had attempted to slit her wrists with a piece of glass.

Secrecy defined the way my family and I coped with my mother's illness and death. Secrecy also dominated how Josh and I dealt with Sophie's illness. We didn't tell people that Sophie had shimmied out of her second story window to meet a pervert or that she'd been hospitalized multiple times. I didn't even tell my brothers. We rationalized our secrecy as protecting Sophie from being ostracized.

Writing this book has been a huge change for me. As I've struggled to come to terms with the demons that haunted my mother and my daughter, I've become more willing to talk about their mental illnesses and the effects they've had on me. But this has been a long and difficult process. When I first told close friends of my plan to write a book about the effects of mental illness on my family, I explained it was a story about being Sophie's mother, still keeping my mother's mental illness secret. Of course, I knew that my story began with my mother's mental illness. Little by little, as I became more comfortable writing about my mother's illness, I began to talk about it. My friends were supportive and thoughtful when I told them the truth. In return, I learned that some of them also had people in their families who suffered from mental illness – people they'd never told me about. In fact, when my friend Lori and I put the pieces of our stories together, we realized that her grandmother and my mother could have been roommates at the Detroit psychiatric hospital.

One morning, my friend Helen, a psychologist I've known for more than thirty years, called me. She asked how work on my book was progressing. I quickly realized I hadn't divulged the book's real story to her.

I wasted little time getting to the point. "Helen, there's more to the book than I've told you. Like Sophie, my mother suffered from mental illness for many years. She eventually killed herself."

Not missing a beat, Helen responded, "That's a very different book than the one I thought you were writing. Tell me about her."

And so I did. I began with the early loss of my mother's mother and told of the cruelty my mother had suffered at the hands of her stepmother. I explained how Mom had excelled in school from an early age and how she'd earned her master's degree in economics and then held several prestigious positions, not common for a woman born in 1924. I told Helen how Mom had abandoned her career when she married my father and how she'd put all her energies into being a first-rate mother. And then I told her about the move to Southfield, how mom started falling apart, and how for the next nine years I watched in horror as she became more and more ill, eventually killing herself.

"So what I'm struggling with now is why didn't I know about her illness until I was twelve and she was forty-two. Were there signs that I missed? I can't believe that would be the case. Was this a new illness? And if so, why did it surface for the first time after we moved?"

There was silence for a moment.

"Do you know about David Gutmann's theory of the psychic immune system?" Helen asked thoughtfully.

"I don't."

"He maintains that people who come unglued in mid and later life decompensate for a reason. To understand that reason, you have to trace back to earlier traumatic memories and meanings. By recreating the historic self, you open up the charged personal narrative that is reactivated by the current stress."

"Helen, too much psychobabble. Explain," I pleaded.

"Gutmann sees the psyche as a kind of immune system – like the physical immune system that seeks to defend the body from viruses and bacterial toxins. Think of the person's earlier traumatic memories and meanings as their reaction to psychological viruses and as triggering their lifelong psychological immunities. Some current stress overloads the capacity of their psychological immune system – which is why they fall apart. Recreating the personal narrative helps us understand and hopefully re-invigorate their psychological immunities."

"And that means?"

"In your mother's case, she never got over the early loss of her mother. She kept looking for the good mother she knew as a little girl for such a brief time. As a student, and then as an employee, she took joy in being rewarded for excelling. With her own children, she tried to become the mother she'd lost, and she was successful as long as you and your brothers were young. Once the youngest was in school all day, the system broke down and she was left with her private demons. On top of that, your family moved out of a neighborhood where she was comfortable and supported."

"Once Brian was in first grade, my mother tried to resurrect her career, but after being out of the workforce for more than a decade, she couldn't re-enter. It was the 1960's when most middle-class women didn't work, and those who did were teachers, nurses, or secretaries. She looked for work, but the only job she could find was as a substitute teacher, not what her education had prepared her for. In several of the letters she wrote to me the year she died, she described her efforts to replace her lost Arista pin."

"Arista pin?"

"It was her high school honor society pin – proof to her that she was a smart person. She was searching for the smart person she and others once saw, her lost self. She wrote several letters to her high school looking for a replacement. At first no one had any idea what she wanted. Finally, they sent her a replacement pin. She was so excited. Who does that more than thirty years after they graduate from high school?"

"Someone trying to reassure herself that she is still the same person she thought she was or maybe someone who was desperately trying to fight her demons."

I thought about my work and how critical the achievement and recognition I received from it had been to defining who I was at every point in my life. When I was young and didn't understand my mother's illness, I threw myself into my schoolwork. My good grades defined me. And it was succeeding at work that kept me sane as I struggled with the challenges of Sophie's mental illnesses. Work and its rewards gave me control and brought order to my world. How would I have reacted without my career?

"So she probably had a genetic predisposition for manic depression that expressed itself once the environment in which she found herself became unsupportive," I pondered out loud.

"That makes sense to me," Helen agreed.

"Helen, I wish we'd had this conversation years ago."

"You weren't ready," Helen said wisely. "But I'm more than happy to help."

Hearing Helen's explanation empowered me to talk with other friends who were clinical psychologists. While the emphasis each put on nature and nurture as explanation for my mother's illness varied, they agreed that it was likely both had played significant roles. Just as nature and nurture explained Sophie's behaviors, so too did they explain my mother's.

Ultimately, mental illness robbed my mother of her life and it robbed Sophie of the life I wanted for her.

Succumbing to a life of silence about my family's mental illnesses has brought me ills of my own. As an adolescent, silence about mental illness distanced me from my peers. I didn't invite kids to my home because I didn't want them to see my mother's strange behaviors. As a young adult, it created walls as I cordoned off parts of myself from my friends. As an adult, it hindered me from securing the support I needed as I schlepped Sophie from one doctor to the next, paid exorbitant sums of money for her care, and tried to keep my family from falling apart. Not telling my friends prevented them from providing me with the support I so badly needed. And perhaps the cruelest irony of all was that the secrets I kept from my friends kept me from truly understanding my mother's illness.

Would Sophie's experience with mental illness have been different had my mother's mental illness and those of her contemporaries not been so well-hidden? Would Congress have allocated more funds to the National Institute of Mental Health if it were clear that so many lives were affected by mental illness? Would we have a better understanding of the causes and treatments of mental illness? Would the stigma of mental illness still exist?

My silence ends. Talking with my friends helped me untangle many of the mysteries of mental illness, made me realize I was not to blame, and gave me the courage to write this book. The toxic stigma, as prevalent now as it was in 1968, has denied the very existence of mental illness and kept it hidden. By hiding mental illness, my family and I helped prevent people who are very ill from getting the treatments they need, and we have abetted the alienation and humiliation of family members.

No more.

CHAPTER **74**

Regrets

Three weeks later.

A few weeks after talking with Helen, I woke up with a crick in my neck. Seeking to relieve the pain and pamper myself with a relaxing massage, I called a local spa, described my problem to the receptionist, and asked if she could recommend a massage specialist. She suggested Maggie.

I wasn't on Maggie's table for more than five minutes when we started jabbering. I learned that she'd been working at the spa for about a year and that she was divorced with two children, a fourteen-year-old son and an eleven-year-old daughter. I told her that I had a fifteen-year-old son and a nineteen-year-old daughter.

She talked about her son. He was a good student, enjoyed playing video games, helped out at home, and had a nice group of friends. She hoped he would become a pharmacist, although he'd set his sights on being a lawyer. I told her about Aaron, his interest in robotics, and his thoughts about becoming an engineer.

What was not said about our daughters was deafening. I waited, not wanting to move our conversation in the direction of Sophie, yet knowing it was inevitable.

As Maggie worked the muscles in my back, she said, "My daughter, she's the troubled one. I really worry about her."

"Why's that?" I groaned. She'd found the muscle.

"Her grades last year were D's and F's. She refuses to study. Her room's a disaster. She's taken up with some bad kids."

"Sounds like my daughter," I confessed. "Does she lie to you?"

"All the time."

"Mine lied to me about important things as well as stupid things – like whether the window was closed. Not being able to trust her drove me wild."

"Last spring I caught my daughter sending sexually explicit texts to a boy, complete with pictures. Luckily she had her clothes on."

"Mine sent nude photos with her texts," I shared.

"At eleven?"

"No, she was fourteen."

"I took her phone and computer away from her and she's not getting them back until her grades improve," Maggie said.

"We did the same thing, but it didn't matter to her. She found other ways to get in trouble."

"That's what I'm afraid of. I'm having her tested for ADHD," Maggie said.

My thoughts returned to the summer of 2003 when Sophie was eleven and we first discovered that she had ADHD. Maggie was living the life I had lived. She was just eight years behind me.

"I'm going to have a tough decision to make if the doctor wants to put her on medication. My ex-husband will go ballistic," she said.

"Why's that?"

"He doesn't believe those medicines do any good."

"My daughter was diagnosed with ADHD when she was eleven," I said. "We put her on medication and at first it seemed to help. After a few years, she developed bipolar disorder as well as borderline personality disorder. Now she's a train wreck."

"That's what my ex is afraid of. He has two sisters with bipolar disorder and he's convinced the medicines they took as kids had something to do with their developing bipolar disorder."

"You know, some of the research I've read suggests that may be the case. It's not an easy decision."

"I think my ex is bipolar. That makes me even more worried about my daughter. I hope she has my genes, but somehow, I don't think that's the case."

Other than the soothing, new age music piping through the speakers, there was silence in the room. I waited for her to ask the question I knew was coming.

"So, what advice would you give me?"

Like me, she saw the similarities in our experiences. What do I say? Run for the hills? Medicate her? Don't medicate her? Tie her to the kitchen table and never let her out of your sight? I thought about all I'd been through with both Sophie and my mother. There were no easy answers. Medical science had little to offer, but I had learned one important lesson during my forty-year struggle with mental illness.

"Talk. Tell your family. Tell your friends. Tell the school. Tell the community. Don't keep it a secret and don't try and fight this on your own. If I could turn back time, the one thing I'd do differently is tell people what I was going through. They would have been supportive and that would have made a big difference. But I bought into the stigma of mental illness and I hid."

She put a hot towel on my neck. My muscles relaxed and I melted onto her table.

Letting Go of the Dream

The daughter I dreamed of went to a first-rate liberal arts college. She became fervent about science, art, and theatre, and earned a bachelor's degree. She worked hard in school, made lots of wonderful lifelong friends, and found her passion. She travelled the world, earned a graduate degree, and launched her career. She met a kind, loving man who brought out the best in her. After a long courtship, she married and started a family of her own. Following a strict medication schedule, she learned to thrive despite the mental illness demons that challenged her to run toward a life of mania. With the help of caring therapists, she battled the evil remnants left by her rapist. She took charge of her life, embraced health, and made herself proud. Along the way, she repaired the relationships she'd torn asunder with Josh, Aaron, and me. We welcomed her back, cautiously at first, and then wholeheartedly. She learned about the importance of honesty and came to value it. She lovingly took care of me in my old age, and when I died, she mourned me.

But magical thinking will not make this a story with a happy ending.

I have not seen Sophie for close to three years. She calls rarely and she drifts farther and farther from Josh and me. The last time she called, she told Josh she was addicted to methamphetamine and was homeless. She continues to refuse treatment.

Unlike fairy tales in which the characters live happily ever after, I work on letting go of my shattered dream. But it is a long, painful process. I mourn for what could have been but was not. I play Monday morning quarterback, telling myself that, if only I'd done this or that, things would have been different. Could I have done anything more for Sophie? Knowing that my worrying doesn't help Sophie but that it harms Josh and Aaron, I work to contain it. I dabble in thoughts of blaming a vengeful deity, but get no solace from doing so. I wear Sophie's Jewish star, comforted by having something she once cherished close to me.

Just as it did when my mother was alive, my heart pounds when the phone rings late at night. I'm convinced that each call will be the one telling me that my daughter is dead. I fight back the tears as yet another of barrage of sadness rushes in, pulling me off-kilter. Knowing that thousands of other families face situations similar to mine doesn't console me, but it does make me want to change the system.

Having survived the deaths of my parents, and the painful void that ensued with each of those premature losses, I know time will heal. In my more rational moments, I know I've done all I could for Sophie. Yet I worry about where she is and what she's doing, and I feel guilty because I can't protect her. But I couldn't even protect her when she was living with me. I could protect Sophie no more than I could protect my mother years ago. This is the legacy of mental illness.

I cling to Josh as we take turns being strong. I lean on my brothers and my lifelong loving friends who, now that they know all I've been through, comfort and support me. I throw myself into work in an effort to numb the pain, and I give thanks for Aaron who challenges me in all the right ways.

References

CHAPTER 4: Ten Years After

1. *Monthly Vital Statistics Report, Annual Summary for the United States, 1976: Births, deaths, marriages, and divorces.* U.S. Department of Health, Education, and Welfare, (PHS 78-1120, Volume 25, No. 13, December 12, 1977).

2. *Silent Grief: Living in the Wake of Suicide* by Christopher Lukas and Henry Seiden. Jessica Kingsley Publishers, Philadelphia, PA, 2007.

3. Life Events and Interdependent Lives: Implications for Research and Intervention. By Rachel Pruchno, Fred Blow, & Michael Smyer, *Human Development*, 1984, 31-41.

CHAPTER 18: The Initial Diagnosis

1. http://www.nimh.nih.gov/health/publications/attention-deficit-hyperactivity-disorder/adhd_booklet_cl508.pdf

CHAPTER 25: Letters

1. Anatomy of an Epidemic: Psychiatric Drugs and the Astonishing Rise of Mental Illness in America. By Robert Whitaker, *Ethical Human Psychology and Psychiatry*, 2005, 7 (1), 23-35.

CHAPTER 52: Finding Normal

1. *The Bipolar Teen: What You Can Do to Help Your Child and Your Family* by David J. Miklowitz and Elizabeth L. George. Guilford Press, New York, 2008.

CHAPTER 57: The Final Piece of the Puzzle

1. http://www.nimh.nih.gov/health/topics/borderline-personality-disorder/index.shtml

Chapter 61: Rock Bottom

1. *The Insanity Offense: How America's Failure to Treat the Seriously Mentally Ill Endangers Its Citizens* by E. Fuller Torrey. W.W. Norton & Company, New York, 2008.

Chapter 73: Coming Out

1. *The Psychic Immune System in Later Life: Thoughts on Late-Onset Disorders* by Allen Gutmann. Paper presented to Conference on Mental Health and Aging, Tel Aviv University, 1995.

Acknowledgments

Writing this book has been a three-year adventure. When Sophie left home, I was raw. There was a sadness that I could not shake. And then I started writing. As I wrote, I first came to understand my daughter's story and only later, my mother's.

At every step of the way, my early readers were my sounding board and my guides. I asked people to be as honest as possible, hoping to use their comments to make the memoir as powerful as it could be.

The first draft was therapeutic. It told my story of being Sophie's mother. My mother, while present, played a very minor role. My readers, Susan D. Chapman, Arnold R. Shore, Ph.D., and Abby Spector, MMHS, wanted to understand how I experienced my mother's illness and how that influenced the way I experienced my daughter's mental illness.

Realizing that I had a powerful story to tell and that I was a reasonably strong writer, I knew I needed help transitioning from my day job as a research psychologist to a memoir writer. And so I read countless memoirs and books about writing memoirs. To help me understand narrative arc, scene creation, and the importance of dialogue, I worked with Sarah Lovett, a published author and professional writing coach. Like no therapist had ever done, Sarah encouraged me to dig into my past and understand my mother's story.

In the second draft, although my mother's story was expanded, my readers felt that the stories about my mother and my daughter were bolted together, rather than interconnected. Readers of this draft included B. Sharon Atteberry, Rosemary Blieszner, Ph.D., Susan D. Chapman, Lisa Ewan, Lucy Feild, Ph.D., R.N., Marguerite Hall, Joanne Marshak Katz, Helen Q. Kivnick, Ph.D., Desiree Marble, Laura Maryanski, Megan McCutcheon, M.A., Thea Singer, Ph.D., Arnold R. Shore, Ph.D., and Sherry Weiss. They found some of the text too graphic, were surprised by how much I – a psychologist – didn't understand about mental illness, and wanted to know more about how my marriage survived and how my son was impacted. Most importantly, they wanted to see more of my thoughts.

I dug deeper, went back to the drawing board, and addressed their concerns. My third group of readers included Steven M. Albert, Ph.D., Nancy P. Kropf, Ph.D., Marcia Pruchno Lawrence, M.Arch., Sheryl Potashnik, Ph.D., Avalie Saperstein, M.S.W., and Michael Smyer, Ph.D. This group complained less about the stories about my mother and my daughter feeling bolted together, but encouraged me to more closely weave them together. They urged me to share more of the touching and poignant moments, and suggested that I muse more about how I survived.

With the fourth group of early readers, I turned an important corner. The experiences I've had with mental illness, first as they were witnessed through the eyes of a child and later as they were experienced as a mother and a professional, came together. My readers were Debra Finch, Ph.D., R.N., F. Joe DeLong, III, Esq., Dawn Gober-Wright, Christina Hansen, M.A., Karen Jung, Barry Lebowitz, Ph.D., Sidney Moss, M.S.W., Miriam Rose, Arnold R. Shore, Ph.D., Linda Teri, Ph.D., Kimberly Van Haitsma, Ph.D., Robert Weiss, M.P.A., Marcia Willing, M.D., Ph.D., and Maureen Wilson-Genderson, Ph.D. They found the story tragic and compelling, and the message clear.

Finally, I am fortunate to have friends who are lawyers, psychologists, psychiatrists, nurses, and social workers who helped me develop ideas about how to make this world a better place for people with mental illness and their families, ideas shared on my website and in my talks about the book. Reviewers included Steven M. Albert, Ph.D., Rosemary Blieszner, Ph.D., William J. Champion, III, Esq., Lucy Feild, Ph.D., R.N., Debra Finch, Ph.D., R.N., Nancy Galambos, Ph.D., Helen Q. Kivnick, Ph.D., Nancy P. Kropf, Ph.D., Barry Lebowitz, Ph.D., Stuart Lev, Esq., Narsimha R. Pinninti, M.D., Denise A. Rubin, Esq., Avalie Saperstein, M.S.W., Arnold R. Shore, Ph.D., Michael Smyer, Ph.D., Stephen M. Scheinthal, D.O., and Kimberly Van Haitsma, Ph.D.

Turning the manuscript over to my editor, Laurie Rozakis, Ph.D., was one of the scariest things I've ever done. She was the first person I didn't know who read my story. I worried about everything from what she would think of my writing ability to what she would think of me as a person. She was, however, the perfect editor for me. She very clearly told me what she liked, what needed work, and why. Her easy sense of humor made me feel that she was an old friend. She helped me strengthen areas that needed more punch and let go of text that did not add to the story.

My last group of early readers included Emily Andreano, M. Cherie Clark, Ph.D., Christine Ferri, Ph.D., Nancy Galambos, Ph.D., Irene Leamon, Jonathan Leamon, and Denise A. Rubin, Esq. Their comments told me I was done writing and ready to begin the next phase of my journey – publishing my book so that other families would be encouraged to tell their stories.

To all of my early readers, my writing coach, and my editor: thank you from the bottom of my heart. Without you, this book would not exist.

As a big sister, it's sometimes hard to acknowledge the important role my two younger brothers have played in my life. This is certainly true with regard to this book. When I first told my brothers about my plans to write about our mother's mental illness, I worried whether they were ready to have the story made public. Their support has been unwavering. They read and commented on various versions of the manuscript, and they filled in details that enriched the story. Learning that I had kept secret so many details about my life with Sophie angered them, but only because they love me and wished they could have helped lessen my pain through their love and support. To both of you: thank you for being the best brothers ever.

Finally, despite all of the trials and tribulations of Sophie's illness, my marriage not only survived, but it has thrived. For this I thank my awesome husband who patiently read and reread each chapter as I wrote it, corrected my grammar, talked with me daily about my progress, made decisions about publication, and edited each version of the manuscript. I know this was difficult, as it made you relive so much of the pain we experienced. Yet you never stopped encouraging me to tell the story. From the night I told you about my mother, you've been by my side, patiently holding my hand. Thank you for your love and your support. I couldn't have done this without you.

Discussion Questions

1. Though *Surrounded By Madness* is brimming with unforgettable stories, which scenes were the most memorable?

2. *Surrounded By Madness* shows so many problems in the way people with mental illness are treated. If we are to become a more humane society, what needs to change? What are the priorities and why?

3. *Surrounded By Madness* provides a glimpse into how people with mental illness have been treated beginning in the 1960's and ending in 2011. Have significant changes been made? What are they? Has the stigma associated with mental illness changed?

4. Discuss the meanings implied by the title *Surrounded By Madness.* Is the title a good representation of the author's experience?

5. How did Pruchno's early experiences with her mother's mental illness influence her approach to parenting a child with mental illness?

6. In what ways did Sophie's mental illness affect her brother Aaron?

7. How was Pruchno's marriage affected by Sophie's mental illness? What kept Rachel and Josh together?

8. What would you have done had you found your teen-aged daughter communicating with a pervert? How do we keep our children safe?

9. How much of a role did adoption play in this book? Would Pruchno have felt any differently had Sophie been her biological child?

10. Do you agree with the message of *Surrounded By Madness* – don't hide mental illness? If you had a child with mental illness, would you hide it? Why or why not?

11. Most memoirs about mental illness have happy endings. How does *Surrounded By Madness* change your understanding about mental illness?

12. Most people with mental illness do not have access to the resources Pruchno and her family had. How might Pruchno's story have been different had she not had the educational and financial resources she had?

13. All of Sophie's doctors agreed she was not competent to make decisions about her medical care. Yet once she turned eighteen she had the legal right to make these decisions. How should autonomy and paternalism be balanced in the context of mental illness?

14. What would you have done if, like Pruchno, you had to make the choice between letting your child with mental illness leave home and providing shelter, security, and support to her as she put you, your home, and your other children at risk?

15. Pruchno never told Sophie about her mother's illness. Should she have told? Would you have told? Would it have made a difference?

16. Pruchno describes both her mother's mental illness and her daughter's. Which was worse? Why?

Participate in online conversations about these and other questions, locate resources for families coping with mental illness, and follow the author's blog at www.surroundedbymadness.net.

CPSIA information can be obtained at www.ICGtesting.com
Printed in the USA
LVOW04s0858170814

399533LV00002B/370/P

9 781457 525599